God's Beauty-in-Act

Princeton Theological Monograph Series

K. C. Hanson, Charles M. Collier, D. Christopher Spinks,
and Robin Parry, Series Editors

Recent volumes in the series:

Anette I. Hagan
*Eternal Blessedness for All?:
A Historical-Systematic Examination of Schleiermacher's Understanding
of Predestination*

Larry D. Harwood
*Denuded Devotion to Christ:
The Ascetic Piety of Protestant True Religion in the Reformation*

Jamey Heit
*Liturgical Liaisons: The Textual Body, Irony,
and Betrayal in John Donne and Emily Dickinson*

Fujiwara Atsuyoshi
*Theology of Culture in a Japanese Context:
A Believers' Church Perspective*

David L. Reinhart
*Prayer as Memory: Toward the Comparative Study of Prayer
as Apocalyptic Language and Thought*

Maeve Louise Heaney
Music as Theology: What Music Says about the Word

Peter D. Neumann
Pentecostal Experience: An Ecumenical Encounter

Ashish J. Naidu
*Transformed in Christ: Christology and the Christian Life in John
Chrysostom*

God's Beauty-in-Act

Participating in God's Suffering Glory

STEPHEN M. GARRETT

☙PICKWICK *Publications* · Eugene, Oregon

GOD'S BEAUTY-IN-ACT
Participating in God's Suffering Glory

Princeton Theological Monograph Series 196

Copyright © 2013 Stephen M. Garrett. All rights reserved. Except for brief quotations in critical publications or reviews, no part of this book may be reproduced in any manner without prior written permission from the publisher. Write: Permissions, Wipf and Stock Publishers, 199 W. 8th Ave., Suite 3, Eugene, OR 97401.

Pickwick Publications
An Imprint of Wipf and Stock Publishers
199 W. 8th Ave., Suite 3
Eugene, OR 97401

www.wipfandstock.com

ISBN 13: 978-1-61097-730-2

Cataloguing-in-Publication data:

Garrett, Stephen M.

God's beauty-in-act : participating in God's suffering glory / Stephen M. Garrett.

xviii + 244 pp. ; 23 cm. Includes bibliographical references and indexes.

Princeton Theological Monograph Series 196

ISBN 13: 978-1-61097-730-2

1. Aesthetics—Religious aspects—Christianity. 2. Balthasar, Hans Urs von, 1905–1988. I. Series. II. Title.

BR115.A8 G39 2013

Manufactured in the U.S.A.

para mi familia

Contents

Preface ix
Acknowledgments xv
Abbreviations xviii

Introduction: The Scandalous Cross?   1

Panel One: No Room in the Inn

1. Beauty as the Theological Beast?   23
2. Re-form-ing Beauty: The Significance of Hans Urs von Balthasar's Theological Aesthetics   58

The Hinge

3. Following a Biblical Trajectory   93

Panel Two: God's Beauty-in-Act

4. The Impossible Suffers as Incarnate Beauty   127
5. Our Dramatic Participation in God's Awful Beauty   162

Conclusion   196

Bibliography   207
Scripture Index   227
Subject Index   235

Preface

PATIENCE WITH GOD. PATIENCE WITH GOD! PATIENCE WITH GOD? THANK God, he's patient with us. Tomáš Halík, a Czech theologian and secretly ordained Catholic priest during Communist occupation, identifies with many contemporary atheists in his culture regarding that confounding "sense of God's absence from the world."[1] These atheists, agnostics, and critics of religion espouse that "God is dead" in an attempt to explain God's apparent absence in a world darkened by the horrors of the Communist regime and other atrocities of the twentieth and now twenty-first century. Such an explanation seems plausible if one understands God as static and uninvolved with his creation. Yet, Halík, in his work entitled *Patience with God*, posits an alternative explanation. There are "three (mutually and profoundly interconnected) forms of patience for confronting the absence of God. They are called *faith*, *hope*, and *love*."[2] Patience with God, he surmises, teaches us how to live with God's mystery and hiddenness, for it is this patience that distinguishes between faith and atheism. Yet, what is it about the manifestation of patience in the life of faith that makes it so attractive, so appealing, so fitting, as to address such non-belief?

Jürgen Moltmann, in an effort to address God's apparent absence, contends that Christian theology and the church face "a double crisis: the *crisis of relevance* and the *crisis of identity*." When theology and the church endeavor to be relevant to the surrounding pluralistic culture, they face a crisis of identity because they are confronted with conflicting viewpoints. Yet, the more they "assert their identity in traditional dogmas, rights and moral notions, the more irrelevant and unbelievable they become."[3] Moltmann and others like Wolfhart Pannenberg and Catherine Mowry LaCugna fault classical theism for this dual crisis because God as the infinitely perfect being, for example, seems untouched or unmoved by the suffering and pain of this world. In response to this dual crisis, some capitulate to the cultural ethos of the day, becoming indistinguishable from

---

1. Halík, *Patience with God*, ix.
2. Ibid.
3. Moltmann, *Crucified God*, 7.

Preface

the culture, while others isolate themselves and withdraw into Christian ghettos failing to engage the culture.[4] Such responses seem indicative of a bifurcation between theology and life, between theory and praxis. How, then, might we connect orthodoxy with orthopraxy, right thinking or right worship of God with right action?

Moltmann attempts to navigate between cultural capitulation and isolation by advocating the way of orthopraxy, not in the sense that we begin with right doctrine (orthodoxy) such that "a particular insight can be demonstrated by what everyone can experience and check by repeating the experience." Rather, the kind of orthopraxy Moltmann has in mind comes "through *verum facere*, what everyone is not yet assumed to be able to experience"[5] such that knowledge of the truth comes through action. This approach is meaningful, though, only if the notion of *relation* is the central idea of Christian theology. Even Moltmann, though, begins with what he believes to be orthodoxy, namely the "dialectic principle: the deity of God is revealed in the paradox of the cross." Thus, to the extent that the "Christian life is a form of practice which consists in following the crucified Christ, . . . a theology of the cross is a practical theory."[6] Although Moltmann seems to identify the problem facing Christian theology and the church, is he able to avoid the extremes of cultural capitulation and isolation as he so desires?

Elaine Scarry implicitly offers us another approach in her book, *On Beauty and Being Just*.[7] In part one of that work, she seeks to ally beauty with truth such that beauty "ignites the desire for truth by giving us . . . the experience of conviction and the experience, as well, of error."[8] Yet, beauty's association with error in that it "brings us into contact with our own capacity for making errors" has led many to disassociate beauty and truth and perhaps is why many have exiled beauty from the field of humanities.[9] Nevertheless, she attempts to redeem beauty, in part two, by refuting the political complaints that insist beauty distracts us from social injustices and even leads us to prolonged stares and gazes that are degrading and

---

4. Ibid., 8–15, 18–23.
5. Ibid., 11, 27.
6. Ibid., 11, 25, 27.
7. Scarry, *On Beauty and Being Just*.
8. Ibid., 52.
9. Ibid., 31, 52–57.

destructive. In the end, Scarry argues that our experience of beauty "radically decenters" us, turning our attention to correct injustices.[10]

Nicholas Wolterstorff, in an essay presented to the National Lilly Fellows Conference in Seattle entitled "Beauty and Justice," critiques Scarry's notion of beauty and how she relates it to justice.[11] He rightly surmises that Scarry's conception of beauty as "unity, equality, and symmetry" echoes the Romantic ideals of a bygone era that championed the "inherent salvific power" of art to reshape society. Such notions, Wolterstorff contends, "are patently false" because of the numerous instances of those who may very well be enamored with beauty but have little regard for justice, not unlike "the Germans who supervised the concentration camps during the day [and] attended concerts during the evening and expanded their art collections with paintings plundered from the occupied countries."[12]

Scarry may very well be on to something, though, in that she has brought beauty into the conversation, forcefully arguing that it is somehow bound up with truth and justice. Wolterstorff seems to concur, although he does not accept the analogies that Scarry sees between beauty and justice. Instead, beauty and justice are "two modes of acknowledging worth, two modes of acknowledging excellence."[13] Nevertheless, both seem to recognize some version of objective realism in which beauty and justice are connected. That being the case, if we are to link orthodoxy and orthopraxy it seems that beauty has a role to play as Graham Ward suggests when he reasons for "the inseparability of a Christian aesthetics from a Christian epistemology, and both from a theological ethics."[14] Yet, what do we mean by theological aesthetics, and how might we incorporate the notion of God's beauty into our theological discourse, particularly given its supposed exilic status?

Ludwig Wittgenstein, in his *Notebooks, 1914–1916*, makes an astute observation regarding the relationship between art and ethics: "The work of art is the object seen *sub specie aeternitatis*; and the good life is the world seen *sub specie aeternitatis*. This is the connection between art and ethics."[15]

---

10. Ibid., 58, 109–24.

11. I am grateful to Joice Pang for providing me with a copy of Wolterstorff's lecture.

12. Wolterstorff, "Beauty and Justice," 6.

13. Ibid., 19.

14. Ward, "Beauty of God," 64.

15. Wittgenstein, *Notebooks, 1914–1916*, 82. Commenting on a previous draft, I am grateful to Kevin Vanhoozer who reminded me of this quotation.

Preface

In other words, Wittgenstein connects aesthetics and ethics through the lens of eternity, similar to Scarry's acknowledgement when she says, "what is beautiful is in league with what is true because truth abides in the immortal sphere."[16] Herein lie the rudiments for addressing the relationship between orthodoxy and orthopraxy—the Way of incarnate Beauty—a way that has received much scrutiny and disdain, particularly in Protestant theology.

Although the burgeoning discipline of theological aesthetics has emerged over the last three decades where beauty appears to be awakening from its slumber, a reticence to integrate God's beauty into Protestant theological discourse still persists. This reticence seems to stem, in part, from fears that associate beauty with human *eros* and with the seduction of humanity into an ornamental and innocuous pleasant or into some ethereal reality in an effort to escape the bane and pain of human existence. Yet, I wonder if we can afford *not* to speak of beauty and continue to perpetuate this gap in our knowledge of God as Karl Barth suggests.[17] In my estimation, greater danger lies in omitting beauty from our theological discourse, furthering the bifurcation between theology and life and diminishing Christian worship, witness, and wisdom.

This book, based on my doctoral dissertation, seeks to contribute to this ongoing renaissance in theological aesthetics that strives to answer Karl Barth's charge, not by merely delineating God's beauty as some have done but by explicating the interconnectedness of his beauty with human action and flourishing to address, in part, this supposed bifurcation between theology and life. To do so, I offer a trinitarian account of God's beauty noting particularly how it artfully renews human imagining, which is essential not only for human being but also for creative expression and ethical action. The key idea, God's beauty-in-act, is understood through the risen Christ's actions in the Spirit by following a biblical trajectory found in the pattern of the Suffering Servant motif in the Old Testament and Christ's death and resurrection in the New. Hence, we see God's beauty-in-act radiating the splendor of God's multifaceted, self-giving, dynamic love that draws perceivers into these divine patterns of living and being. These fitting movements of the risen Christ in the Spirit serve as the patterns that educate and form the imaginations of properly perceiving

---

16. Scarry, *On Beauty and Being Just*, 31. Scarry maintains, though, that acquiescing to "the existence of an immortal realm" is not necessary because beauty's enthralling self-showing "incites in us the longing for truth" as it "brings us into contact with our own capacity for making errors" (ibid.).

17. Barth, *CD* 2/1, 651–52.

subjects, enabling them to envision their role and to perform their parts creatively and fittingly in God's drama of redemption. In doing so, human beings flourish as they jettison false identities and realities of their own making that are incommensurate with God's purpose found in Christ by the Spirit.

Acknowledgments

WHILE WORKING ON THIS PROJECT, I WAS FORTUNATE TO HAVE WITNESSED and experienced several fitting performances, which I must acknowledge, in the midst of a variety of difficult circumstances that almost eclipsed this project's completion. Like many, I stretched myself to the limits, probing the boundaries of my finitude and falling exhausted in my efforts to maintain a work-life balance while raising a family, writing full-time, and working part-time as an engineer. Throughout the process, Balthasar's remarks reverberated in my mind: "It is not possible to make a clean break between [writing and living]."[18] So, writing and living and living and writing never seemed to separate as various themes of this project surfaced in my life and my life surfaced in various aspects of this project. Fortunately, I was a part of several supportive communities that provided council and encouragement along the way, without which I would not have been able to complete this work.

The value and importance of living in community with the people of God has no greater voice than Willem VanGemeren, whose pastoral and scholarly wisdom brought comfort on more than one occasion, both in private and in public. I owe him a debt of gratitude for his insistence that we live in community and not attempt to walk this academic path alone. His words would often be the impetus for making sure I stayed connected with my peers even when I was no longer living in the Chicagoland area. I owe much to the doctoral community at Trinity Evangelical Divinity School for my spiritual and academic formation. Another important member of my community to whom I extend my sincerest appreciation is Graham Cole, whose sharp intellect and apt ability to ask just the right question often stimulated my thinking beyond the classroom. His writings on the Holy Spirit and research on religious experience have left an indelible impression as this book shows. And to Ben Mitchell, who gave more of his time than I am sure he had to give to listen to and counsel with me on numerous ecclesial matters. His familiar face while we were at Oxford, for the briefest of times, brought the assurance of conviction as I wrestled

---

18. Balthasar, *My Work*, 17.

Acknowledgments

with various doctrinal matters, learning better to extend grace than "be right." Many thanks as well to Fr. Francis Caponi who graciously provided insightful and instructive comments on my interpretations of relational theism and Hans Urs von Balthasar while preparing the manuscript for publication.

To my *Doktorvater*, Kevin Vanhoozer, I am grateful for and shaped by his modeling of the intellectual virtues as he patiently and wisely guided me through this process. His concern, prayers, words of encouragement, and constructive criticisms were always fitting. His influence on my life extends beyond the classroom and this project, as his family—Sylvie, Mary, and Emma—has shaped mine, giving us a sense of what it looks like to live with a Gospel-formed imagination.

Particular mention must be made of the care rendered by two churches: Christ Church, Lake Forest and Tabernacle Baptist Church. Christ Church loved my family immeasurably and shared life's burdens with us while we were at Trinity. We are grateful for the lasting friendships and the continuing community. To Tabernacle Baptist Church who welcomed a stranger into their midst by providing a quiet and spacious place to write and keep my research. I would not have been able to complete this book without these provisions.

Para mi familia—I use the Spanish language because of the cultural implications associated with the importance of family within the Hispanic community, from which my childhood was formed. There is little doubt that I would have finished if it were not for the Henry and Garrett families. While having their support throughout, both families came along side of my family particularly during the writing phase that gave me the freedom to devote my energies to writing without having to worry about the necessary essentials for living. To my aunt, Anna Melton, whose generosity still never ceases to amaze as she took an abiding interest in my work, praying and encouraging until the end.

To my wife Rebecca, who has faced and continues to deal with some of life's chronic afflictions, I know of no other person I would rather share this life with than her. Her constant encouragement, loveable sense of humor, and insistence on having tea while reading poetry kept our hearts knit together, for which I am immensely grateful. And to my son, Owen, whose love for life, endless questions, and colorful artwork that adorns my office always brings joy. Such are the reasons why I dedicate this book to all of them.

Acknowledgments

I have endeavored to make sense out of the practical shapes of words by fashioning them in such a way to explore a particular aspect of the frameworks and structures of meaning within which we live and understand our everyday experiences. I hope to have communicated in a way that is clear, relevant, and meaningful for graduate students interested in dissolving the supposed bifurcation between theology and life and for academic specialists interested in the inter-relatedness of the doctrine of God, theological aesthetics, and theological ethics. I, and I alone, am fully responsible for the errors and misjudgments that arise within this work. My desire is that this book honors the triune God, be of some service to followers of Christ, and to those in the public square interested in contemplating the implications of God's beauty for human flourishing.

Abbreviations

CD	*Church Dogmatics*
GL	*Glory of the Lord*
KB	*Theology of Karl Barth*
NIDNT	*New International Dictionary of New Testament Theology*
NIDOTT	*New International Dictionary of Old Testament Theology*
ST	*Summa teologica*
TD	*Theo-Drama*
TDNT	*Theological Dictionary of the New Testament*
TL	*Theo-Logic*

Introduction

The Scandalous Cross?

Does the cross of Christ, construed as an instrument of suffering and torture, present a dilemma for classical theism? Contemporary theologians like Jürgen Moltmann, Wolfhart Pannenberg, Catherine Mowry LaCugna, and others believe that it does. They contend that classical theism creates a metaphysical gap between who God reveals himself to be *ad extra* in Christ as the One who suffers on our behalf and who he really is *in se* as the infinitely perfect being untouched or unmoved by such suffering. Such commitments, they contend, render the Gospel impotent in a modern world. With all the suffering and turmoil of the twentieth century in mind, these theologians wonder how a loving God cannot suffer *ad intra* with his creation, freely limiting his sovereignty to be immanently present with them. Inherent within this question are concerns to safeguard God's love, which is rooted in a relational ontology, and to present God as one who cares for his creation. Why, though, do these "relational theists" attempt to levy such damning charges against classical theism?

The Scandalous Cross: Relational Theism's Assessment of Classical Theism

Many relational theists have noble apologetic concerns regarding Christianity's place in the modern world. During the latter part of the nineteenth and early twentieth centuries, when modern science was flourishing and the world had suffered two world wars, God was declared dead while others sought the historical Jesus. In a postwar era fueled by historical critical methods of biblical interpretation, theologians questioned the classical understanding of God because of its inability to address the contemporary problems of the modern era. The Western church and her classical theism "faced a growing crisis of relevance and credibility," Moltmann remarks.[1] This crisis of relevance, according to Moltmann, is due to the church's inability to reform itself and respond to modern concerns because the church "simply continued its previous form and ideology, [which] was in the process of losing contact with the scientific, social, and political reality of the world around it, and in many respects had already lost it."[2] The modern Western church's obstinate adherence to classical theism, relational theists contend, guarantees Christian theology's irrelevance in the world and the church. They assert that nothing less than the Gospel, with its socio-political and economic implications, is at stake in this growing crisis. Something must be done in its defense.

Classical Theism Defined According to Its Critics

A summary description of relational theism's understanding of classical theism is important to articulate before detailing their apologetics for Christianity. Relational theists depict classical theism as conceiving first of God's oneness and then of his threeness. Such a starting point allows classical theism to argue not only for divine unity but also for the rational existence of God. In doing so, God is a single unified substance, a single unified subject. Conceiving of God in this manner, Christianity at its earliest stages was able to import Greek philosophical concepts like, infinity, immortality, immutability, and impassibility, ". . . certain characteristics of the cosmos, and these are marked by negation. That is the *via negativa*."[3] Most notably, the Greek mind prized the immutability of God absent any form of human passion, from which God's impassibility, "the doctrine that God being perfect, nothing can affect the divine nature," was derived.[4]

---

1. Moltmann, *Crucified God*, 8.

2. Ibid. See Moltmann's extended discussion regarding the Western church's irrelevance, "Identity and Relevance of the Faith," 7–29.

3. Moltmann, *Trinity and the Kingdom*, 11. Moltmann offers a succinct description of the development of classical theism, arguing that it has its roots in early patristic thought, which is rooted in Hellenistic philosophy (10-20). Huw P. Owen, a modern proponent of classical theism, seems to concur with relational theism's definition: "belief in one God, the Creator who is infinite, self-existent, incorporeal, eternal, immutable, impassible, simple, perfect, omniscient and omnipresent" (*Concepts of Deity*, 1).

4. Owen, "Does God Suffer?," 177. Although not a proponent of relational theism, Graham Cole, an evangelical Anglican, agrees with relational theism's assessment in his article, "Towards a New Metaphysic of the Exodus," 75–84 where he attributes classical theism's metaphysical underpinnings to Platonic and Aristotelian ideas that climax in two streams of the Christian tradition—Augustine and Aquinas. What is at

These brief statements encapsulate the perspective of relational theists regarding classical theism and its roots in classical Greek philosophy. These are the ideas, relational theists contend, that are smuggled into the Christian tradition through Augustine, Anselm, and Aquinas, evidenced most notably in the doctrine of impassibility. Consequently, relational theists cite classical theism as the culprit for Christianity's contemporary identity crisis and lack of relevance in a pluralistic world.

Relational Theism's Critique of Classical Theism

Relational theologians who identify with the concerns of Christianity's irrelevance in the modern era embark upon a theological project that first identifies when the church's theology "fell from grace" and then proceeds to a theological solution that attempts to avoid these historical pitfalls while addressing the concerns of modern society. This project, according to Wolfhart Pannenberg, begins with Albert Ritschl and has as its goal "to purify [Christian theology] from the various metaphysical influences that the so-called Hellenization of Christianity had on the Christian doctrines of God, world, and humanity."[5]

Historically, the argument begins by suggesting that the starting point of the Church Fathers, *una substantia*, is problematic as well as the division between *De Deo uno* and *De Deo trino*. Consequently, "if the real God is known as one, the tacking on of his threeness simply appears as an unnecessary complicating of the simple belief in God," as Colin Gunton surmises.[6] Moltmann, for example, contends that Augustine's and Aquinas's belief in the one supreme subject and single divine substance as the necessary supposition to the three divine persons allows both to import Greek notions of divinity, identifying the divine as "one, necessary, immovable, infinite, unconditional, immortal, and impassible."[7] Moltmann identifies further evidence of this in theological textbooks, both Catholic and Protestant, that divide the doctrine of God, first, into a treatment on *De Deo uno* and then on *De Deo trino*, particularly Aquinas. In doing so, natural theology with its cosmological proofs takes precedent over divine revelation, thereby establishing a generic structure into which one pours

---

stake in this discussion is what these terms mean and how they function within the doctrine of God, particularly during the patristic and modern eras.

5. Pannenberg, *Metaphysics and the Idea of God*, 3.
6. Gunton, *Promise of Trinitarian Theology*, 3.
7. Moltmann, *Trinity and the Kingdom*, 10–19.

divine revelation; yet, divine revelation has no influence on that structure. By allowing divine unity to precede divine threeness, salvation history is deemed irrelevant, Moltmann maintains, leading to "the disintegration of the doctrine of the Trinity in abstract monotheism."[8]

LaCugna also argues that the artificial distinction between the ontological and the economic Trinity adhered to by classical theism detracts from the Gospel. The quintessential doctrine that demonstrates this artificiality is the doctrine of impassibility. While criticizing the mysticism of the Cappadocians regarding God's ineffability, LaCugna remarks, "How could the immutable, impassible God become incarnate and suffer in Christ? [This] God could not." How did the Cappadocians come to this conclusion? LaCugna answers, "Greek patristic theology took over from Greek philosophy the classical divine attributes . . . and applied them to the God incarnate in Christ," thereby denying any real suffering in the Logos and asserting that Christ suffers in his humanity, not in his divinity. She concludes that this decision to preserve both divine impassibility *and* the Nicene dogma of *homoousios* contributes to the demise of the Trinity and allows "the attributes of God taken from philosophy to remain intact, rather at odds with the living God of the Bible."[9] How do relational theists attempt to address the irrelevance of trinitarian theology as well as this supposed metaphysical gap between who God is *in se* and who he is *ad extra*?

Solving Christian Theology's Crisis of Relevance

Each relational theist mentioned has a unique contribution to this question, yet all seem to follow the same general approach—*De Deo uno* is derived from *De Deo trino*. In other words, as Moltmann says, "We are beginning with the trinity of the Persons and shall then go on to ask about the unity."[10] The formal principle for this approach to God's nature is Rahner's rule: "The economic Trinity is the immanent Trinity, and *vice versa*."[11] Although each nuances Rahner's Rule and departs from it in

---

8. Ibid., 17. See also LaCugna's *God for Us*, 21–205, and her article "Relational God," 647–63; Pannenberg's *Systematic Theology*, I.280–327 and his article "Father, Son, and Spirit," 250–57; Gunton's *Promise of Trinitarian Theology*, 30–55 and his article "Augustine, The Trinity, and the Theological Crisis of the West," 33–58; and Rahner's *Trinity*, 17–19, 115–20.

9. LaCugna, *God For Us*, 300–301. See also Moltmann, *Crucified God*, 267–78.

10. Moltmann, *Trinity and the Kingdom*, 19.

11. Rahner, *Trinity*, 21. See the following selections where each of these theologians

various ways, each affirms, as LaCugna surmises, that "the God of Jesus Christ whom we come to know in the Spirit *is* the eternal, free, absolutely mysterious God who exists as the mystery of love and communion."[12] In doing so, there is no *deus absconditus* lurking behind the *deus revelatus* as there is in classical theism.

Moltmann builds upon Rahner's Rule by attempting to develop a social doctrine of the Trinity. He reasons that "we understand the scriptures as the testimony to the history of the Trinity's relations of fellowship, which are open to men and women, and open to the world. This trinitarian hermeneutic leads us to think in terms of relationships and communities."[13] Two assumptions buttress this move toward a relational ontology. First, the flow of redemptive history becomes *constitutive* of God's being when relational theists employ Rahner's "vice versa" to equate the economic and the immanent Trinity. Moltmann argues that "the economic Trinity not only reveals the immanent Trinity; it also has a *retroactive effect on it*," which is why "the meaning of the cross of the Son on Golgatha reaches right into the heart of the immanent Trinity."[14] Thus, God's being is in his *becoming* and is constituted by relations—relations to himself and to the world.

---

subscribes to Rahner's Rule yet offer various nuances: Moltmann, *Trinity and the Kingdom*, 144–48, 160; LaCugna, *God For Us*, 209–41; and Pannenberg, *Systematic Theology*, I.327–36. It is important to note that, although, Rahner's Rule is the formal principle relational theists use to address their reservations about classical theism, Barth's emphasis on God's triunity appears to be the material principle as relational theists rightly seek to recover a trinitarian understanding of God (See Grenz, *Rediscovering the Triune God*, 33–162).

12. LaCugna, *God For Us*, 211.

13. Moltmann, *Trinity and the Kingdom*, 19. See also LaCugna, "Re-Conceiving the Trinity as the Mystery of Salvation," 1–23 and LaCugna, "Returning From 'The Far Country,'" 191–215.

14. Moltmann, *Trinity and the Kingdom*, 159–60. Emphasis added. Pannenberg also remarks, "Today we see that differentiating the eternal Trinity from all temporal change makes trinitarian theology one-sided and detaches it from its biblical basis. This situation obviously calls for revision." What revision does he have in mind? He suggests that "viewing the immanent and the economic Trinity as one presupposes the development of the concept of God which can grasp . . . the eternal self-identity of God . . . in the process of history, along with the decision made concerning it by the consummation of history" (Pannenberg, *Systematic Theology*, I.333). Similarly, Robert Jenson brings temporality back into the Godhead, making redemptive history constitutive of God's being and asserting that God in his fullness will not come until the eschaton with the consummation of all things, including God himself (Jenson, *Triune God*, 207–23).

Second, these relations presume that God's eternal nature is love, a self-giving love, and is thus God with and for us. As Moltmann observes, "If we follow through the idea that the historical passion of Christ reveals the eternal passion of God, then the self-sacrifice of love is God's eternal nature."[15] God's love is not self-absorbed or arrogant but is teeming and abundant, seeking communion with all his creation. This kind of love makes God vulnerable to and capable of suffering because "God, as perfect love, is at the same time perfectly selfless, he loves himself in the most extreme and complete self-forsakenness. God lays God open for his future."[16]

LaCugna takes this kind of love a step further by insinuating that God is not God unless he is with us in the economy of redemption: "Revealed there is the unfathomable mystery that the life and communion of the divine persons is not 'intradivine;'" rather, God is "... overflowing love, outreaching desire for union with all that God has made. The communion of the divine life is God's communion *with us* in Christ and as Spirit."[17] The essence of God is fundamentally linked, then, to his relationship with creation. The turn toward relationality that dominates current trinitarian theological discourse can be attributed, in part, to how relational theists use Rahner's Rule and their methodology, which conceives of God by moving from three persons to divine unity.[18]

Challenges to the Solution Offered by Relational Theism

There is a growing body of literature, though, that challenges the assumptions, methods, and conclusions of relational theism, proceeding generally along historical and theological lines. Historically, patristic scholars like Lewis Ayres, Fergus Kerr, and Paul Gavrilyuk contest the theory of "Theology's Fall into Hellenistic Philosophy" by demonstrating that Hellenistic philosophy did not consist of a unified notion of divinity characterized as one, infinite, impassible, removed, and unemotional, but rather was an eclectic, often conflicting, array of conceptions. To say otherwise creates a false dilemma and produces a convenient caricature as an antagonist for relational theism's theological reconstruction.[19] Theologically, schol-

---

15. Moltmann, *Trinity and the Kingdom*, 32. See also Moltmann, "Passion of Christ and the Suffering of God," 19–28.

16. Moltmann, *Trinity and the Kingdom*, 33.

17. LaCugna, *God For Us*, 15 and LaCugna, "Relational God," 647–63.

18. Grenz, describes the current discussion in trinitarian theology as "The Triumph of Relationality" (*Rediscovering the Triune God*, 117–62).

19. Gavrilyuk, *Suffering of the Impassible God*, 21–46. Patristic scholars Kearsley,

Introduction: The Scandalous Cross?

ars like Paul Molnar, John Cooper, and Ted Peters contend that relational theism domesticates God by blurring or eliminating the Creator-creature distinction.[20] Such notions seem to subscribe to pantheistic or panentheistic conceptions of God, which make God dependent upon his creation, compromising his divine freedom and making God in our own image.[21]

What seems to be uncontested, however, is relational theism's assessment of the current irrelevance of the Trinity. The Trinity does seem to have little bearing on Protestant theology, particularly the doctrine of God, and the Christian life; yet, it is essential to the Gospel. If this assessment is correct regarding the Trinity's irrelevance and these recent critiques are enough to cause concern regarding relational theism's project, what might be the culprit for this current trinitarian crisis of irrelevance?

The answer is complex and should be nuanced with the appropriate developments regarding the contemporary trends toward the atomization of knowledge, individualism, the supposed superiority of human reason, the emphasis on pragmatism, and the relativistic nature of truth, yet it is beyond the scope of this project to do so. The answer to this question, in part, can be found, ironically, in the writings of these same relational theists. Moltmann and Pannenberg, for example, cite René Descartes as one who furthers and expands the classical theism they oppose, yet they persist in faulting Augustine, Anselm, and Aquinas for this current situation.

Taking my cue from these relational theists, there seems to be more of Enlightenment deism, and specifically perfect being theology, in their

---

"Impact of Greek Concepts of God on the Christology of Cyril of Alexandria," 307–29 and Rowe, "Adolf von Harnack and the Concept of Hellenization," 69–98 attempt to refute Harnack's theory of "Theology's Fall into Hellenistic Philosophy." Kerr in *After Aquinas*, Ayres in *Nicaea and Its Legacy*, Dodaro and Lawless in *Augustine and His Critics*, Pecknold in "How Augustine Used the Trinity," 127–41, Barnes in "Augustine in Contemporary Trinitarian Theology," 237–50, and Charry in "The Soteriological Importance of the Divine Perfections," 129–47 also contest Greek philosophy's induction into Christian theology via Augustine, Anselm, and Aquinas.

20. See Torrance, *Christian Doctrine of God*; Powell, *Trinity in German Thought*; Cooper, *Panentheism*; Placher, *Domestication of Transcendence*; Molnar, *Divine Freedom and the Doctrine of the Immanent Trinity*; and Vanhoozer, *Remythologizing Theology*.

21. Moltmann and Pannenberg desire to retain some form of the Creator-creature distinction, yet critics see more panentheistic tendencies and tritheism in their work. LaCugna's approach places God closer to his creation, further blurring the Creator-creature distinction to the point that some charge her with pantheism and with reducing God to human experience. See Ted Peters, *God as Trinity*; Gunton, "Review of *God For Us*," 136–37; Finan, "Review Symposium: *God For Us*," 134–35; and Muller, "Science of Theology," 311–41 (I am grateful to Fr. Francis Caponi for drawing my attention to Muller's perceptive review of LaCugna).

understanding of classical theism, rather than Hellenistic philosophy. What I am suggesting is that Descartes and the tradition of perfect being theology, with its notions of perfection, transcendence, and the infinite, *reconstructs* the classical understanding of God. It is this understanding that relational theists *read back into* the Christian tradition, creating a false dilemma between classical theism and the living God of the Bible.[22] What Gavrilyuk only suggests in saying that "enlightenment deism should not be read into the philosophical climate of late antiquity,"[23] I attempt to make clear in the next section.

Golgotha: Perfect Being Theology as the Foil of Relational Theists

Golgotha, for Moltmann, is the essential point in redemptive history that reveals "the eternal heart of the Trinity" and "is the inescapable revelation of [God's] nature in a world of evil and suffering," which is why, he believes, the cross becomes a scandal for classical theism.[24] Perhaps, though, Golgotha continues to be a scandal, but for relational rather than classical theism, since relational theists conflate perfect being theology with classical theism and trade one notion of perfection (i.e., a transcendental ontology) for another (i.e., relational ontology). Does talk of God's unity *first* necessarily lead, then, to depicting God as static, unemotional, etc. as purported by relational theists?

Ens Perfectissimum: *What Is Perfect Being Theology or What Makes God, God?*

Operative among the assumptions of relational theists is the notion that classical theism is "perfect being theology" and *vice versa*. Perfect being theology defines God *first* as a being of infinite perfections and then

---

22. This may be one of the reasons why more work has been done on the doctrine of God by philosophical theologians than systematic or dogmatic theologians. See Sanders's article "State of the Doctrine of the Trinity in Evangelical Theology," 153–75.

23. Gavrilyuk, *Suffering of the Impassible God*, 35. Placher also argues that 17th century theological discourse on divine transcendence so influenced contemporary theology that many have misconstrued the classical theism of Aquinas, Luther, and Calvin (*Domestication of Transcendence*, 1–20). For an incisive example of philosophers reading Aquinas through the lens of Descartes's modern ontology, see Franks, "The Simplicity of the Living God," 275–300.

24. Moltmann, *Trinity and the Kingdom*, 31–32.

considers how these perfections manifest themselves in his interactions with the world. Perfect being theology has a storied and convoluted history that is often assumed to be synonymous with classical theism yet as recent scholarship has shown the two are rather dissimilar.[25] Whither then did perfect being theology arise?

Anselm is often cited as a source of perfect being theology because of his maxim regarding the nature of God: "We believe that you are a being than which nothing greater can be conceived." Typically, Anselm's ontological argument is perceived to prove—heard with a modern ear—God's existence with "analytic precision" to the unbelieving. Yet, Anselm, at the outset of *Proslogion*, acknowledges humanity's inability to understand God apart from divine revelation and presupposes that one has faith before understanding.[26] His argument intends, as Philip Clayton notes, "to lift this obvious truth to the status of a rational, even necessary, inference." Why Anselm's intentions are later misconstrued by moderns, Clayton rightly observes, is due to the "secularization of society and the methodological atheism of the natural sciences," for it was "only after the immediacy of the intuition that God exists had become questionable did the arguments' inability to produce such intuitions become obvious."[27] Anselm, when read in context, yields his understanding of God to divine revelation rather than beginning with some *a priori* notion of perfection. His conceptual use of the "most perfect being" seems to function differently from the Enlightenment thinkers of five centuries later.

Turning now to Descartes, as a representative progenitor of perfect being theology, we find that he conceives of God by first beginning with the finite and then proceeding to the infinite. In his *Meditations*, Descartes acknowledges his finitude and thus his inability to grasp the infinite; yet the only way he can perceive of such an idea is by way of negation: "I do not perceive the infinite by a true idea, but only by the negation of the finite." Furthermore, he connects infinity and perfection with the very idea of God: "I understand God to be actually infinite, so that He can add nothing to His supreme perfection, . . . for we can imagine nothing more perfect than God, or even as perfect as He is." He identifies God further as "a substance that is infinite, eternal, immutable, independent, all-knowing,

---

25. See Richard Muller's article, "Incarnation, Immutability, and the Case for Classical Theism," 22–40 for further evidence of this dissimilarity and the refutation of Harnack's thesis.

26. Anselm, *New Interpretive Translation of St. Anselm's Monologion and Proslogion*, 221–27.

27. Clayton, *Problem of God in Modern Thought*, 263–64.

all-powerful, and by which I myself and everything else, if anything else does exist, have been created."[28]

Clayton concurs that Descartes should be a common reference point for the modern discipline of perfect being theology because Descartes's theology intertwines premodern notions of divine infinity and perfection, which is known today as "ontotheology."[29] The thrust, then, of perfect being theology is on the "systematic analysis of the divine attributes beginning with the concept of God as limitless perfection,"[30] thereby conceiving God by maximizing, negating, or reasoning from human conceptualities rather than beginning with God's particular revelation.[31]

Relational Theism and Perfect Being Theology

If we examine relational theism's description of classical theism in the previous section, we find notions of perfect being theology imbedded within their depiction, suggesting they have read classical theism in light of perfect being theology. Taking a closer look at Moltmann and Pannenberg, we find that both actually identify Descartes as the one who "succeeds in equating the idea of the infinite as such with the traditional concept of God" because of Descartes's notion that "our views of finite objects are formed by limitation of the infinite."[32] Yet, in my estimation, both underestimate the influence of Descartes's theology and theological method on subsequent generations, which at best intertwines aspects of perfect being

---

28. Descartes, *Meditations on First Philosophy*, 23.

29. Clayton, *Problem of God in Modern Thought*, xii, 51–116. See Clayton's extended discussion on the development of the modern discipline of perfect being theology that begins with the premodern ideas of divine infinity and perfection that come together in Descartes (117–82) and culminate in Leibniz (183–262). Ingraffia, "Deconstructing the Tower of Babel," 284–306 also attributes the roots of ontotheology to Descartes and the rationalist tradition, citing Kant as the first to label this trajectory "ontotheology."

30. Rogers, *Perfect Being Theology*, 4.

31. Vanhoozer, *Remythologizing Theology*, 94–98 furthers the discussion by distinguishing between an Anselmian and Cartesian ontotheology and by their *use* of the concept of the most perfect being. He contends that Anselm's theological project is a *ministerial* use of the concept because he submits his conception of God to the canonical judgments of Scripture whereas Descartes's *magisterial* use is controlled by *a priori* notions of perfection.

32. Pannenberg, *Systematic Theology*, I.350. See also Pannenberg, *Systematic Theology*, I.82–95, 350–59 and Moltmann, *Trinity and the Kingdom*, 13–16.

theology with the Gospel and at worst conceives of God apart from divine revelation all together.

Instrumental in this assertion is an examination of relational theism's insistence that theology *must* begin with God's threeness *before* discussing his oneness, otherwise theology will degenerate into the distant, uninvolved, unemotional, removed God of "classical theism" (read here perfect being theology). Must this be the case? Aquinas is often cited for severing *De Deo uno* from *De Deo trino* because of how he orders them in his *Summa*.[33] Examining Aquinas's idea of persons as derived from relations elucidates how Aquinas understands *De Deo uno* in light of *De Deo trino*. In question twenty-seven, Aquinas asks what we can know of "what belongs to the Trinity of the persons in God." He answers that we can know about the divine processions of *generatio* and *spiratio* on the basis of redemptive history, which demonstrates that Aquinas does *not* divorce talk of the Trinity from the economy.[34]

God's oneness and threeness are intimately connected in Aquinas and Augustine for that matter, suggesting that beginning with God's oneness does not *necessarily* lead to the dire outcomes suggested by relational theism. Descartes dissolves the relationship between *De Deo uno* and *De Deo trino*, though, by wedding notions of the infinite and the perfect with the one God, irrespective of God's threeness, proffering the kind of God relational theism adamantly and rightfully opposes.

Relational theism's turn to and championing of a relational ontology, though, has led critics to conclude that the current consensus is no more than "a 'kinder-gentler' substantionalist metaphysics."[35] In fact, John Cooper suggests that relational theism has exchanged one god of the philosophers for "the other god of the philosophers," arguing that the ancient philosophy of panentheism governs much of contemporary theology.[36] In my estimation, relational theism wrangles with one notion of perfect being theology while adopting another. God is still a maximally perfect

---

33. Aquinas, *ST*, I.1–26, I.27–43; See Rahner, *Trinity*, 15–17; LaCugna, *God For Us*, 145; LaCugna, "Relational God," 647–63 as examples of this accusation.

34. Aquinas, *ST*, Ia. 27. See also Cunningham, "Participation as a Trinitarian Virtue," 20–23 and Benner, "Augustine and Karl Rahner on the Relationship between the Immanent Trinity and the Economic Trinity," 24–38 where both argue that Augustine and Aquinas are not guilty of dividing *De Deo uno* from *De Deo trino* as Rahner and relational theists like Moltmann, Pannenberg, and LaCugna maintain.

35. Cunningham, "Participation as a Trinitarian Virtue," 9.

36. Cooper, *Panentheism*, 13–30, 237–318. See also Brierley, "Naming a Quiet Revolution," 1–18 and Tracy, *On Naming the Present*, 36–46.

being, just a perfectly related being rather than a static one. In doing so, relational theism's understanding of love and relationality are akin to human conceptualities rather than God's self-revelation. The antagonist of relational theism seems to be the perfect being theology stemming from Descartes and Enlightenment theology that unifies premodern notions of divine infinity and perfection, severs God's oneness from his threeness, and thus portrays God as distant, uninvolved, and unemotional.[37]

It can be problematic, then, to begin with threeness and move to oneness and problematic to move from oneness to threeness, but it is not necessary to begin with either so long as the two are not separated and divine revelation remains normative for understanding God's identity and life. Stanley Grenz, along with others, makes an important distinction: the *ordo essendi* and *ordo cognoscendi*.[38] God is who he is eternally, yet our understanding of the eternal and living God comes by divine revelation attested to in Holy Scripture. In short, the order of being *precedes* the order of our knowing. What perhaps are some of the implications for insisting we begin with either God's oneness or his threeness?

Making God in Our Own Image: Why Perfect Being Theology Is a Problem

If perfect being theology conceptualizes God by maximizing, negating, or reasoning from human conceptualities rather than beginning with God's particular revelation, then Ludwig Feuerbach's critique seems applicable. Feuerbach, in his *Essence of Christianity*, argues for the elimination of God-talk since our understanding of God is nothing more than the projection

---

37. Part of the confusion within contemporary theology may be in fact that several who defend perfect being theology, like philosophical theologian Katherin Rogers, link their approach to the Christian tradition and claim to be classical theists. Rogers's book, for example, which defends perfect being theology, bears no mention of the Trinity. Philosophers of religion, like Eleonore Stump and Norman Kretzmann, contribute to the confusion too as they claim to follow Aquinas when arguing for divine simplicity irrespective of Aquinas's commitments to the Creator-creature distinction, the Incarnation, and the doctrine of the Trinity as Franks documents in his article, "Simplicity of the Living God," 282–284 (cf. Holmes, "'Something Much Too Plain to Say,'" 137–54 and Kerr, *After Aquinas*, 35–51, 73–96). This is not to say, though, that philosophical theology is a bankrupt endeavor. On the contrary, I concur with LaCugna that analytic philosophers and theologians have *much* to say to each other ("Philosophers and Theologians on the Trinity," 169–81; cf. McCall, *Whose Trinity? Which Monotheism?*).

38. See Grenz, *Rediscovering the Triune God*, 196.

Introduction: The Scandalous Cross?

of our human conceptions. Commenting specifically on ontotheology, he says, "'we cannot conceive God otherwise than by attributing to him without limit all the real qualities which we find in ourselves.'" Feuerbach further asserts that "our positive, essential qualities, our realities, are therefore the realities of God, but in us they exist with, in God without, limits."[39] Further evidence of Feuerbach's critique among perfect being theologians is the lack of consensus regarding what a perfect being is: "Inconsistencies have been alleged between almost all the 'perfect-making properties,' even by perfect-being theologians."[40] If Feuerbach is correct, then theology is nothing more than anthropology—post-Enlightenment idolatry.[41] How can *this* God bear the suffering of twenty-first-century humanity, much less rise from the dead?

Some contemporary conceptions of perfect being theology also seem to require a kind of scientific precision for their theological discourse that arranges a set of propositions into a particular system, what David Tracy sees as "a series of seemingly endless debates on . . . the correct set of abstract propositions which name and think God."[42] This requirement for precision, although noble in its pursuit of clarity, appears to apply a modern scientific positivism akin to the precision attempted in analytic philosophy. Carl Raschke attributes such notions to a modern epistemology where "the goal of thought is to obtain a clear and precise picture of what one is viewing," in this case God.[43]

This suggests overconfidence in human reason to develop an airtight, interlocking *systematic* theology not unlike those who follow the methodology of the great Princetonian theologian Charles Hodge who considers the Bible to be "a storehouse of facts" such that theology is "the exhibition of the facts of Scripture in their proper order and relation."[44] Consequently, the perfect being theology of this sort often privileges the propositions of Scripture and principlizes other genres, eclipsing the *form* of God's communicative action, thereby distorting its meaning.[45] Such notions can lead

---

39. Feuerbach, *Essence of Christianity*, 38.
40. Clayton, *Problem of God in Modern Thought*, 134–35.
41. See Marion, *God Without Being*, 25–52.
42. Tracy, "Literary Theory and Naming God," 307.
43. Raschke, *Next Reformation*, 213.
44. Hodge, *Systematic Theology*, I.10, 19. See also Vanhoozer's essay "On the Very Idea of a Theological System," 125–82 where he analyzes and offers an alternative approach to the task and purpose of systematic theology.
45. Clark, *To Know and Love God*, 91–98.

God's Beauty-in-Act

to the domestication of God, maligning his wholly otherness.[46] Merold Westphal warns that Christian theology, particularly philosophical theology, "can easily lapse, both in appearance and in fact, into trying to make everything clear, thereby producing a God not obviously related to prayer, worship, and witness."[47]

Hans Urs von Balthasar draws a similar conclusion while suggesting a different consequence. He contends that theology, to the extent that it is enamored with the exactness of modern science, diminishes our understanding of reality, namely of being itself:

> And since the exact sciences no longer have any time to spare for [beauty] (nor does theology, in so far as it increasingly strives to follow the method of the exact sciences and to envelope itself in their atmosphere), precisely for this reason is it perhaps high time to break through this kind of exactness, which can *only pertain to one particular sector of reality*, in order to bring the truth of the whole again into view—truth as a transcendental property of Being, truth which is no abstraction, rather the living bond between God and the world.[48]

Implied in this quotation is an assumption that modern scientific methodology has the tendency to *reduce* reality to extended matter in motion governed by verifiable laws that reasons from the self, to the world, and then to God (if, in fact, God exists). Modern science and analytic philosophy assume the existence of reality without ever inquiring as to why something exists rather than nothing. To the extent that theology imbibes these suppositions and this methodology, it fails to offer a thick description of reality and ultimately of God's being.

It appears, after reflecting on the concerns of relational theists like Moltmann, Pannenberg, and LaCugna that perfect being theology has become their antagonist. Yet, is it enough to say that they have misplaced their critique and absolve classical theism of any wrongdoing, or do their concerns still resonate despite their misapplication? Perhaps these theologians are reticent towards *contemporary* conceptions of classical theism that pander to aspects of perfect being theology. It is beyond the scope of this work, though, to examine this supposition. Their concerns do appear

---

46. See Placher, *Domestication of Transcendence*, 181–82 where he articulates three troubling consequences, namely that God becomes an *"enemy of science, . . . human freedom, . . . [and] transformative justice."*

47. Westphal, "Onto-theology, Metanarrative, Perspectivism, and the Gospel," 146–47.

48. Balthasar, *GL* I, 18. Emphasis added.

to have validity, especially in light of the millions who continue to suffer today, as Christian doctrine continues to find itself on the periphery of the Christian life, not to mention humanity's common life together. Furthermore, the concern of relational theists regarding God's actuality in Christ is of supreme importance since Christ's identity turns on being God in the flesh. Finally, God's love for and relationship to his creation is also significant since the living God of Scripture does not wind up his creation, let it go, and remain uninvolved.[49]

"Radicalizing" Rahner's Rule, however, by collapsing the immanent into the economic Trinity, does not appear to be the way forward because such notions not only fashion God in our own image but also identify God's being in his becoming, making redemptive history constitutive rather than communicative of his identity.[50] Those who wed modern scientific methods to perfect being theology, whether explicitly or implicitly, possess a distorted view of reality, atomizing and fragmenting our understanding of God, the world, and ourselves. Vigorous theological debates about the true and the good ensue, but wherefore art thou beauty? *There seems to be no room for beauty, much less God's beauty, in the inn of perfect being theology.*

A Proposal

Recent discourse on the doctrine of God has seen a revival in trinitarianism, as previously mentioned. In the last three decades, discussions regarding theological aesthetics have also surged but have yet to find its place among theological discourse and praxis for a variety of reasons.[51]

---

49. If we are to recover the term classical theism, then the doctrine of the Trinity is essential to doing so, as Gerald Bray asserts: "If classical theism is meant to be equated with traditional Christian orthodoxy, then it cannot be separated from the doctrine of the Trinity, which is the key to understanding" ("Has the Christian Doctrine of God Been Corrupted by Greek Philosophy?," 109). With this in mind, Westphal's claim that Christian theology is actually more a "sustained critique of onto-theology than an instance of it" makes much more sense ("Onto-theology, Metanarrative, Perspectivism, and the Gospel," 141–56).

50. See Sanders, *Image of the Immanent Trinity*, 47–82 for a discussion on the background and origin of Rahner's Rule as well as his apt categorization of those who employ it, namely those who "radicalize" and those who "restrict."

51. Theological aesthetics is a broad and diverse discipline ranging from theological accounts of beauty and the imagination to the ever popular discussions between theology and the arts (See my entry in *Encyclopedia of Christian Civilization*, s.v. "Theological Aesthetics"). There are few accounts, though, of God's beauty as an aspect of his being within this renaissance. What seems to be lurking in these discussions is a

God's Beauty-in-Act

Theological aesthetics, at its core, acknowledges that reality consists of more than simply axiomatic propositions or relative personal experiences. Rather, beauty, as a dimension of reality, is discerned by the imagination; and by implication, it follows that logic and science themselves do not know the whole of reality.[52] How might we understand, then, the peculiar beauty of the cross in light of God's drama of redemption—the economic Trinity as the summary of the gospel—in order to address some of the concerns of relational theists regarding the contemporary irrelevance of the Trinity and the safeguarding of God's love *without* domesticating it?

The theological method of perfect being theology, which begins with human conceptualities and reasons back to an understanding of God, provides an excellent *contrast* to the theological method of this project. If we are to understand anything regarding the being of God, we must privilege his self-revelation—God's revealing of himself through himself, which presumes that God speaks (i.e., divine triune discourse)—amidst the polyphonic voices of the biblical authors.

We begin by critically appropriating Hans Urs von Balthasar's focus on Jesus Christ as the Lord of Glory (*Herrlichkeit*) and as the distinct speaking and doing form (*Gestalt*) of God's beauty, a splendorous form of divine communicative action that demands a response. Accordingly, beauty, as an aspect of God's trinitarian being, is normed by his free and compassionate act in Christ's redemptive-creative suffering and glorious resurrection for us—the nexus of God's being, beauty, and Christian living. Christ, as incarnate Beauty, elucidates the contours of God's impassible suffering by demonstrating his sovereign compassion as he triumphs over death, all befitting actions of God who loves in freedom. Therefore, I propose that beauty is the connection between theology and ethics whereby *God's beauty is the fittingness of the incarnate Son's actions in the Spirit to the Father's will. This fittingness radiates God's glory and enraptures properly perceiving subjects, transforming the imagination through the shaping power of the Spirit and drawing them to participate in God's drama of redemption.*

The peculiar beauty of the cross on this side of the resurrection reveals God's beauty-in-act, a self-giving act of love for our benefit. Such beauty reveals a compassionate and holy God who acts fittingly in accordance with who he is rather than our construal of some "maximally

---

properly theological account of God's beauty and its implications for Christian theology, although some have taken up the task as previously mentioned.

52. See Scruton, *Culture Counts*, 28–44.

Introduction: The Scandalous Cross?

perfect being." In this sense, the cross is not a dilemma for classical theism as relational theism contends. Rather, Christ's actions in the Spirit manifest the splendor of God's self-giving, triune love that transforms the imagination, engenders hope, and draws beholders out of themselves in order to participate fittingly by faith in God's drama of redemption. The Trinity is no longer irrelevant but essential to the Christian life. To the extent that the church participates fittingly in God's triune life, she radiates the beauty of God's trinitarian love to the world. Let us turn now to the structure of my argument to develop this proposal further.

Diptych Structure and the "Bargello Diptych"

The "Bargello Diptych: The Adoration of the Magi and Crucifixion" (Unknown French Master, fourteenth century) is an apt depiction of the structure of my argument and portrays in visual form the essence of Christ's glory and suffering as a way to contemplate the thrust of my proposal.[53] The left panel, with its exquisite detail and color, depicts the infant Jesus sitting in the lap of the Virgin Mary who is seated on a canopy style bed resembling a throne. At their feet are the Magi who have come from afar to worship the Christ child as they remove their crowns as a sign of honor and humility. A bright star centered and high on the left panel shines down onto the infant Jesus, indicating Christ's glory and preeminence. The right panel depicts the crucifixion of Christ, giving it prominence by placing the cross at the top-center and foreground of the panel. On the bottom left, a once jubilant Mary is now full of sorrow as she laments the suffering of her Son, evidenced by the blood spewing from his side, hands, and feet.

How can such themes of adoration, glory, sorrow, and suffering be brought together in this diptych? Is the artist's rendering an attempt to glorify suffering? Or, is there a profound wisdom expressed by contemplating these themes together? Much like poetry, we should not read visual art in a literalistic manner; to do so inhibits our understanding, as form has no bearing on content. Rather, we should consider how the various parts are understood in light of the whole, paying careful attention to the sensations evoked by the artist's use of color, light, technique, etc. This book is obviously not a piece of visual art, yet it is an attempt to think theologically

---

53. The Bargello Diptych, "The Adoration of the Magi and the Crucifixion," reproduced in Snyder, *Northern Renaissance Art*, figure 2.8, 2.9.

God's Beauty-in-Act

about an aspect of God's being by connecting various parts together within the whole of God's drama of redemption, giving form its just due.[54]

The diptych-like structure of my argument consists of two parts, the first containing two chapters and the second containing two with a conclusion. The two parts are joined together with a single chapter acting as a hinge in between. Part one, in light of the posed theological problem, attempts to locate the status of beauty and the imagination within contemporary theological discourse. In doing so, we identify several common reasons why much of contemporary theological discourse discards the rhetoric of beauty. Such actions, we come to learn, diminish Christian worship, witness, and wisdom (chapter 1). The next chapter critically appropriates Balthasar's notion of Christ as *Übergestalt* and *Herrlichkeit*, both of which become the theological loci for retrieving a theology of beauty. In the end, the place of theological aesthetics begins to emerge *between* theology and ethics (chapter 2).

The "hinge" chapter develops a relevant biblical motif through the thematic patterning of the Suffering Servant in the Old Testament. We turn to a specific instantiation of this motif in Jeremiah, analyzing his laments to Yahweh, its connection with wisdom, and his embodiment of that wisdom. We proceed to interpret theologically the nexus of μυστήριον, δόξα, σοφία, and πάθημα in Col 1–2:5 where this relevant biblical motif suggests that God's actions in Christ elucidate God's beauty as the fittingness of the incarnate Son's actions in the Spirit to the Father's will. Finally, we attempt to discern the important relationship between God's glory and his beauty (chapter 3).

Part two is the constructive proposal to the problem presented in the introduction where we conceptually expand upon the idea of God's beauty-in-act through the notion of incarnate Beauty. There we learn of Christ's redemptive-creative suffering where Christ's *redemptive* love is manifested in his obedience to the Father and the Spirit's *creative* new beginning comes at the resurrection. Next, we examine the communication of God's beauty to the world, parsing its objective, subjective, and relational components. We conclude with a brief case study appraising the

---

54. Plantinga writes an illuminating essay suggestive of the profound wisdom found in the beauty of the cross, entitled "Deep Wisdom," in *God the Holy Trinity*, 149–55. At one point he remarks, "'The hour has come for the Son of Man to be glorified,' says Jesus. How can this be? Being glorified on a cross? Is that like being enthroned on an electric chair? Is it like being honored by a firing squad? Glory in the cross of Jesus Christ sounds almost grotesque." Yet, "the Gospel wants us to find glory in this disaster, and we want to know what this mysterious glory is, and why we should see it in Jesus' terrible suffering" (151–52).

doctrine of impassibility in light of God's beauty (chapter 4). The final chapter details the implications of God's beauty-in-act for the church and the world. It is suggested that the imagination, as a viable mode of human understanding necessary for fitting action, is transformed by participating in the beauty of God's trinitarian life revealed in incarnate Beauty (2 Cor 3:18). In doing so, we manifest fitting performances in the dramatic theater of God's glory—*perfect-fit theology* (chapter 5).

This project is designed to address a contemporary problem within the doctrine of God (i.e., perfect being theology) that anesthetizes God's beauty and stifles the imagination thereby hindering people from flourishing and participating fittingly in God's drama of redemption. God's beauty is necessary to our theological discourse; to ignore the beauty of God in his triunity, as Karl Barth remarks, is to ". . . have a God without radiance and without joy (and without humor!)."[55] We turn now to understanding why most contemporary Protestant theological discourse seems so disinterested in God's beauty.

---

55. Barth, *CD* 2/1, 661.

Panel One

No Room in the Inn

Beauty as the Theological Beast?

THE CARTESIAN VARIETY OF PERFECT BEING THEOLOGY THAT CONCEIVES of God as limitless perfection by maximizing, negating, or reasoning from human conceptualities severs *De Deo uno* and *De Deo trino*, rendering God as static and aloof from or dynamic and entangled with his creation. God, on both accounts, is unable to act on our behalf, because of either his static, uninvolved nature or his self-limitation that precludes his sovereign freedom. Furthermore, contemporary notions of perfect being theology, enamored with modern scientific concerns for exactitude, seem to perpetuate a fragmented reality, leaving us to wonder whether beauty lurks in the background, lies dormant, or is lifeless. Yet, do Protestant theologians relegate beauty to the margins, limiting their understanding of reality and perhaps ignoring beauty's potential to address some of the concerns of relational theism; or, does beauty have a part to play in their theological discourse? Simply, what is beauty's status in contemporary Protestant theology?

Edward Farley assesses that beauty has a beastly reputation in a variety of contemporary disciplines, particularly aesthetic and theological ones: "Beauty has ceased to be an important notion both in discourses that interpret 'the way the world is' and in discourses that express primary human values—those of human experience, the arts, ethics, and religion."[1] Beauty is often omitted from these discourses for its association with idolatry, hedonism, elitism, an oppressive metanarrative, or vain imaginings, to name a few.[2] Is Farley's assessment, though, accurate for contemporary Protestant theology?

1. Farley, *Faith and Beauty*,1.
2. Ibid., 1–2. Note the decline of beauty in the following disciplines: aesthetics and the arts, see Beardsley, "Theories of Beauty Since the Mid-Nineteenth Century," 207–14 and Graham, *Philosophy of the Arts*; humanities, see Scary, *On Beauty and*

PANEL ONE: No Room in the Inn

Beauty has not always had such a negative connotation. Ancient and medieval thought assign beauty a prominent place in its thinking. Plato, in *The Republic* and *Symposium*, develops his metaphysical *theory of forms* of which beauty is a part. Forms are not seen with the eyes but are grasped with the intellect alone and exist in a separate reality from the empirical world. Concrete beauty possesses essential qualities without which an object cannot be beautiful—*symmetron* (symmetry) and *metron* (measure)—and has its existence through its participation in absolute beauty.[3] Aristotle, in his works *Metaphysics* and *Poetics*, disputes Plato's dualistic metaphysics and contends that form cannot be separated from matter, because the absolute is discerned through the material and not by jettisoning it. Beauty, he surmises, contains order, symmetry, and definiteness, thereby producing the most pleasure. One apprehends absolute form in the material. By doing so, Aristotle ascribes ultimate value to the material, contra Plato. Herein lies the significance of Aristotle's metaphysic.[4]

The concept of beauty is not foreign to the theologians of the early church either (e.g., Justin Martyr, Irenaeus, Origen, Basil, John Chrysostom, etc.).[5] Gregory of Nyssa describes beauty in tangible terms as the impression of form onto matter. This combination of form and matter appeals to the human senses where an amalgam of color harmoniously arranged is most beautiful.[6] Augustine's understanding of beauty has two components, objective and subjective. The objective aspect of beauty is apparent to the senses while the subjective appeals to the affections of the perceiving subject. God is the source of all truth, beauty, and goodness and is seen only by the faithful who are pure in heart.[7] Both theologians

---

Being Just, 57; analytic philosophy, see Wittgenstein, *Lectures and Conversations*, §7–9 as well as Austin, "Plea for Excuses," 183. Hart makes a similar assessment in *Beauty of the Infinite*, 1–34.

3. Plato, *Republic*, 376d–402c, 595a–608b; Plato, *Symposium* 201c–212a.

4. Aristotle, *Metaphysics*, 639b–640a, 1046a–b, 1070a–b, 1078a–b; Aristotle, *Poetics*, 1447a–1462b.

5. See Justin Martyr, *Dialogue with Trypho*, §128 and *First Apology*, §9–10; Irenaeus, *Against Heresies*, 1.25.6, 2.13.3–4, 2.32.2, 4.20.6, 5.16.1–2; Origen, *De principiis*, 1.2.4–5, 1.2.6–8; Basil, *On Psalm 29 (Homily 14)*, and *Exegetical Works, On the Hexameron (Homily 1)*; and Chrysostom, *On the Incomprehensible Nature of God (Homily 12)*; Tertullian, *De anima*, 17.1–6, 8, 10–11, 13–14; 18.6–8, 11–13.

6. Gregory of Nyssa, *Life of Moses*, 1.49–50, 2.170–73; Gregory of Nyssa, *Ascetical Works: On Virginity*, 38–44; Gregory of Nyssa, *Ascetical Works: On Perfection*, 110–19.

7. Augustine, *Confessions*, 2.5.10, 4.13.20–15.24, 6.16.26, 10.34.55–57, 12.27.37; Augustine, *De Trinitate*, 6.10.11, 8.4.6, 14.17.23, 14.19.25. See my essay "Beauty and the Baptists," 104–24 where I compare and contrast Augustine's and Gregory's

understand beauty christologically and contend that believers can become beautiful by faith in and imitation of Christ through the power of the Holy Spirit.

The medieval divines (e.g., Anselm of Canterbury, Nicholas of Cusa, Bonaventure, and Thomas Aquinas)[8] build largely on the work of the early church fathers and Pseudo-Dionysius, who in his *Divine Names* writes particularly about beauty. Aquinas identifies those things as beautiful and pleasing which possess *integritas* (proportion), *claritas* (splendor of proportion), and *consonantia* (harmony of proportion).[9] The medieval theologians locate earthly expressions of beauty eternally in the mind of God and retain an objective notion that produces subjective responses in the perceiver. The primary shift from the patristic to the medieval period is to the analogical beauty of creation where beauty is the divinely impressed proportions of the world.[10]

Beauty's royal status, however, begins to diminish as the new science, inaugurated by Copernicus and Galileo, offers alternative explanations for reality that challenge the medieval synthesis of authority, not to mention other realms of thought that make similar challenges. These discoveries and new inquiries of thought, albeit slowly, begin to elevate human reason to a superior status amidst the ongoing renaissance in science, literature, the arts, education, and politics. Consequently, these challenges create an authorial vacuum as traditional structures of authority, from ecclesiastical to political, begin to dissolve, and are reinstituted through an emphasis on methodology and the human subject in an effort to stave off skepticism.[11]

---

theology of beauty regarding its definition, purpose, and significance.

8. See Anselm, *Proslogium*, §16–17 and *Monologium*, §11; Nicholas of Cusa, *On the Vision of God*, 5.13, 6.17–21, 8.30, 10.40–41, 12.47–48, 22.94, 98, 100 and *On Learned Ignorance*, 2.13.75, 2.13.177–178; Bonaventure, *Soul's Journey into God*, 2.1, 4–8, 13 and *Tree of Life*, §35.

9. Aquinas, *ST*, I.2–11, I.33–44, I.2.22–30, I.2.141–154, 3.38–45; *De veritate*, 1.1, 21.1; *I Sententiarum, dist.* 8. Beauty as a transcendental in the thought of Aquinas is the subject of an ongoing debate. See Aertsen, "Beauty in the Middle Ages," 68–97 and Gilson, "Forgotten Transcendental," 159–63 for an introduction.

10. See Garrett, "Beauty," 218–20 where some of the previous two paragraphs appear. Farley describes this ancient and medieval synthesis as the "Great Theory of Beauty" (*Faith and Beauty*, 17–27).

11. Historians typically identify this period as the Renaissance or "rebirth," beginning roughly in the 14th century and ending in 17th century. Some historians debate the usefulness of the term Renaissance, seeking to demonstrate its continuity or discontinuity with the Middle Ages. See Brotton, *Renaissance* or Kristeller, *Renaissance Thought and Its Sources*.

This chapter offers an excerpt from the tale of beauty as its value in interpreting the world begins to wane during the modern period and eventually is disparaged in much of postmodern thinking.[12] The purpose is to suggest a few reasons why beauty no longer figures into much of Protestant theological discourse regarding our explanations of the real, particularly God's divine reality. After this account, I suggest why the dismissal of beauty from Protestant theological discourse is problematic, and why it is significant for Christian theology. These explanations echo the recent renaissance in theological aesthetics, noting how to further the conversation.

Towards an Understanding of Beauty's Broad Dismissal and Postmodern Demise

Distinct challenges to the ancient and medieval theology of beauty begin, albeit ever-so slowly, with the advent of the Renaissance where significant shifts in thought occur throughout large swaths of intellectual pursuits. These shifts are characterized by the revival of learning predicated on classical sources, the development of perspective in art, new scientific discoveries, political innovations, and ecclesiastical reforms, as a new humanism emerges. Descartes inaugurates, with good intention, a methodological shift that gives prominence to human reason in order to overcome the rising skepticism and open new avenues for human progress. In doing so, he sets a rationalistic trajectory that defines reality in terms of mathematical first principles, laying the foundation for locating beauty within the subjective cognitive faculties of humanity. Ironically, though, we learn that this rationalistic trajectory severs beauty from any sort of objectivity. Likewise, across the English Channel, Sir Francis Bacon seeks to overthrow the skepticism of this period with a new methodology by reasoning inductively from material existence and experience. In turn, he spawns an

---

12. See the following for more detailed historical accounts of beauty and the imagination: Bredin and Santoro-Brienza, *Philosophies of Art and Beauty*; Beardsley, *Aesthetics*; Bernstein, *Fate of Art*. My account attempts to weave together several primary sources pertinent to elucidating the contemporary situation regarding beauty and the imagination. I am sure to omit relevant thinkers but believe those presented here are representative and tell an insightful story, in part, of why beauty and the imagination have disappeared from theological discourse. I hope to have done so without mischaracterization.

empiricist tradition that would later locate beauty in the ambiguous realm of human feeling and emotion.[13]

Anticipating the skeptical conclusions of this subjectivist turn, Immanuel Kant attempts to incorporate his predecessors's ideas, including aspects of ancient and medieval synthesis on beauty, into his "analytic of beauty" in his landmark work *The Critique of Judgment*. His efforts stave off beauty's demise until the late 19th and early 20th century but further problems emerge as beauty is sequestered to the realm of aesthetics, leading to an aesthetic humanism. Subsequent thinkers like Friedrich Nietzsche, Martin Heidegger, and Jacques Derrida pervert this trend, finding beauty in one's "will to illusion." Beauty, along with its siblings the true and the good, meet their demise as notions of referentiality succumb to relativism. Let us return, now, to the period of the Enlightenment as we try to discern the status of beauty among contemporary Protestant theology.

Beauty and the Enlightenment: The Journey toward Subjectivity

Alexander Baumgarten, the father of modern aesthetics, serves as a paradigmatic example of the rationalistic tradition as he attempts to understand the arts, particularly poetry, through Descartes's notion of "clear and distinct" ideas.[14] Aesthetics, according to Baumgarten, is the *scientia cognitionis sensitivae* (science of sensory cognition)[15] or "the science guiding sensate discourse to perfection," which distinguishes "between *things perceived* and *things known*."[16] The things known are discerned by the superior cognitive faculty of logic whereas the things perceived by the inferior

---

13. Why tell the tale of beauty from the Enlightenment forward? Is the Enlightenment the root of all evil, the cause of all our theological problems today? No, our human finitude and fallenness will suffice. Does this mean that beauty is not despised before the Enlightenment or praised after it? No, on both accounts. In fact, some attribute beauty's low status to streams of thought prior to the Enlightenment (e.g., the humanism of the Renaissance or even the nominalism of Ockham). Nevertheless, the intellectual developments of the Enlightenment are the clearest references that demarcate a paradigm shift, revealing valuable lessons. Yet, these lessons gain importance only once we situate them within the "grand story" of the Gospel. See Bartholomew and Goheen, *Drama of Scripture*, 15–27 how situating stories within God's story yields understanding.

14. Descartes, *Discourse on the Method*, 9 and his sixth meditation in *Meditations on First Philosophy*, 38–47.

15. Baumgarten, *Aesthetica*, §1.

16. Baumgarten, *Reflection on Poetry*, §115–16.

Panel One: No Room in the Inn

cognitive faculty of perception. In addition, Baumgarten defines aesthetics as *ars pulchre cogitandi* (the art of thinking beautifully) and *ars formandi gustum* (the art of forming tastes).[17] In short, aesthetics is the science of human perception that has as its end the perfection of sensate cognition, which is beauty. Beauty is not an objective property of a thing or a subjective feeling but the *perfection* of one's sensate knowledge.[18] The establishment of aesthetics as a separate discipline with its own laws has significant consequences for later thinkers like Kant as aesthetics gains independent status from ethics and logic within the realm of human cognition, albeit the "lower" faculties of the imagination, intuition, and perception.

Descartes's rationalism has a twin brother in the empiricism of Sir Francis Bacon, whose method of analysis is a "form of induction which shall analyze experience and take it to pieces, and by a due process of exclusion and rejection lead to an inevitable conclusion."[19] Bacon is obsessed with practical matters and technological progress so much so that beauty is of little significance. Function, not form, is preeminent: "Houses are built to live in, not to look on; . . . Leave the goodly fabrics of houses, for beauty only, to the enchanted palaces of the poets; who build them with small cost."[20] Beauty, according to Bacon, is a matter of felicity and feeling—a function of the imagination that is predicated on fascination and emotion rather than reason.[21]

Following the empirical tradition, although not in complete opposition to rationalism, John Locke roots knowledge and its verification in the senses, seeking pragmatic and utilitarian ends. For Locke, "the mind, in all its thoughts and reasonings, hath no other immediate object but its own ideas, which it alone does or can contemplate; it is evident that our knowledge is only conversant about them." These ideas in the mind are simple and are "conveyed in by the senses as they are found in exterior things or by reflection on its own operations" and are only *representative* of

---

17. Baumgarten, *Aesthetica*, §1. Baumgarten defines the goal of aesthetics: *Aesthetices finis est perfectio cognitionis sensitivae, qua talis. Haec autem est pulchritudo* (The goal of aesthetics is the perfection of sensate cognition, as such. This perfection, of which I speak, is beauty).

18. Thiessen, *Theological Aesthetics*, 156. García-Rivera, *Community of the Beautiful*, 9–11 also identifies Baumgarten as the one who reverses the pre-modern supposition of humanity's capacity to receive divine beauty thereby methodologically ignoring its source in God.

19. Bacon, *New Organon*, 19.

20. Bacon, *Selected Writings*, 114.

21. Bacon, *Advancement of Learning*, 69, 119–21.

reality.²² The mind arranges these simple ideas into complex ones through a process called "composition."²³ Assembling these simple ideas together takes "judgment" (i.e., reason) so that one carefully separates ideas and is not "misled by similitude and by affinity to take one thing for another." Through the assembling process in the mind, "beauty appears at first sight, and there is required no labor of thought to examine what truth or reason there is in it."²⁴ Therefore, beauty, according to Locke, is a complex idea perceived in the fancy (i.e., the imagination) of one's mind, bringing delight to the beholder.²⁵ Like all other ideas in Locke's schema, beauty is disconnected from reality. It exists only in the pleasurable perceptions of the imagination. Locke's empiricism continues beauty's journey toward subjectivism; only this time, the failure of both the rationalist and empiricist projects to achieve the certainty they claim sets the conditions for the skepticism of David Hume.

Hume's contributions to aesthetics and the concept of beauty would serve as the impetus for much of aesthetic thought from this point forward, as he draws from John Dennis's, Joseph Addison's, and Francis Hutcheson's notions of beauty, sentiment, and taste, further entrenching beauty into human subjectivity.²⁶ Hume contends that any being's existence "can only be proved by argument from its cause or its effect, and these arguments are founded entirely on experience."²⁷ As such, "beauty . . . is felt, more properly than perceived" and is not a quality of objects

---

22. Locke, *Essay Concerning Human Understanding*, 161, 299.

23. Ibid., 81.

24. Ibid., 80. This excerpt is from an important distinction that Locke makes regarding "wit" and "judgment." It is important to note Locke's disdain in this passage for the imagination (what he calls fancy) because he believes that the imagination is the way of metaphor and illusion that leads to the pleasantry of wit. His distinction separates two supposed faculties of the mind that lead to opposing ends—wit toward the pleasurable and fanciful world of entertainment and judgment toward the toilsome and noble world of knowledge. Language associated with the latter must be clear and precise, while language associated with the former is of the lesser order of metaphor, figures of speech, and poetry, which Locke sees as "perfect cheats" because he desires to "speak of things as they are" (Locke, *An Essay Concerning Human Understanding*, 289). Thus, the imagination and its associated language of metaphor deal with the non-real while reason addresses the real.

25. Locke, *Essay Concerning Human Understanding*, 86.

26. Dennis, *Large Account of the Taste in Poetry*; Dennis, *Grounds of Criticism in Poetry*; Addison, "Pleasures of the Imagination;" Hutcheson, *Inquiry into the Original of Our Ideas of Beauty and Virtue*.

27. Hume, *Enquiry Concerning Human Understanding*, 113.

but "belongs entirely to the sentiment internal and external."[28] Yet, in his ambiguous style, Hume says he can see "obvious beauties that strike the senses," implying some sort of objectivity.[29] He never definitively articulates, though, what beauty is or where it resides. It is as if he teeters between the subjective and objective.

Immanuel Kant, "aroused from his dogmatic slumbers" by the writings of Hume, seeks answers to three fundamental questions: What can I know? What ought I to do? What can I hope for?[30] These questions serve as the basis for his trilogy, *Critique of Pure Reason*, *Critique of Practical Reason*, and *Critique of Judgment*, respectively. In the last of his trilogy, we find his most mature thoughts on aesthetics, particularly that of beauty and the imagination. His work serves as a turning point in the discipline that reverberates into the twentieth century.[31] Kant, in an effort to resolve the dilemmas facing the rationalist and empiricist traditions, combines elements from both by proposing a new method for the validation of scientific inquiry. In this way, he is distinctly modern in his approach to rational inquiry in that method is prior to content. Rather than assuming that our minds conform to reality, he presumes that reality conforms to our minds since our minds possess innate and universal ordering principles that shape the experiential data of the phenomenal world. The form of things comes from the mind while their matter comes from experience. There is no knowledge of the world as it is in itself, only as it appears to the human mind.[32] Metaphysics becomes a study not about the structures of reality but rather a study about the structures of the human mind.[33]

Kant establishes distinct first principles and methods that steer us to the truth (theoretical reason) and guide us in our pursuit of the good (practical reason). Mediating between the theoretical and the practical is judgment. Put another way, judgment mediates between the realms of fact

---

28. Ibid., 114.

29. Hume, *Standard of Taste*, 11.

30. Kant, *Prolegomena*, 4.

31. Guy Sircello attributes twentieth century skepticism regarding beauty to Kant, who "started it all by declaring that the judgment of beauty is not determined by concepts. He meant that no criteria of beauty can be given in terms of features of the objects to which 'beautiful' is applicable; and he thus opened the gates of subjectivism" (*New Theory of Beauty*, 4). Francesca Murphy also sees Kant and his predecessors as contributing to beauty's dismissal from theological discourse today due to Kant's association of beauty with the non-real and its subjectivist nature (*Christ the Form of Beauty*, 28).

32. Kant, *Critique of Pure Reason*, 1–16.

33. Kant, *Prolegomena*, 1–3.

(nature/knowledge) and value (freedom/desire) by enabling us to see the world as if it had purpose. How this mediation takes places depends on Kant's notion of "purposiveness" that functions as an *a priori* principle *and* as a feeling of pleasure.[34] Theoretical reason possesses the ordering principles necessary for understanding the sensations of the phenomenal world. It is limited to these cognitive categories (form) and sensations (matter). Practical reason, as an *a priori* act of reason, transcends theoretical reason and the phenomenal world, offering universal and certain claims to how we ought to live.[35] Yet, aesthetic judgments involve *neither* cognition nor sensation but the imagination:

> If we wish to discern whether anything is beautiful or not, we do not refer the representation of it to the object by means of understanding with a view to cognition, but by means of the imagination (acting perhaps in conjunction with understanding). We refer the representation to the subject and its feeling of pleasure or displeasure. The judgment of taste, therefore, is not a cognitive judgment, and so not logical, but is aesthetic, . . . *it is one whose determining ground cannot be other than subjective*.[36]

Kant walks with his Enlightenment predecessors, locating beauty in the subject where personal feelings and taste determine the beautiful. He breaks stride, though, because he gives aesthetic judgments a universal quality: "Beauty is what, without concept, is liked universally" because feelings are common to all.[37] Beauty and the imagination become sequestered to their own world—separated from any sort of objectivity—and consequently blossom into the aesthetic humanism of the Romantic Period.[38]

An important bridge between Kant and the 20th century is the Romantic period, which most historians identify as occurring from the late 18th century through the 19th century. Although some historians contend that Romanticism is a reaction to the rationalism of the Enlightenment,

---

34. Kant, *Critique of Judgment*, 10–14.
35. Ibid., 3–4.
36. Ibid., 20. Emphasis added.
37. Ibid., 29.
38. I understand aestheticism as the abdication of any sort of authorial/artistic intention such that meaning arises from the free interplay between interpreter and a particular text where textual signs have no reference point beyond themselves. The focus is on the textual signs themselves because of the lack of reference to an objective reality. Thus, it is the pursuit of beauty for beauty's sake that seeks to escape from the realities of the real world.

Jaroslav Pelikan argues that "there is much to be said for an interpretation of the Enlightenment that sees Rationalism and Romanticism in it side by side almost from the beginning of the eighteenth century, at least in Germany."[39] Monroe Beardsley further contends that Romanticism values novelty, nostalgia, emotional intuition, and an acute awareness of feelings and emotions, all within an autonomous realm of poetic discourse.[40] As such, we see these qualities in the writings of Samuel Taylor Coleridge, William Wadsworth, Percy Bysshe Shelly, William Blake, and Johann Wolfgang von Goethe. Beauty and the imagination play a significant role in aesthetic discourse during the Romantic period, conveying the ideal side of the arts as Friedrich Schelling notes in his *Philosophy of Art*.[41] The beauty of Romanticism, however, is that of sentimentality, which "misrepresents reality through evading or trivializing evil, is emotionally self-indulgent, and avoids appropriate costly action."[42]

If this is the case, Kant's subjectivism does not merely continue into the 19th century but turns further in on itself, providing the impetus for two kinds of relativism present today—individualistic and communitarian.[43] This ethos becomes the backdrop for philosophers like Arthur Schopenhauer and Friedrich Nietzsche who laid the foundation for a *postmodern aestheticism*.

Beauty and Postmodernity: The Journey toward Its Demise

The reverberations of this aesthetic humanism from the Romantic period send beauty towards its demise in the twentieth century. As postmodernity dawns through the writings of Nietzsche, Heidegger, and Derrida, an increasing skepticism emerges regarding meaning and reference. Furthermore, the fabric of postmodern culture begins to dull our sensibilities for the real with its incessant reality-indifferent messages that reinforce its norms of deconstruction, relativism, plurality of meaning *ad infinitum*,

---

39. Pelikan, *Fools for Christ*, 148.
40. Beardsley, *Aesthetics*, 244–82.
41. Schelling, *Philosophy of Art*, 24. C. M. Bora details these same Romantic tendencies in *The Romantic Imagination*. Aesthetic theory, during this period, incorporated beauty and the imagination into its self-understanding, evidenced in the following works: Tolstoy, *What Is Art?*; Schlegel, "Limits of the Beautiful;" Hegel, *Aesthetics*; and Schiller, "Letters on the Aesthetic Education of Man."
42. Begbie, "Beauty, Sentimentality, and the Arts," 45–69, here 47.
43. Murphy, *Christ the Form of Beauty*, 29.

and nostalgia.⁴⁴ Beauty becomes irrelevant and the imagination restricted to the human cognitive ability that plays with a variety of textual signs in order to create one's own reality.

Friedrich Nietzsche, in his provocative work, *Thus Spake Zarathustra*, announces in prophetic tone that "God is dead!"⁴⁵ What, though, does Nietzsche mean by this bold assertion? Why is it not simply *his* interpretation or "most enduring lie?"⁴⁶ Surely, Nietzsche draws his conclusions from within a particular frame of meaning? This in fact is his sneering criticism of modernity as he attempts to throw off traditional forms of authority: historical, political, religious, moral, and authorial. Not even science with its claims to neutrality is unbiased, for "there simply is no science 'without presuppositions.'"⁴⁷ There are no facts, only interpretations. There is no single meaning but meanings *ad infinitum*, what Nietzsche calls "perspectivism."⁴⁸

Nietzsche's perspectivism desires to overcome the supposed chasm that separates this world and the "true" world, not unlike what many contemporary theologians express concerning God's actions and who he is in himself. In doing so, humanity must give shape and form to the world through its imaginative "will to power," yet how humanity does so is not through referential language but through the language of metaphor. Chaos is accessorized with human speech to hide the horrors of this world,

---

44. Defining postmodernity is illusive and highly contested (See Jenks, *What Is Postmodernism?*). Edward Farley offers an apt definition that includes two important and interrelated senses: the radical critique of and cultural shift away from modernity (Farley, *Faith and Beauty*, 2–6). Many also identify this shift as the "postmodern turn or condition" (See Jameson, *Postmodern Turn* and Lyotard, *Postmodern Condition*). To understand beauty's fate in contemporary theology, we must come to grips with this shift (See Vanhoozer's "Theology and the Condition of Postmodernity," 3–25.

45. Nietzsche, *Thus Spake Zarathustra*, 2. The main idea of Schopenhauer's aesthetic, found in *Welt als Wille und Vorstellung*, is that art and beauty are an escape from the evil travails and misery of existence, which makes life tolerable. Schopenhauer's thought seems to echo through Nietzsche, bequeathing a reticence for beauty into the postmodern psyche.

46. Nietzsche, *Gay Science*, 283. In an attack on science's claim of objectivity and neutrality, Nietzsche undermines this notion by saying that science works from within a particular perspective and that "it is still a *metaphysical faith* upon which our faith in science rests." Such metaphysical faith beckons back to "that Christian faith which was also the faith of Plato, that God is the truth, that truth is divine. But what if this should become more and more incredible . . . if God himself should prove to be our most enduring lie" (283).

47. Ibid., 281.

48. Nietzsche, *Will to Power*, §481.

Panel One: No Room in the Inn

"for it is only as an *aesthetic phenomenon* that existence and the world are eternally *justified*."[49] For Nietzsche, there is no ultimate reference point, no unity of being that grounds the true, the good, and the beautiful—"God is dead!" Reality consists of strife and destruction, in which beauty has no part. Beauty arises according to one's personal "will to illusion," creating a façade that masks our painful existence, *á la* Arthur Schopenhauer.[50]

Martin Heidegger, in his later writings, counters some of Nietzsche's assertions regarding the demise of being by reasserting being as the grounds of existence while incorporating elements of Nietzsche's perspectivalism.[51] Heidegger contends, contra Kant, that being and time should be considered together. In doing so, he understands being phenomenologically as "presence"[52] and concordantly truth as "unconcealedness" where truth "is neither an attribute of factual things in the sense of beings, nor one of propositions" but "a happening."[53]

In his work, "The Origin of the Work of Art," Heidegger contends that all art has a poetic essence and the essence of poetry is the unconcealedness of beings, namely the grounds of truth. Art is the *locus classicus* for the unveiling of truth because art projects a world in which we are invited to enter. Art is the grounds upon which all human existence depends. This projection is not the result of a subjective artist but is the projection of being itself and continues to produce new prospective meanings long after the original work of the artist. In that way, "art breaks open a place, in whose openness, everything is other than usual."[54]

Heidegger views beauty, then, as an aspect of truth that happens—as unconcealdness.[55] Beauty "is understood here neither as mere appearance nor as a reality behind appearance. Rather, in beauty the being of beings is lit up *in and through* an appearance, where 'appearance' is nothing 'mere,' but is the coming to light of the being of beings in and through an entity."[56]

---

49. Nietzsche, *Birth of Tragedy*, §5. For a summary of Nietzsche's aesthetic, his *Will to Power*, §794–853 or Stern's *Study of Nietzsche*.

50. Nietzsche, *Birth of Tragedy*, §1–4, 16–17. See also Sikka, "On the Truth of Beauty," 244–48.

51. See Macquarrie, "Heidegger's Earlier and Later Work Compared," 3–16, Dreyfus and Wrathall, eds., *Companion to Heidegger* and Thiselton, *Two Horizons*, 327–30, on relating Heidegger's early and later thought.

52. Heidegger, *Being and Time*, 64–73.

53. Heidegger, "Origin of the Work of Art," 176.

54. Ibid., 184.

55. Ibid., 178.

56. Sikka, "On the Truth of Beauty," 251. In "Origin of the Work of Art," Heidegger

This coming to light, though, never ceases because being, according to Heidegger, is perspectival.⁵⁷ Art "is a novel event, which never ceases to be novel, which is never completely exhausted by interpretations. Long after its original creation it continues to generate new possibilities."⁵⁸ Beauty, for Heidegger, is not the product of illusion, as Nietzsche contends, but is an instrument of truth. Nevertheless, beauty sinks into a sea of ever changing perspectivalism, despite its revelatory qualities.⁵⁹

Jacques Derrida's philosophy of deconstruction affirms with Nietzsche "the play of the world and innocence of becoming, the affirmation of a world of signs without fault, without truth, and without origin which is offered to an active interpretation."⁶⁰ For Derrida, such affirmations acknowledge the "loss of the center" of reality. After this loss, "it was probably necessary to begin to think that there was no center, that the center had no natural locus, that it was not a fixed locus . . . a sort of non-locus in which an infinite number of sign-substitutions came into play." In doing so, "everything became discourse."⁶¹ This discourse, consequently, has no reference to or connection with anything outside itself. It only refers to itself. The world becomes an aesthetic array of superficial signs such

---

illustrates his notion that "art is truth setting itself to work" with a well-known Van Gogh painting entitled "A Pair of Shoes" (1886). Their beauty arises when, "more simply and authentically, the shoes are engrossed in their nature" (178). This happens not when we imagine the shoes as simply pieces of leather sewn together for the purpose of covering our feet, but when we envision the laborer who toils in these shoes. Yet how does this happen? Heidegger contends: "Not by a description and explanation of a pair of shoes actually present; not by a report about the process of making shoes; and also not by the observation of the actual use of shoes occurring here and there; but only by bringing ourselves before Van Gogh's painting. This painting spoke. In the vicinity of the work we were suddenly somewhere else than we usually tend to be" (162–66).

57. Heidegger, *Will to Power as Art*, 214–17.

58. Bredin and Santoro-Brienza, *Philosophies of Art and Beauty*, 102.

59. In his "Lamp in the Labyrinth," 37, Vanhoozer rightly notes how this occurs: "It is most significant that in an essay titled 'The Origin of the Work of Art' Heidegger omits any discussion of the artist or author. The poet is the one who listens to the language rather than speaks it; the artist is passive." It is the absence of the artist/author that unleashes the infinite multiplicity of meanings.

60. Derrida, *Writing and Difference*, 292. For a survey of the philosophy of deconstruction, see Caputo, ed., *Deconstruction in a Nutshell*.

61. Derrida, "Structure, Sign, and Play," 248. Regarding the absence of a center, Caputo remarks that there is "no *Wesen* and no *telos* but only *différance*, no deep essence to keep things on course but a certain contingent assembly of unities subject always to more radical open-endedness that constantly runs the risk of going adrift" (*Deconstruction in a Nutshell*, 117).

that humanity playfully interprets those signs *ad infinitum*, constructing reality as it sees fit. Where is beauty in the midst of Derrida's intertextual "sign system"? Beauty is in the eye of the beholder, resulting in the loss of objectivity and the ability to convey meaning beyond the realm of personal taste.[62]

Tracing beauty's history from the Enlightenment to the contemporary situation reveals beauty's slow dismissal from the real and later to its demise. From the Enlightenment to the Romantic period, beauty remains a part of the conversation, albeit in a room by itself contemplating the structures of the human mind, pleasing sentiments, and nostalgic memories. These subjectivities turn further inward as notions of referentiality and metanarratives succumb to relativism at the hands of Nietzsche, Heidegger, and Derrida.

The conception of the imagination as a lesser human cognitive faculty continues along a similar trajectory, despite the incessant bombardment of images within postmodern culture, as Richard Kearney notes: "One of the greatest paradoxes of contemporary culture is that at a time when the image reigns supreme the very notion of a creative human imagination seems under mounting threat." There is no reality, only vain imaginings, for "we are at an impasse where the very rapport between imagination and reality seems not only inverted but subverted altogether."[63] Does contemporary Protestant theology, though, follow this trajectory, omitting beauty from theological discourse and relegating human imagining to the non-real?

Beauty and Contemporary Protestant Theology: Sleeping Beauty or Sleeping Beast?

Roland Delattre says that "the concept of beauty has rarely found an important—not to speak of secure—place in Christian theology, especially with the mainline of Christian orthodoxy and even more especially within Protestant Reformed orthodoxy."[64] Anders Nygren offers a stinging rebuke of any who would dare speak of the beauty of God: "Eros is of a markedly aesthetic character. It is the beauty of the divine that attracts the eye of the soul and sets its love in motion. . . . To speak of the 'beauty' of God

---

62. See Hart, "Without Derrida," 419–29.
63. Kearney, *Wake of the Imagination*, 3.
64. Delattre, *Beauty and Sensibility*, 118.

in the context of Agape, however, sounds very much like blasphemy."[65] Edward Farley states that "all the types (historical, practical, philosophical, systematic) and approaches (neo-Reformation, apologetic, feminist, African-American, liberationist, correlational) share at least one thing in common, *a disinterest in beauty*."[66] Patrick Sherry offers a spectrum for assessing beauty:

> At best, beauty has often been treated as a Cinderella, compared with the attention paid by theologians to its two sisters, truth and goodness, an attention manifested in theology's predominant concern with doctrine and ethics, and resulting in the intellectualization of religion in recent centuries. . . . At worst, beauty has been treated as a meretricious Hellenistic import, who will distract and indeed corrupt good Christians.[67]

Taking these assessments together, it seems that a theology of beauty resides among some contemporary Christian theologies.[68] Overall, though, beauty in Protestant theology seems to possess a beleaguered status. Little credence is given to it as a "deep symbol," those "cultural values such as the 'real,' the holy, tradition, nature, obligation, and law" by which theologians endeavor to make sense of the world.[69] Why, then, do some contemporary Protestant theologians meet beauty with reticence and at times with disdain?

Common Reasons for Discarding Beauty in Theological Discourse

Sherry offers two succinct reasons: 1. a reaction to "high" culture and 2. philosophical skepticism.[70] Karl Barth also expresses concern because of beauty's common association with hedonistic desires, concluding that "the concept of the beautiful seems to be a particularly secular one, not

65. Nygren, *Agape and Eros*, 223–24.
66. Farley, *Faith and Beauty*, 7–8. Emphasis added.
67. Sherry, *Spirit and Beauty*, 18–19.
68. See Balthasar, *GL*; Jenson, *Triune God*; Farley, *Faith and Beauty*, Sherry, *Spirit and Beauty*; and Hart, *Beauty of the Infinite*.
69. Farley, *Faith and Beauty*, 6. Cf. Farley, *Deep Symbols*, 1–12.
70. Sherry, *Spirit and Beauty*, 22. Farley cites three tendencies within the Christian tradition, "monotheistic revolution and its ensuing iconoclasms; otherworldliness and moral asceticism, and apocalypticism," that work to remove "beauty as a primary value from faith's ritual, ethical and theological discourses" (Farley, *Faith and Beauty*, 8–12).

Panel One: No Room in the Inn

at all adapted for introduction into the language of theology, and indeed extremely dangerous."[71] Some express the fear that beauty will become an object of worship, a substitute for worshipping in spirit and truth (John 4:20–24), because the delight found in the created order becomes the object of our desires, mistaking the created for the Creator (Gen 3:6).

Such fears and concerns are often associated with contemporary trends in the artistic scene where purveyors of the arts, and particularly the visual arts, find the contemplation of art for art's sake to be a religious experience. Nicholas Wolterstorff warns of the dangers of the "religion of aestheticism" as such experiences of the beautiful become substitutes for the Gospel of Jesus Christ.[72] He indicts our institutions of high art that display artists's work in revered places like museums, concert-halls, and theaters that encourage by their very nature "disinterested contemplation" where such contemplation becomes the highest value, taking the place of our adoration for God the Creator.[73] Artistic works have become "a salvation from the everyday routines of life," as the sociologist Max Weber notes.[74]

The aforementioned fears and concerns do have a historical precedent in the iconoclastic debates of the early church and the Protestant Reformation. During the 8th century, Emperor Leo III and his son Constantine V order the destruction of icons in Byzantine places of worship. Iconoclasts argue that any lifeless rendering of Christ is an anathema. Lifeless images are incapable of rendering the divine nature of Christ, since only the human is represented, thereby separating Christ's divine and human natures (nestorianism). Or lifeless images may confuse the two natures of Christ, considering them as one (monophysitism). The dispute seemingly finds resolution in the Second Council of Nicaea (AD 787), affirming the fittingness of icons for Christian worship such that "the incarnation of the Word of God is shown forth as real and not merely phantastic."[75] Yet, have the iconoclastic debates ended?

Nearly eight hundred years later, several Protestant Reformers of the likes of Andreas Bodenstein von Karlstadt, Ulrich Zwingli, and John

---

71. Barth, *CD* 2/1, 651.

72. Wolterstorff, *Art in Action*, 50. He roots this religious aestheticism in the Romantic period, citing, at length, the works of Walter Pater and Gustave Flaubert as indicative of Romanticism (50n28).

73. Ibid., 49–50.

74. Gerth and Mills, eds., *From Max Weber*, 342.

75. Leith, *Creeds of the Churches*, 55. See Brubaker and Haldon, *Byzantium in the Iconoclast Era* for a survey of the iconoclastic debates in the early church.

Calvin brought about their own *Beeldensturm* as images, icons, and various works of art are "cleansed" from churches across Europe. These Reformers argue that God commands his people to make no graven images (Exod 20:1–6), thereby making the veneration of images comparable to idol worship. John Calvin remarks: "We must cling to this principle: God's glory is corrupted by an impious falsehood whenever any form is attached to him."[76] Yet, Martin Luther takes a nuanced position, finding himself at odds with the iconoclastic Reformers: "Nor am I of the opinion that the gospel should destroy and blight all the arts, as some of the pseudo-religious claim. But I would like to see all the arts, especially music, used in the service of Him who gave and made them."[77] The tensions apparent within the Reformation regarding the use of images in Christian worship still find resonance today, contributing to the dearth of theological discourse on beauty and its human cognitive counterpart, the imagination.

Sherry's second reason for the contemporary theology's reticence toward beauty, philosophical skepticism, can be seen in the aforementioned synopsis from the story of beauty. With the onset of the Enlightenment, beauty takes a subjectivist turn where the judgments of beauty are simply a logical or psychological analysis of the human being that ultimately culminates in an expressivist ideal. This subjectivist-expressivist trajectory leads to the skepticism of the postmodern condition as Francesca Murphy notes: "Beauty, [according to Kant], is said to reveal the supra-material basis of the artist's subjectivity. We are again referred back into the depths of the subject. . . . This idea of beauty neither supplies a bond to the external world, nor provides a path leading to a meaning outside the self."[78] What emerges is an aestheticism focused on forms that are detached from the way things really are. Beauty is only in the eye of the beholder.

---

76. Calvin, *Institutes*, 1.2.1. For a survey of the iconoclastic elements within the Protestant Reformation, see Dillenberger, *Theology of Artistic Sensibilities* or Coulton, *Art and the Reformation*. Zachman, in his book *Word and Image in the Theology of John Calvin*, contends that although Calvin rejects the "dead images" that were typical of the iconoclastic debates, Calvin does so to point us to "living images of God" that we see when we hear the Word of God (7–9). Consequently, Calvin's theology does attend to God's beauty in that "we need the truth of God to be able to discern the beauty of God in God's works; but we also need the beauty of God to be sweetly allured and gently invited to God, so that we might be ravished with admiration for the beauty of God's goodness, and seek God from the innermost affection of our hearts" (3).

77. Luther, *Liturgy and Hymns*, 316.

78. Murphy, *Christ the Form of Beauty*, 28. See also Brown, *Religious Aesthetics*, 5–6, 24–30 who not only traces beauty's decline to the Renaissance but also attributes contemporary eschewals of the term to modern secularism that sought to expunge religion from its ranks.

PANEL ONE: No Room in the Inn

Underlying these reasons for discarding beauty in theological discourse is an understanding of form, what Hans Urs von Balthasar calls *Gestalt*, that is either disconnected from reality or limited to a particular part of it. Form, according to Balthasar, always has particularlity and is "fundamentally a sign and appearing" in that "the appearance of the form, as the revelation of the depths, is an indissoluble union of two things. It is the real presence of the depths, of the whole of reality, and it is a real pointing beyond itself to these depths."[79] Balthasar's notion of *Gestalt* differs from Plato's theory of forms (*eidos*) because Plato jettisons particularlity in order to ascend to some ethereal ideal. He differs from Aristotle's notion of form (*morphe*) in that form is not the pinnacle of being but rather revelatory of it.[80] If theological discourse is to do justice to God's self-revelation and thus speak truly of God, it must attend to the particularity of his self-revelation while also accounting for his universality and singularity. Let us examine two trends in contemporary Protestant theology, which have little regard for beauty as valuable for interpreting the way the world is, while also noting their implicit assumptions regarding the nature of form.

Exemplars of Aesthetic and Amorphous Theology

Almost thirty years ago, a surge of publications surfaced within the theological academy interested in exploring the fruitfulness of categories like narrative, metaphor, poetry, the imagination, and other aesthetic concepts for theology, what some have identified as *aesthetic theology*.[81] The thrust

---

79. Balthasar, GL I, 118. Drawing from Balthasar, I understand *Gestalt* as a dynamic appearance that expresses a unified whole found in the interrelation of parts in an external medium. The splendor of the internal depths of reality radiates through the external such that the whole is greater than the sum of its parts, producing a unified meaning inconceivable in the parts alone. This expression of the invisible in and through the visible not only reveals but also conceals such that the invisible is not exhausted in the appearing. Chapter 2 further explores Balthasar's notion of *Gestalt* applied to *Herrlichkeit* and *Übergestalt*.

80. Describing Aristotle's understanding of form, Gilson says that the highest principle for his metaphysics is "form . . . whereby a substance is what it is, and if a being is primarily or, as Aristotle himself says, almost exclusively *what* it is, each being is primarily and almost exclusively its form." Therefore, "the distinctive character of a truly Aristotelian metaphysics of being lies in the fact that it knows of no act superior to the form, not even existence" (*Being and Some Philosophers*, 47). Balthasar, following Aquinas, emphasizes the act that precedes form because "it is through action, and only through action, that real beings manifest or 'unveil' their being, their presence." Thus, "it is the very nature of real being, existential being, to pour over into action that is *self-revealing* and *self-communicative*" (Clarke, *One and the Many*, 31–32).

81. See, for instance, McFague, *Speaking in Parables* and her *Metaphorical Theology*;

of these publications portray an aestheticism that values the formalism found in literary criticism as well as the linguistic-logical impulse of analytic philosophy, all the while lacking commitment to some form of objective reality.

Gordon Kaufman's comments are paradigmatic: "It is a mistake to take over traditional [theological] vocabulary and methods uncritically, since these were worked out largely on the assumption that God-language was directly objectivist or referential." Since a "more adequate understanding of the human function and the logical standing of religious and theological language" exists today, the task of theology "is to work out, to construct an image/concept of God appropriate to contemporary life."[82] Kaufman's aesthetic theology not only parallels the anti-realism of Don Cupitt but also allows the imagination of the interpreter to play with the vast array of culturally instantiated theological signs such that the concept of God is disconnected from the reality of God's self-revelation. Theology becomes anthropology, succumbing to Feuerbach's criticism—what Moltmann identifies as cultural capitulation.

Another trend within contemporary Protestant theology that contributes to the disinterest in and dismissal of beauty as a deep symbol for theological discourse is what I am calling *informis theologia* or *amorphous theology*. Amorphous or *form*-less theology acknowledges an objective reality, contra aesthetic theology, yet limits theological discourse about that reality to the true and/or the good. In doing so, a theological atomization of knowledge ensues not unlike the perfect being theology we discussed in the introduction.[83] To the extent that theology subscribes to scientific methodologies or its ethos of exactitude, God's beauty is excluded because such methods distort their understanding of reality. The imagination, if even acknowledged, is shunned because of its supposed fancy for the unreal and proclivity toward vain imaginings. Consequently, the aptitude "to *see* what is right and fitting in a particular situation given one's under-

---

Martin, "Significance of Aesthetics for Theology as Imaginative Construction," 81–85; Tracy, *Analogical Imagination*; and Kaufman, *Theological Imagination*.

82. Kaufmann, *Theological Imagination*, 29–30, 279.

83. Amorphous theology is similar to perfect being theology in its view of reality, its exaltation of reason, its search for precision, and its commitment to theological reasoning based purely on inductive and deductive methodologies. Amorphous theology is different from perfect being theology, though, because it may privilege divine revelation rather than maximizing human conceptualities per se. Nevertheless, God's beauty is absent from its theological discourse, for a variety of reasons but primarily because beauty and the imagination are associated with human eros, the non-real, or some form of aestheticism.

Panel One: No Room in the Inn

standing of the larger whole of which it is a part" is diminished, lacking wisdom.[84]

T. Chris Crain offers a few examples, criticizing evangelical systematic theology as "beastly" because "it has neglected one aspect of the triumvirate of transcendentals," namely beauty.[85] He examines Louis Berkhof's, Millard Erickson's, and Wayne Grudem's systematic theologies and indicts evangelical systematic theology for turning beauty into a beast on the basis of beauty's conspicuous absence from their texts and/or failure to incorporate God's beauty into other doctrines all the while integrating God's truth and goodness.[86]

In light of these fears and concerns, should we continue to avoid the rhetoric of beauty in our theological discourse, particularly by not ascribing beauty to God's divine reality? Has the notion of beauty been so adulterated with platonic conceptions, or connected with hedonistic pleasure that its incorporation into Protestant theology is too dangerous and perhaps even heterodox—a beastly ordeal? Are we not, on the grounds of the Christian tradition, in good company to shy away from or even shun the rhetoric of beauty?

Perhaps, there is, at a minimum, room to develop a theological *aesthetic* that gives a Christian perspective on the arts.[87] Yet, the proposal I am suggesting goes much deeper than those discussions, as important as they are.[88] Certainly, we must proceed with caution and perhaps even more so,

---

84. Vanhoozer, "Praising God in Song: Beauty and the Arts," 116. Emphasis added. W. T. Dickens also details the atrophy of the imagination in contemporary biblical studies (*Balthasar's Theological Aesthetics*, 1–24).

85. Crain, "Turning the Beast into a Beauty," 27. See also Stackhouse, "True, the Good, and the Beautiful Christian," 60–61.

86. Crain, "Turning the Beast into a Beauty," 29–31. I find it interesting that North American Evangelicals would not have a greater respect for God's beauty, particularly given their love affair with Jonathan Edwards who spoke often of God's beauty and identified God as "the foundation and fountain of all being and beauty" (*Religious Affections*, 15; cf. Edward's *Nature of True Virtue*, 15).

87. The likes of Umberto Eco, Aidan Nichols, Robin Jensen, Richard Viladesau, William Dyrness, Jeremy Begbie, and others rightly employ beauty in theological discourse, ascribe epistemic validity to the imagination, and articulate a theological basis for beauty. Most move quickly, though, to a Christian understanding of the arts. As important as this discussion is, beauty and its cognitive counterpart, the imagination, have little resonance within contemporary Protestant theology, particularly North American evangelical theology.

88. Farley offers an important distinction between a "theology of the arts" and "the place of beauty in the life of faith" (*Faith and Beauty*, vii–x), identifying theological beauty as the *grounds* for a theology of worship and the arts.

given beauty's beleaguered story. Yet, as with Barth, the pressing question is "whether we can hesitate indefinitely, whether we can avoid this step." Will our reticence, reluctance, or even our refusal perpetuate "a gap in our knowledge [that] can be filled only in this way? Finally and above all, does biblical truth itself and as such permit us to stop at this point because of the danger, and not say that God is beautiful?"[89] Can we afford not to speak of God's beauty? Indeed, we cannot. What, then, are the costs for abdicating beauty and the imagination from our theological discourse?

The Deleterious Effects of the Demise of Beauty and the Imagination

To be sure, the contemporary rhetoric associated with beauty, ascribing to it sentimental, nostalgic, and hedonistic motifs, should be avoided. Such rhetoric presumes a subjectivist ideal where beauty loses its ability to convey meaning beyond the realm of personal taste, relegating it to the ornamental and innocuous pleasant. The imagination constructs its own reality with no consideration for the way things really are, signifying the beautiful as an escape from our painful existence. Yet, the concern for "the aestheticism which threatens here is no worse than the other 'isms' or any 'ism.' They are all dangerous," as Barth notes.[90] Greater danger, still, lies in the omission of God's beauty from theological discourse and the ascription of the imagination to the non-real thus diminishing Christian worship, witness, and wisdom.[91]

The Diminishing of Christian Worship

Balthasar makes a bold claim against those who dismiss beauty as unimportant for discerning the way things are: "Whoever sneers at [beauty] as if she were the ornament of a bourgeois past—whether he admits it or

---

89. Barth, *CD* 2/1, 651–52. Barth's decision to incorporate the rhetoric of beauty into the doctrine of God acknowledges the aforementioned concerns. Yet, Barth insists that "we speak of God's beauty only in explanation of His glory. It is, therefore, a subordinate and auxiliary idea which enables us to achieve a specific clarification and emphasis" (*CD* 2/1, 653). When we speak of God's beauty we must do so not in abstraction but in light of God's self-revelation (*CD* 2/1, 656–66).

90. Barth, *CD* 2/1, 652.

91. See also my essay "Beauty and the Baptists" where I argue why the omission of beauty from our theological discourse is detrimental for the sacramental ordinances, Scripture, and the Gospel within the Baptist tradition.

Panel One: No Room in the Inn

not—can no longer *pray* and soon will no longer be able to *love* [God or neighbor]."[92] Balthasar's assertion ties God's beauty to prayer and love—the instrument and impetus for worship. Yet, why is it that one can no longer pray or love if one dispenses with God's beauty? Prayer is the means by which we are permitted to communion with God through an intimate dialogue where we listen to God's Word (Matt 17:5) and respond in love with the totality of our being (Matt 22:37–39). In doing so, we are "bathed in this light which radiates upon us from God," and in turn "we ourselves become light and transparent before him."[93]

When we encounter God through prayer, we experience the triune God in a living, dynamic encounter, one that shames our understanding of God, the world, ourselves, and others. To exclude God's beauty from our understanding of that encounter makes his truth and goodness unattractive, lifeless, boring, and cold. In fact, by ignoring or sneering at God's beauty, we actually delimit our understanding, closing off the possibility of experiencing the triune God himself. If, however, his beauty attracts, persuades, and draws us out of ourselves and into something greater—participation in his divine life—then his beauty shapes and forms our imaginations such that we can envision how to perform our part in his drama of redemption, all by the power of the Holy Spirit (John 6:65).

When beauty is no more, we are no longer overawed and humbled by God's majesty and holiness nor convinced he can satisfy our deepest longings. We fail to be still and listen to God's Word because we cannot envision why it matters or the life God intends for us to live. Instead, we are overwhelmed by the vicissitudes of life, often becoming impatient and frustrated with the things we cannot control. Prayer becomes nothing more than a manipulative tool motivated by egocentric desires, inundating God "with problems, with demands for information, for clues, [or] for an easier path" because "we cannot go on living unless [our requests] are answered."[94] Prayer and ultimately our worship become about us, "instances of natural egocentrism and even idolatrous self-securing."[95] Our love becomes self-centered rather than other-centered. In light of God's beauty, though, prayer and worship can order our affections as the *beauty*

---

92. Balthasar, *GL* I, 18. Emphasis added.

93. Balthasar, *Prayer*, 15. See also his "Toward a Theology of Christian Prayer," 245–57 and his "Christian Prayer," 15–22.

94. Balthasar, *Prayer*, 16.

95. Farley, *Faith and Beauty*, 106.

Beauty as the Theological Beast?

of his holiness shines into the darkness of our hearts, transforming us to love God and neighbor rather than merely ourselves (Matt 22:37-39).

On a more pragmatic note, many Protestant churches today are engrossed in "worship style wars" as the church growth movement with its buildings, budgets, and baptisms desires to attract "seekers" into their services. The logic usually goes like this: we need to be sensitive to the tastes of nonbelievers so that our services will attract them to our church. Then, once they come, the preaching of the gospel will change their lives. What often results is an emotive, sentimental, and nostalgic worship service that mimics pop culture in order to attract these seekers; sermons are crafted to the lowest common denominator; and buildings are designed to look like shopping centers. In these instances, the church professes to be wise but has exchanged God's glory for a lie (Rom 1:20-25).

At its core, this argument fails to consider God's beauty because it assumes that the form or medium in which the Gospel is presented remains neutral, having no affect on the message or those who hear it.[96] In other words, the way in which the Gospel message is packaged within a particular cultural form actually matters to how the message is received. To be sure, effective communication of the Gospel properly interprets the surrounding culture in order to understand what is vying for our attention, what cultural narratives are competing or complimentary of the Gospel story, and where we are situated in the flow of redemptive history.[97] Yet, when the Gospel is set within a nostalgic, sentimental, and emotively driven worship service, church leaders fail to evaluate how their use of popular culture impacts the message and fail to consider the *manner* in which God reveals himself.[98] The focus is often on the truth and good-

96. Hodges, "Aesthetics and the Place of Beauty in Worship," 63-66.
97. See Vanhoozer, "What is Everyday Theology?," 15-60.
98. Church leaders often argue that they are being "incarnational" when using various cultural artifacts, technology, etc. in their worship services. Such argumentation, though, fails to wrestle with the deeper implications of *why* God took on human flesh. Hodges offers important insights as to how church leaders can consider God's beauty in worship: "In our decisions about worship, we need to put into practice a good understanding of beauty. Realize that the music we choose is first and foremost to be our best we can offer, not merely what the surrounding culture will bear. The liturgy should be in a language the unbeliever can understand, but should also offer something he cannot find anywhere else in his world: order, fittingness, mature sensibilities, and beauty.... Beauty can speak to the heart in a way that logical reasoning and moral teaching cannot. Our musical and liturgical choices in worship can display an aspect of God that is often ignored. We must ask ourselves, how can we whet the congregation's appetites now for the satisfactions that will be theirs in God for eternity?" ("Aesthetics and the Place of Beauty in Worship," 73).

ness of God without consideration for God's beauty. This kind of worship may satisfy in the immediate but fails to touch the deepest recesses of our being. God did not disclose himself as a proposition or as a virtue. God disclosed himself as a person, the Lord Jesus Christ. To ignore the form of God's self-revelation seeks to understand God *in abstracto*. What do we do, though, when we find ourselves in houses of worship where God's beauty is held in low esteem?

We must remember that we live between the two advents in light of the resurrection where the eschatological has broken into history. This eschatological component of God's beauty, which we will discuss in chapter four, reminds us, in the here and now, to worship in spirit and truth (John 4:20–26) all the while longing for that beatific vision where the community of God will worship in true beauty (Rev 4).[99] No matter how well worship is performed where God's beauty is taken seriously, all of our worship falls short. Our attempts are futile when our affections are self-centered rather than God-centered because God does not delight in superficial worship (Isa 1:11–20; Hos 6; Matt 23:13–36).

Nevertheless, as Barth argues, "form is necessary to the content because it belongs to it." The perfect content of God's being, his triune life, "makes his form perfect." In other words, "the perfection of His form is simply the radiating outwards of the perfection of His content and therefore God Himself."[100] Form matters. To neglect God's form of self-revelation is to ignore an aspect of God, thereby diminishing our worship. Therefore, let us heed Augustine's exhortation to worship with understanding "and let not the weakness of the flesh turn away [our] eyes from the splendor of His beauty."[101]

The Diminishing of Christian Witness

Those who omit beauty from theological discourse often do so because of beauty's supposed association with egocentric pleasures and the satisfaction of human desires—in short, hedonism. They fear the delight found in the beauty of the created order (both creation and human creation) will become the object of our desires, mistaking the created for the Creator. This proclivity to possess the object of our desire, though, stems from our sinful nature, actually doing violence to God's beauty by confusing the

---

99. See Jüngel, "Even the Beautiful Must Die," 59–82.
100. Barth, *CD* 2/1, 659; cf. Balthasar, *GL* I, 20.
101. Augustine, *Expositions of the Psalms*, 237.

subjective elements with the objective. We should caution ourselves regarding the order of our affections, yet there is no need to dismiss God's beauty because it appeals to our desires. After all, as C. S. Lewis notes, given "the staggering nature of the rewards promised in the Gospels, it would seem that Our Lord finds our desires not too strong, but too weak." We are often too content and pleased by vain pleasures because "we are half-hearted creatures, fooling about with drink and sex and ambition when *infinite joy* is offered us, like an ignorant child who wants to go on making mud pies in a slum because he cannot imagine what is meant by the offer of a holiday at the sea. We are far too easily pleased."[102]

Omitting God's beauty hinders, what many medieval divines knew as *fruitio Dei*, turning our delight in the Lord into a duty and nullifying the hope we must witness to in our narcissistic and nihilistic culture. Holy Scripture exhorts us to delight in the Lord (Pss 34:8, 37:4; Prov 23:26), to rejoice in the Lord always (Matt 25:11, Phil 4:4), and to delight in the Law and ways of God (Pss 1:2, 112:1, 145:16; Rom 7:22). Joy in the Lord arises not from an egocentric desire to gain personal satisfaction, nor can it "be conjured up at will by an obsessive desire for happiness." Rather, the joy of Christ comes "only from our deliverance out of a private abyss of illusion,"[103] reorienting our affections toward God and giving us hope (Rom 5:1–5; Jas 1:2–6). This is the beauty of the gospel that quenches humanity's thirst for something greater than us.

J. R. R. Tolkien also remarks that "the birth of Christ is the eucatastrophe of human history. The resurrection is the eucatastrophe of the incarnation. This story begins and ends in joy."[104] If we are to proclaim the good news of this cataclysmic event, then we must bear witness to the truth in joy. Yet, where does this joy come from? What attracts us to this joy in the Lord? It is the *form* of God's glory, namely his beauty revealed in and through the incarnate Christ by the power of the Spirit. When our hope is in this joy, "there is a transcending of egocentric pleasure into the life of the other" as we participate fittingly in God's drama of redemption.[105] Yet, if we continue to disregard God's beauty, especially when bearing witness to the Gospel in our speech and actions, we "will always have in a slight or dangerous degree something joyless, without sparkle or humour, not to

---

102. Lewis, "Weight of Glory," 26. Emphasis added.
103. Leiva, translator's note to Balthasar's, *Heart of the World*, 9.
104. Tolkien, "On Fairy-Stories," 83.
105. Farley, *Faith and Beauty*, 106.

say tedious and then finally neither persuasive nor convincing."[106] Hence, as beauty of the Gospel is ignored, truth and goodness becomes distorted and inevitably disappears, which is why "the fool says in his heart, 'There is no beauty,' and thus refuses to see the fittingness of the gospel. Things fall apart; wisdom is no more."[107]

The Diminishing of Christian Wisdom

The British painter Cecil Collins, known for making "the fool" a distinct motif of his paintings, sketches a pen and brown ink drawing of the crucifixion, entitled "The Crucifixion, 1952." In this drawing, the crucified Christ is prominently at the center with several stilted and distant figures ordered in linear fashion, possessing sharp weaponry, on the right and a line of dancing fools in jester like costumes, playing the drums and coming to comfort the clinging woman at the foot of the cross, on the left. The crucified Christ's downward and leftward gaze gives tacit approval to the dancing fools as his bent left knee seems to indicate that he is about to join their dance.[108] This sketch could be aptly subtitled, "Fools for Christ," as Collins gives a visual rendering of the beauty of God's wisdom, which is often considered foolishness in today's world. To disregard God's beauty makes God's wisdom distant, prickly, and stiff, similar to the stilted figures on the right side of Collins's sketch. To embrace God's beauty is to enter into the "foolishness" of the cross, envisioning how to act fittingly in God's drama of redemption.

Contemporary aesthetic theology is "a theology that makes use of [aesthetic] concepts" thereby "betraying and selling out theological substance to the current viewpoints of an inner-worldly theory of beauty."[109] Such theology lacks wisdom because it lacks "the capacity to see what is [really] there, without illusion, self-indulgence, fantasy or denigration;" consequently, aesthetic theology will ultimately lose its "capacity to love."[110] Amorphous theology, while acknowledging the real, limits its understanding of it to the true and/or the good.[111] Enlightenment modes of thinking

---

106. Barth, *CD* 2/1, 655. Emphasis added.

107. Vanhoozer, "Praising God in Song," 19.

108. See Anderson, *Cecil Collins*, 81 for an easily accessible print of Cecil Collins's "The Crucifixion" (1952) and brief interpretation.

109. Balthasar, *GL* I, 38.

110. Harries, *Art and the Beauty of God*, 106.

111. Brown, *Restoration of Reason*, 142.

captivate their imaginations, whether deductive (rationalism) or inductive (empiricism), such that the absolute certainty of the knowledge of God is derived from a particular theological method. The imagination has no seat at the table of scientific reason.[112] Wisdom, consequently, is impeded as theology splinters into numerous theological disciplines, furthering the divide between theology and life. Theology is no longer seen as a "peculiarly beautiful science" but as a high-minded discipline done in the pristine, whitewashed, ivory towers of academia disconnected from the dingy and dirty mess of daily living.[113] Such mischaracterizations stem from these modes of thinking. Yet, God's beauty transforms the imagination, enabling it to see how to act fittingly in an unjust world. Such actions take wisdom, for wisdom "integrates the true, the good, and the beautiful."[114]

To the extent contemporary Protestant theology either denies an objective realism or omits beauty from its purview, it subscribes to a deformed portrait of God's beauty. This image has captivated the contemporary Protestant theological imagination with serious implications for Christian worship, witness, and wisdom. During the last three decades, however, beauty seems to be awakening from its slumber as theologians like Hans Urs von Balthasar, Robert Jenson, Edward Farley, Patrick Sherry, John Milbank, Graham Ward, and David Bentley Hart attempt to integrate God's beauty into their theological discourse. The significance of beauty's awakening should not go unnoticed, particularly in light of the parallel renaissance of trinitarian theology.

---

112. See Lewis's *Surprised by Joy* where he chronicles his struggles on how to unite reason and the imagination. Here is a brief snippet: "Such, then, was the state of my imaginative life; over against it stood the life of my intellect. The two hemispheres of my mind were in the sharpest contrast. On the one side a many-island sea of poetry and myth; on the other a glib and shallow 'rationalism.' Nearly all that I loved I believed to be imaginary; nearly all that I believed to be real I thought grim and meaningless" (170). Lewis would ultimately unite these two cognitive faculties together, finding that the imagination also gave him access to reality.

113. Barth, *CD* 2/1, 656. Barth chastises theologians who do not enjoy their work: "Indeed, we can confidently say that [theology] is the most beautiful of all the sciences. To find the sciences distasteful is the mark of the Philistine. It is an extreme form of Philistinism to find, or to be able to find, theology distasteful. The theologian who has no joy in his work is not a theologian at all. Sulky faces, morose thoughts and boring ways of speaking are intolerable in this science" (656).

114. See Harries, *Art and the Beauty of God*, 65–79 and Vanhoozer, "Praising God in Song," 115.

PANEL ONE: No Room in the Inn

Re-form-ing Beauty: Sleeping Beauty Awakes

Some attribute beauty's awakening in theology to its covert entry via the arts, creation, and postmodernity's infatuation with image while others contend it has reemerged due to a sustained attention to cultural life.[115] It seems to me that God's beauty resounds within the corridors of this burgeoning discipline called theological aesthetics, in part, for more properly theological reasons, found in the parallel resurgence of trinitarian theology. Barth makes the point well: "the triunity of God" appears to be "the secret of His beauty. If we deny this, we at once have a God without radiance and without joy (and without humour!); a God without beauty."[116] The connection between the two trends appears to be the common emphasis on particularity, and more specifically on the inseparability between form and content.[117]

Of the transcendentals, "beauty, more than unity, goodness, and truth, oscillates between the sensible and the intellectual, the concrete and the universal. It totters more precariously on the precipice between complete abstraction and total particularity."[118] Trinitarian theology has similar resonance as it focuses on the particularity of God's one being as the Father, Son, and Holy Spirit. The incarnation of the Logos becomes the point of embarkation for much of theological aesthetics, which is why

---

115. See Farley, *Faith and Beauty*, 67 and 79n3 and Treier et al., *Beauty of God*, 8. I am not sure how "natural" a theology of beauty has reemerged among North American evangelicals, if it even has, but Treier and company offer sage advice for articulating one: "If the doctrines of creation, incarnation and sacrament are to have authority for Christian approaches to aesthetics, then we must attend to the reality of the Fall; the dynamics of the life, death, and resurrection of Jesus; and the workings of the Spirit in the life of the church" (10–11).

116. Barth, *CD* 2/1, 661. Although Barth's *Church Dogmatics* is largely attributed as the progenitor of this trinitarian renaissance, the surge in literature on the Trinity begins in the 1970s and early 1980s with the likes of Karl Rahner, Walter Kasper, W. J. Hill, John D. Zizioulas, Robert Jenson, and Jürgen Moltmann, all parallel to theological aesthetics. See Gunton's *Promise of Trinitarian Theology* and Grenz, *Rediscovering the Triune God* for a survey and bibliography.

117. See my article "God's Beauty-in-Act" where I give a fuller explanation of Barth's take on beauty and further warrant for suggesting a correlation between the renaissance in trinitarian theology and theological aesthetics.

118. Gallagher, "Analogy of Beauty." Carol Harrison, speaking about the tension between the dangers of beauty and its ability to evoke wonder and awe, asks the question: "Again, why is this? Is it because, of the three transcendentals, beauty is the most embodied, the most incarnate, the one which is virtually inseparable from matter—from the created, temporal, mutable, realm" that makes the point (*Beauty and Revelation*, 271).

Balthasar places beauty first (as we will see in chapter two). Yet, we also see an oscillation between God's particularity and his universality—stated differently, between *De Deo uno* and *De Deo trino*—not unlike beauty's oscillation between the intellectual and the affective. The key, in both instances, is to keep the two in balance, not emphasizing one over the other, collapsing one into the other, or severing them from each other. Perhaps these affinities with trinitarian theology have given rise to theological aesthetics and, more specifically, a return to a theological understanding of beauty. The following taxonomy not only seeks to trace the contours of beauty's awakening but also to situate this project further in hopes of addressing some of the aforementioned concerns of relational theism.

Assessing Theologians of Beauty

There appear to be three general approaches among those attempting to recover theological notions of beauty: 1. the transcendental/iconic, 2. the anthropocentric, and 3. the christocentric. The transcendental/iconic category understands beauty to be a transcendental notion that is mediated through the material, whether through nature or human creation. God's beauty is understood by reasoning, usually analogically, from these various media back into the Godhead.[119] Patrick Sherry's work, *Spirit and Beauty*, is representative, particularly regarding the transcendental. Although Patrick Sherry attempts to root his understanding of beauty in the Trinity, he ultimately follows this pattern because he derives his understanding of beauty by assuming its perfection in God and God's working that perfection into the world. The Holy Spirit, then, is the locus and mediator of God's beauty. He works God's perfect beauty into creation and is the primary source for ascertaining it that serves as a way to God.[120] Although Sherry does not dwell long on defining beauty, he insists on beauty's ob-

---

119. Robert Jenson discusses beauty as a transcendental of being in volume one of his *Systematic Theology*, following much of the medieval transcendental tradition as well as appropriating Jonathan Edwards (His appropriation of Edwards is one of the few). He understands God's beauty as "the perfect harmony of the triune communal life." In other words, "the actual living exchange between Father, Son, and Spirit, as this exchange is perfect simply as exchange, as it *sings*" (235). His correlations between God's beauty and music are insightful, yet God's beauty is still in his *becoming*, as a fugue thereby entangling God's identity with creation and redemptive history.

120. Sherry, *Spirit and Beauty*, 121–41. See also Sherry's article "Sacramentality of Things," 575–90 for further evidence of his transcendental/iconic approach where he argues that "we can perceive signs-by-likeness of God in the world, especially in beauty" (575).

jectivity and subjectivity since creation possesses a realist component that produces delight in a subject. He also connects God's beauty to earthly beauty by the Holy Spirit's work in inspiring human creativity through wonder and the imagination, and contends that beauty has an eschatological element due to the Holy Spirit's role in the resurrection.[121]

Sherry's transcendental/iconic approach to reviving theological discourse on beauty offers several important contributions with one significant drawback. Sherry is right to proffer a theological understanding of beauty by placing beauty within the Godhead, connecting the Holy Spirit and God's beauty. This is significant because any theological account of God's beauty must account for the Spirit. His insistence on objective and subjective components of beauty and his emphasis on its eschatological character also give God's beauty an important role in redemption and the consummation of the world. The primary drawback for Sherry's proposal, though, is his lack of christological control, which has implications for his theological method as well as his conception of God's beauty. By locating God's beauty in the Holy Spirit as evidenced in creation, Sherry contends that humanity has a pathway to God, blurring the lines between the human spirit and the Holy Spirit. Ironically, such an approach places beauty in the hands of personal taste, which Sherry demurs in his assessment of contemporary notions of beauty.[122]

Radical Orthodoxy's (RO) discussion of beauty and the sublime also seems to fit best within the transcendental/iconic motif, although it does have some overlap with the other two categories.[123] In the collection of essays, entitled *Theological Perspectives on God and Beauty*, John Milbank remarks that "modern beauty after Kant is therefore a 'raped' beauty" because modern beauty is no longer associated with the sublime, "the terrible aspect that is the wounding excess of the visible that pierces our everyday defenses." Milbank continues, noting the objective and subjective aspects of divine beauty: "Given this simultaneous objectivity and subjectivity of the experience of the beautiful, we can say that to see . . . the beautiful

---

121. Sherry, *Spirit and Beauty*, 43–48, 109–113, 142–59.

122. Sherry does mention that "in associating beauty with the Holy Spirit we are not ruling out a connection with the other Persons of the Trinity" (78). Yet, he does not indicate how this is so nor detail what relationship the Son or the Father has in discerning God's beauty. Further development of these relationships may have served to eclipse the ambiguity regarding the relationship between the human spirit and Holy Spirit (See his chapter 5, "Inspiration and Imagination" and 6, "Reflections of Divine Beauty").

123. For a superb introduction to the "spirit" or "sensibility" of Radical Orthodoxy, see Smith, *Introducing Radical Orthodoxy* and Milbank, et al., *Radical Orthodoxy*.

is to see the invisible in the visible."[124] Like Milbank, Graham Ward also speaks ill of contemporary conceptions of beauty, indicting modernity's conception of the world as "opaque, inert data" for beauty's secularization. Consequently, he understands God's beauty as "iconic" where "the beauty of Christ makes manifest His own watermark within creation" that "calls forth praise, doxology."[125]

RO's efforts to rehabilitate the concept of beauty for theological discourse by retrieving a notion of the sublime are noble and needed in order to reassert, in part, the wholly otherness of God. Their theological realism is refreshing as they attempt to usurp the common Kantian dualisms that plague much of contemporary theology and reassert an objective and subjective account of God's beauty. Moreover, Ward's emphasis on discipleship—that necessary disciplining of the whole self—as essential to discerning God's beauty rightly weds aesthetics and ethics without collapsing one into the other. It is difficult, though, to discern exactly *why* RO thinks God is beautiful. If RO desires to recover a theological realism, then a cogent rendering of God's objective beauty needs articulation, no matter how sketchy it might be because of their concern for incorporating the sublime.[126] Other points of clarification are also needed, particularly regarding the pneumatological aspects of God's beauty and the noetic affects of sin on humanity's perception of the beautiful.

The second category, the anthropocentric approach, attempts to recover a theological notion of beauty through the experience of the redeemed community of faith. Edward Farley follows this pattern by purporting that beauty should be defined in light of the redeemed *imago Dei*—the life of the community of faith understood as "redemptive existence."[127] Farley contends that although God's creation and the intratrinitarian relationships are beautiful, they "do not tell us how and why beauty is intrinsic to redemptive transformation;" in fact, "do [they] not all . . . presuppose the fact of redemptive transformation?" That being the case, beauty predi-

---

124. Milbank, "Beauty and Soul," 3–6. Cf. Rossi, "Metaphysics of the Sublime," 101–111.

125. Ward, "Beauty of God," 36, 43–44. Ward, in a recent essay "*Kenosis, Poiesis, and Genesis*," 165–75, intimates at the rudiments of my proposal, revealing some overlap between these various categories. Coming to these conclusions independent of Ward, this book seeks to develop similar lines of thought and flesh out Ward's suggestion of a "theological aesthetics of suffering" (173).

126. Perhaps some of the ambiguity lies with their implicit ascription to a platonic ontology, what James K. A. Smith calls "Radical Orthodoxy's New Plato" in his essay "Will the Real Plato Please Stand Up?," 61–72.

127. Farley, *Faith and Beauty*, 83–100.

cated on the life of faith presumes "the need of redemption (sin) and the possibility of redemption (*imago Dei*)." Farley concludes that any understanding of beauty should be through the renewal of the *imago Dei* found in the redemptive existence of the community of faith.[128]

Farley's anthropocentric approach draws our attention to the presupposition for the existence of the community of faith—the fact of redemption, which entails the problem of sin and possibility of redemption. He missteps, though, by predicating his understanding of beauty on his notion of redemptive existence because this existence is the *result* of divine redemptive action and not the *action* itself. Furthermore, Farley never articulates why redemption of the *imago Dei* is beautiful. Is it because of the sheer attractiveness of going beyond oneself—yet what makes going beyond oneself attractive? If it is because the *imago Dei* mirrors God's self-transcendence and compassion, as he seems to suggest, then Farley defines beauty by beginning with a particular doctrine, which he attempts to avoid at the onset. So either Farley is inconsistent by rooting his understanding in God and claiming not to or he follows an anthropocentric formulation that privileges human action over divine action. The latter seems to be his intent.[129]

Moving Forward with Hans Urs von Balthasar

The final category, the christological approach, attempts to recover a theological notion of beauty by beginning with God's communication of himself through himself in Jesus Christ. Hans Urs von Balthasar follows this pattern by declaring that Christ is the *Übergestalt* and thus all have meaning and are held together in him. Balthasar is quick to distinguish his approach from other aesthetic approaches by arguing that these secular aesthetic models are smitten with human constructions, which rupture the analogical relationship between theological beauty and earthly beauty, thereby jettisoning any notion of objectivity.[130] Christ is the neces-

---

128. Ibid., 84, 93. Other works that could be placed in this category include Brown, *Religious Aesthetics* and Martin, *Beauty and Holiness*.

129. Farley derives his understanding of beauty on the life of faith by following a theological method that attempts to uncover interdependent systems comprising various phenomenon rather than one that privileges a particular doctrine, say the doctrine of God or Christology (viii). This is why he turns primarily to the western story of beauty to derive his understanding of divine beauty rather than to God's actions in Christ by the Spirit.

130. Balthasar, *GL* I, 38–39. Other works that could be placed in this category

Beauty as the Theological Beast?

sary objectivity—the perfect form and content who brings together the heavenly and earthly to articulate a theological aesthetic. God's beauty, for Balthasar, centers on perfect concordance, which refers "primarily to the concordance between Christ's mission and existence." This is rooted in "the fact that he does not do his own will but that of the Father." As such, they "'are in tune' with one another and no one can accuse him of any disharmony."[131]

The difficulty, however, with Balthasar's approach lies primarily in his attempts to reconcile what traditionally separates Catholics and Protestants—*analogia entis* vs. *analogia fidei*, as two ways of understanding God's singular revelation. His attempts at reconciliation lead him to posit a closer relationship between nature and grace whereby vestiges of God as impressions of his being are present within creation. Yet, Balthasar still maintains that these natural forms arrive first by grace and are meaningful only in Christ. So is natural revelation a viable alternative to knowing God, or is God's particular revelation necessary for understanding natural revelation? It seems to me that Balthasar's synthesis is closer to a Protestant understanding of general revelation because of his christocentric focus, although his restatement is in traditional Catholic terminology.[132] I also

---

include Navone's *Toward a Theology of Beauty*; Viladesau's *Theological Aesthetics*; and Hart's *The Beauty of the Infinite*, which is an "extended marginalium" (29) to Balthasar's work. Hart ascribes particularly to Balthasar's creative-redemptive approach and understanding of the *analogia entis* (241). He is right to acknowledge beauty's elusiveness while recognizing its objective nature and subjective appeal to human desire (18). Yet, he ironically has little to say about what beauty actually is, ascribing beauty to God often because God's self-revelation is intrinsically pleasing (266). Perhaps, a thicker explanation of the beauty of Christ and the Spirit's communicative role would serve as a remedy. Without such specificity, it is difficult to determine how the rhetoric of beauty factors into his "*dogmatica minora*" (153). Moreover, it seems Hart's work could benefit from a fuller account of the relationship of beauty to the morally good rather than merely the aesthetic, particularly since he adamantly contends for an ontology of peace. Nevertheless, Hart's work is indeed commendable as he affirms the indispensability of beauty for Christian theology predicated on God's dynamic trinitarian existence.

131. Balthasar, *GL* I, 469.

132. If nature and grace are as close as Balthasar presumes, it seems he would give credence to other world religions as viable ways to God. Yet, Balthasar is not amenable to them because Christ is "the measure, both in judgment and redemption, of all other religious forms of mankind" (Balthasar, *GL* I, 171, 216–17, 437, 479–80, 496), which seems to affirm that he is closer to a Protestant restatement of the doctrine of general revelation than to the traditional understanding of *analogia entis*. Can he really argue, then, for the kind of sharp distinction between aesthetic theology and theological aesthetics, if nature and grace are as close as he presumes? We will explore this issue further in chapter two.

PANEL ONE: No Room in the Inn

wonder whether he has afforded nature greater significance by advocating a *mutual* relationship between Christ and creation that seems to suggest that creation "images" God in the same way that Christ does. Balthasar also predicates his understanding of the *analogia entis* on the ontological infinite difference between the divine persons—what I call a divine eternal kenosis—that seems to place him close to tritheism.[133]

How God's beauty is understood depends, in part, on how we define the God-world relation, and as such, will be an underlying theme in the remaining chapters. For example, if one presumes God is maximally perfect beauty, then beauty in creation is a *refraction* of his beauty. If one reasons from the beauty of creation, then created beauty is *analogous* to God's beauty. If the redemptive community is the basis, then God's beauty is a *reflection* of that community. No matter the approach, a Christian understanding of beauty affirms its place in reality alongside the true and the good, has objective and subjective qualities, is seen when properly related, and is an aspect of God. All of these approaches within our typology offer valuable accounts to understanding God's beauty. Yet, if Christ, who brings together the heavenly and earthly, is God's distinct speaking and doing form of his beauty, which presumes a communicative God-world relation, then the *drama of redemption* attested to in Scripture should be the *norming norm*, ordering the other accounts. If this is our approach to rendering a trinitarian understanding of God's beauty, where in the economy of God's self-revelation do we begin?

God has revealed himself most fully in his Son, Jesus Christ—the Word made flesh—who is the radiance of God's glory and the exact representation of his being as attested to in Holy Scripture (John 1:1–14; Col 1:15–20; Heb 1:1–4). To be sure, we can gain knowledge of God from other aspects of his self-revelation because he spoke long ago to our forefathers, Abraham, Isaac, and Jacob, as well as through the prophets (Heb 1:1). Yet, it is through Jesus Christ that we gain a fuller understanding about what God is saying and doing (Heb 1:1–4). Jesus Christ is definitive for discerning God's beauty, which is why in chapter two we attempt to appropriate critically Balthasar's notion of Christ as *Übergestalt* and *Herrlichkeit*.[134] Let us examine, now, how Balthasar derives these conclusions,

---

133. See also Goodall, "Hans Urs von Balthasar," 425–26 and Williams, "Balthasar and the Trinity," 37–50. We will explore this notion of "divine eternal kenosis" further in chapter four.

134. Dellatre declares that the key to unlocking Jonathan Edwards's theology is his notion of beauty, particularly since he equates it with God's glory (*Beauty and Sensibility*, 1). If beauty is such a central theme for Edwards, why not chose Edwards

providing us with the theological loci for retrieving a theology of beauty and the imagination.[135]

---

as a primary dialogue partner? Edwards's theology of beauty is commendable when he argues for beauty's objectivity, subjective receptivity, and for the inherent ethical implications that follow from beauty, giving way to his notion of the beauty of holiness. His linking of beauty to the Trinity also resonates with the thrust of this project. Yet, he is keen to locate divine beauty with the Holy Spirit, not unlike the transcendental/iconic approach, identifying the Spirit as the Beautifier rather than with Christ in whom beauty appears.

135. I am under no illusion that my attempts to reform our understanding of God's beauty will result in some pristine notion unscathed by my finitude and fallenness. Rather, as I converse with the Christian tradition both past and present, while privileging the biblical text, I hope what emerges is a sage understanding of God's beauty and its significance for Christian theology and human imagining. I am in substantial agreement with John Webster's astute advice for such a project: "All talk of God is hazardous. Modern constraints bring particular challenges which can be partially defeated by attending to a broader and wiser history, but there is no pure Christian past whose retrieval can ensure theological fidelity" ("Theologies of Retrieval," 596–97).

2

Re-form-ing Beauty

The Significance of Hans Urs von Balthasar's Theological Aesthetics

BEAUTY AND THE IMAGINATION, AS WE LEARNED IN CHAPTER ONE, HAVE a precarious standing in contemporary Protestant theology. Many still consider beauty and the imagination to be fruitless subjectivities left to the poets while serious theologians deal only with the hard sciences of exegesis, historiography, and logical reasoning. Still others implicitly embrace beauty as they attend to narrative, poetic, metaphorical, and other literary forms. Yet, these forms are considered to have little to do with the way things really are. Balthasar's concerns about the broadening gap between theology and life still resonate today as relational theists maintain. Yet, while relational theists contend that Christian theology's irrelevance is due to classical theism, Balthasar argues that it is actually due to a dysfunctional view of reality.

Balthasar identifies several reasons for this divorce between theology and life and the subsequent dismissal of the beautiful, not unlike those detailed in the tale of beauty found in chapter one. Two primary sources for this caesura stem from what Balthasar calls "the cosmological reduction" and "the anthropological reduction." The cosmological reduction comes about at the hands of a metaphysical shift away from the supernatural (not necessarily a Christian understanding of it) to a natural one, reducing reality to merely the material. The anthropological reduction makes human beings the measure of all things whereby they give the world its structure and are able to transcend the world via human reason.[1] Balthasar

---

1. Balthasar, *Love Alone Is Credible*, 15–50. I am grateful to conversations with Fr. Edward Oakes who first directed me to this book as well as Balthasar's *Heart of*

roots the reduction of being in the *esse univocum* of Duns Scotus (Being as a Concept) and Meister Eckhart (Being as God).[2] These roots bear fruit as this reductionism takes shape in the thought of René Descartes and Immanuel Kant when "the turning from Being to mental concepts, from things (and God) existing *in themselves* to things conceived as existing 'for me' and 'from me.' From now on, the subject can regard itself as legislative reason."[3] At this point, Christian theology adopts modern scientific methods, fragmenting into numerous specializations where "not only the faith but the heart, too, is wrapped up in a spiritless, conscientious and ultimately Pharisaical practice, a religion of dogmas and an enthusiasm for dogmas (the more that are defined, the better), a zeal for everything that can be seen, that is limited, calculable, and controlled."[4] Many theologians have attempted to bridge this chasm, only to fall short because they presume the validity of this bifurcation at the outset.[5]

Balthasar's theological aesthetics attempts to counteract the cosmological and anthropological reductions by advocating a theological understanding of beauty that draws perceivers out of themselves and into an encounter with God, eliciting a response and demonstrating the interconnectedness between aesthetics and ethics. This chapter critically engages the heart of Balthasar's theological aesthetics where he identifies Christ as *Herrlichkeit* and *Übergestalt,* christocentric terms that allude to Christ's

---

the World and *God Question and Modern Man* as entry points into the Balthasarian adventure.

2. Balthasar, *GL* V, 9–47.

3. Balthasar, *GL* V, 28. Cf. Balthasar, *GL* I, 72. Although Balthasar attributes the demise of western metaphysics to Duns Scotus and Meister Eckhart (*GL* V, 12–20), he notes that "only with Descartes does philosophy become dependent on the scientific ideal of the rising natural sciences, thereby beginning its rift with theology" (*GL* I, 72), lending further support to our previous arguments in chapter one.

4. Balthasar, *Creator Spirit*, 502. See also Balthasar, *GL* II, 11–17 where he maintains that theology after Aquinas became a "specialized" discipline similar to that of the sciences.

5. See Balthasar, *Spouse of the Word*, 181–209. Balthasar considers the Reformation and its emphasis on Scripture as a noble attempt to overcome this chasm between scholastic and spiritual theology yet ultimately detrimental because of its individualistic tendencies. He believes the neoscholasticism of the Counter-Reformation, far from bridging the gap, actually furthers the divide because of its inattention to divine revelation. Balthasar mentions more contemporary examples like liberation theology as it tries to bridge the divide by uniting faith with social and political activism. Although Balthasar concurs with liberation theology's central thrust to take up the cause of the disenfranchised, he faults it for focusing only upon the good to the neglect of the beautiful (Ouellet, "Message of Balthasar's Theology to Modern Theology," 270–99).

singularity, God's divine freedom and trinitarian nature, and the inherent connections between creation and redemption.

Underlying these claims, though, are questions regarding Balthasar's doctrines of sin and prevenient grace, which are based on a divine eternal kenosis, that blur the lines between justification and sanctification and seemly undermine the efficacy of his claims. Yet, if we maintain a clear distinction between justification and sanctification and retain the biblical ascription of kenosis to the Son (which I will discuss in chapter four), these christological terms become the theological loci for retrieving a theology of beauty, preserving the efficacy of God's glory. Let us begin by briefly sketching Balthasar's theological aesthetics in light of his metaphysical concerns.

Aesthetic Theology or Theological Aesthetics?

The rift between theology and life primarily stems, according to Balthasar, from the demise of Western metaphysics and theology's defunct view of reality, resulting in the dearth of beauty in theological discourse. Also contributing to beauty's conspicuous absence is an understanding of aesthetics (the science of perception) as an *independent* discipline with its own scientific methods pursued irrespective of the true and the good. Balthasar faces a dilemma as to whether beauty can be disassociated from hedonistic motifs or whether the notion should be abandoned all together.[6] It is patently obvious how Balthasar answers this dilemma as he has written seven volumes to developing what he means by theological aesthetics, hardly an abandonment of the concept. To understand, though, what he means by *theological* aesthetics, we need to understand what he intends to avoid, namely an *aesthetic* theology.

Aesthetic Theology According to Balthasar

Balthasar acknowledges the difficulties for reintroducing beauty into theological discourse not only because of the pejorative connotations surrounding the term but also because of the tendency to identify what is beautiful with the inner subjective feelings of pleasure. If beauty finds its meaning in the inner subjectivity of human persons, then the object of contemplation begins with human experience rather than God, seeking some pristine, unadulterated understanding of beauty that is then applied

---

6. Balthasar, *GL* I, 79–80.

to him. God's beauty is reduced to and constrained by "an inner-worldly theory of beauty," never able to reach beyond the realm of personal taste.[7]

The problem with this approach, Balthasar contends, is two-fold. First, aesthetic theology is fundamentally at odds with Christian spirituality because it seeks to create a world that evades the ugly and dark sides of human existence. Balthasar declares that "every aesthetic which simply seeks to ignore the nocturnal sides of existence can itself, from the outset, be ignored as a sort of aestheticism" because such approaches live beyond the realities of ordinary human life as an escape from the bane of human existence.[8] Second, the Romantic theology, upon which this aestheticism is built, fails because it does not properly adhere to the Creator-creature distinction, thereby rupturing the analogical relationship between God's beauty and worldly beauty.[9] When aesthetic theologies collapse the Creator-creature distinction, there is an *esse univocum* whereby God becomes subject to human projections, subsumes all of creation into his very being, or simply does not exist. Hence, it is as if the world belongs to human beings who then determine its structures, content, and limitations.[10]

Balthasar does not follow the path of aesthetic theology; rather, he conceives of beauty as "derived from God himself. Furthermore, what we know to be most proper to God—his self-revelation in history and in the Incarnation—must now become for us the very apex and archetype of beauty in the world, whether men see it or not."[11] This notion serves as the primary basis for Balthasar's theological aesthetics.

---

7. Balthasar, *GL* I, 38, 79.

8. Balthasar, *GL* I, 460.

9. Balthasar, *GL* I, 104. The *analogia entis*, for Balthasar, is the notion that despite the similarity between the world and God, there is a far greater dissimilarity, *á la* his mentor Erich Przywara. Edward Oakes asserts that at the heart of Balthasar's doctrine of being is Aquinas's doctrine of the "Real Distinction" between *esse* and *essentia* (Oakes, *Pattern of Redemption*, 180–81; Cf. Aquinas, *De ente et essentia*, chapter IV and Wippel's *Metaphysical Thought of Thomas Aquinas*, 94–176). Balthasar christologically appropriates Aquinas's Real Distinction (*KB*, 261–63; Cf. *GL* IV, 393–412), connecting the incommensurability of God's divine glory and the transcendental of beauty through the doctrine of analogy and properly proportional language (See Clarke, *One and the Many*, 44–52).

10. Balthasar, *GL* I, 69.

11. Ibid. Aquinas's notion of God as First Cause is operative here for Balthasar. This notion should not be construed, though, in the mechanistic terms of the scientific rationalism transmitted through the Enlightenment, but rather as God being the Source of all that is. It is also important to note that the Incarnation and the Trinity aptly inform Aquinas's doctrine of creation as seen in Aquinas's discussion of creaturely reality *after* discussing the processions within the Godhead (*ST* I.27–42) and the

Panel One: No Room in the Inn

A Sketch of Balthasar's Theological Aesthetics

Balthasar owes much of the impetus for his theological aesthetics to his contemporary Karl Barth, who "rediscovers the inner beauty of theology and revelation itself" by "contemplating the data of Scripture, especially God's 'glory' (*Herrlichkeit*)," concluding that beauty is serviceable only "as [an] 'auxiliary concept.'"[12] Yet, Balthasar wonders what Barth has actually achieved, since Protestant theology, at the time, failed to integrate beauty into its theological discourse. Lurking within Balthasar's assessment are questions regarding the reception of Barth's theology, his theology of beauty in particular, and the adequacy of Barth's relegation of beauty to an auxiliary category of God's glory.[13] In response to these lingering questions and perceptions, Balthasar begins, as Fergus Kerr notes, "a slow, patient and much more elaborate working out of Barth's conception of divine beauty."[14]

By beginning with beauty, Balthasar countermands the philosopher, particularly Immanuel Kant, who relegates beauty to the realm of the non-real, the realm of subjectivity and taste. He also seeks to counteract the deadening exactitude of the sciences, particularly when it perceives itself as laying claim to the whole of reality. To the extent theology imbibes such scientism theological discourse becomes arid and fragmented, creating a false dichotomy between theology and ethics. Positively speaking, Balthasar leads with beauty because beauty brings the whole of reality

---

divine missions (*ST* I.43). Yet, one can make the case that Aquinas does not make the connections explicit (cf. Kerr, *After Aquinas*, 35–51 and Franks, "Simplicity of the Living God," 275–300). Such will be the deficiency Balthasar attempts to rectify through his christocentrism.

12. Balthasar, *GL* I, 53, 80. Cf. Barth, *CD* 2/1, 651.

13. Balthasar, *GL* I, 56. Along with Balthasar, I demur from Barth's description of God's beauty as an "auxiliary concept" because if form and content are inseparable, then beauty is an aspect of God's being as the splendor of God's triune life. Barth all but acknowledges this, yet his Romantic notion of beauty and its associations with our hedonistic pleasure and desire preclude him from doing so. Moreover, by subsuming beauty under God's glory, I wonder if Barth continues to leave a gap in our knowledge of God. We can agree with Barth, though, in saying that "God is not beautiful in the sense that he shares in an idea of beauty superior to him, so that to know it is to know him as God. On the contrary, it is as he is God that he is also beautiful, so that he is the basis and standard of everything that is beautiful and of all ideas of the beautiful" (*CD* 2/1, 656).

14. Kerr, "Foreword: Assessing this 'Giddy Synthesis,'" 9. For further theological connections between Barth and Balthasar, see Wigley, *Karl Barth and Hans Urs von Balthasar*. Cf. Balthasar, *GL* I, 18.

back into our purview by reinstituting beauty as a transcendental property of being and advocating an analogous God-world relationship, albeit one with a christological focus. It is precisely at these two interconnected points, however, where Balthasar and Barth most disagree. Balthasar contends that Barth has so christologically narrowed theology that he has equated it with revelation and that Barth has not only misunderstood Erich Przywara's doctrine of *analogia entis* but is, in his *analogia fides*, actually in essential agreement with the theological basis for the Catholic doctrine of analogy.[15]

According to Balthasar, theological aesthetics does not "primarily work with extra-theological categories of a worldly philosophical aesthetics" but with "the data of revelation itself with genuinely theological methods," all the while acknowledging the important role of human perception for "seeing" God's self-revelation.[16] Moreover, this subjective aspect gives value to the created order. Unless we acknowledge this, Balthasar argues, we will not only lack a spiritual understanding of creation but will also fail to perceive God's self-revelation in the Incarnation. Thus, Balthasar advocates for the interconnectedness of creation and redemption, predicated on a distinct yet mutual relationship between nature and grace.[17]

Balthasar's emphasis on the value of the created order is not, in his estimation, without theological justification because the glory of God has entered into creation, taking on created forms. Balthasar maintains that "God's Incarnation perfects the whole ontology and aesthetics of created Being."[18] The incarnate Son takes the form of a servant who bears witness to God as a *human being* throughout the entire spectrum of human existence, from birth to death. The incarnate Son "is what he expresses—namely God—but he is not whom he expresses—namely, the Father. This incomparable paradox stands as the fountainhead of the Christian aesthetic, and therefore of all aesthetics!"[19] It is precisely this "incomparable

---

15. Balthasar, *GL* I, 17–23 and 441–62; Balthasar, *KB*, 86–167; Balthasar, *GL* IV, 11–42. See the following sources regarding the dispute over the viability of the analogy of being for theology, whether Barth actually misunderstood Przywara, and Balthasar's case that Przywara's view was not Catholic orthodoxy: McCormack, *Karl Barth's Critically Realistic Dialectical Theology*, 1–28; Betz, "Beyond the Sublime," 1–50; Wigley, *Karl Barth and Hans Urs von Balthasar*, 9–48; and Johnson, *Karl Barth and the Analogia Entis*, 191–201.

16. Balthasar, *GL* I, 117.
17. Balthasar, *Epilogue*, 46.
18. Balthasar, *GL* I, 29.
19. Ibid.

Panel One: No Room in the Inn

paradox" that is at the heart of Balthasar's theological aesthetics and why it is not an aesthetic theology.[20]

In short, Balthasar's theological aesthetics attempts to piece together the fragments of Western metaphysics by establishing a metaphysical point of contact (i.e., beauty) with God's divine glory in order to relate them analogically, for "if a concept that is fundamental to the Bible has no kind of analogy in the general intellectual sphere, and awoke no familiar echo in the heart of man, it would remain absolutely incomprehensible and thereby a matter of indifference."[21] Balthasar stresses this subjective-objective (what I call a creative-redemptive) order to allow for a positive account of human sensibilities because the reverse order, according to Balthasar, tends to consider them in a "negative fashion, by showing their inadequacy and by striving in practice to eliminate them."[22] Nevertheless, both are necessary if communication is to occur, which is why Balthasar grounds his metaphysics in the incarnate Christ as the one through whom the transcendent God of the universe *communicates* himself to us. How, then, does Balthasar come to associate *Herrlichkeit* and *Übergestalt* with the incarnate Christ?

---

20. Chia, in his article "Theological Aesthetics or Aesthetic Theology?," 75-95, characterizes Balthasar's theological project as an aesthetic theology because of Balthasar's commitments to platonism and the *analogia entis*. To be sure, Balthasar has great respect for Plato and the ancient Greek philosophers in that they first consider the question, "Why is there something rather than nothing?" Yet, Balthasar's project is not platonic because of his commitments to the doctrine of the Incarnation and the *analogia entis*. Balthasar seeks a *via media* between his mentor's (Erich Przywara) position and his dear friend Karl Barth's position. In light of his christocentrism, Balthasar subsumes the *analogia entis* under the *analogia fides*, called the *analogia amoris* that emphasizes the interpretation of being as love. Such a move, ever so subtle, has implications for Balthasar's theological aesthetics, ones that Chia does not consider, rendering his best argument suspect.

21. Balthasar, *GL* IV, 14. This enables Balthasar to demarcate between God's glory and earthly beauty in order to preserve God's wholly otherness and the Creator-creature distinction (See also Balthasar, "Weltliche Schönheit und göttliche Herrlichkeit," 513-17).

22. Balthasar, *GL* I, 429. Balthasar desires to render a positive account of human sensibilities by beginning with a discussion of the "subjective elements" found in the apprehension of any object (*GL* I, 131-428). Yet, there *is* an object to apprehend and we must allow the object to speak for itself (*GL* I, 429-684).

The Beauty of Jesus Christ as *Herrlichkeit* and *Übergestalt*

Since God's glory has entered into created existence most fully in his Son, Balthasar identifies Jesus Christ as *Herrlichkeit*—the Lord of Glory, which is why a christocentrism permeates his theological aesthetics.[23] This designation assumes three things. First, God in his infinite freedom creates this world and is wholly other than his creation, thereby controlling the form and content of his communicative actions. Second, while interpreting Romans 1:19, Balthasar affirms the revelatory nature of creation that points to God's glory and not the world's. Such an understanding underscores the utter dissimilarity between God and his creation, while emphasizing the fact that God's glory shines in and through the form of creation such that it can be seen by his creatures. Third, the revelation of God in Christ "is not simply . . . the prolongation or intensification of the revelation in creation." Rather, it brings together the "heavenly and earthly, which is thus endowed by grace with a crown, the radiance of whose glory belong[s] to the *Kyrios* of the world." Hence, God's revelation in creation prepares the way for his self-revelation in Christ.[24] This self-revelation of God in Christ is the definitive restatement of all things in heaven and on earth as the one who is "the measure of all measures."[25] These three theological presup-

---

23. *Herrlichkeit* means splendor, glory, or magnificence, yet Balthasar intends here two different play on words. The first occurs with the German *Herr* meaning lord or master and *Herrsein* meaning lordliness, rendering the term, what English translators of his *magnum opus* attempt to capture as "The Glory of the Lord." The second play on words is with *Hehrsein* meaning sublimeness, identifying God's glory with the sublime (See Balthasar, *GL* I, 116 and Balthasar, *GL* VI, 10). These play on words encapsulate the relationship between God's glory and earthly beauty that is explored further in chapter three.

24. Balthasar, *GL* I, 429–31. Balthasar, within the same context, makes an important distinction regarding God's revelation in his creation: "God in his entirety is meant [to be] seen from one particular standpoint. Thus, Paul is not saying that basically only one 'part' of God is knowable, or that only one aspect of him is 'invisible;' rather, the 'vision' of the invisible God through the mediation of creatures allows us to 'grasp' his divine Being, different though it is from all creatures, and his eternal might, which is revealed in his act of creation" (431).

25. Ibid., 432. Some may perceive that Balthasar attempts to establish the conditions necessary within nature for grace to occur. This perception is contrary to what Balthasar intends and is manifested in his differences with Karl Rahner. Rahner, on the one hand, views humanity as essentially transcendent such that grace merely fulfills the potential present in humanity (See Balthasar, "Current Trends in Catholic Theology," 77–85). Balthasar insists, however, nature is a medium that communicates God's grace in a way that humanity would never expect. After all, how could humanity ever describe God as love without divine revelation? Balthasar's approach allows the object, in its existential reality, to speak for itself (See Oakes, *Pattern of Redemption*, 95–98).

positions serve as the basis for Balthasar's understanding of *Gestalt*. Yet, what does he mean by *Gestalt*, how do we perceive it, and how do these elements factor into his theological aesthetics?

The Meaning and Perceiving of Gestalt

Balthasar admits, at the outset of his theological aesthetics, the difficulty in translating the term *Gestalt*, stating that it could mean form, figure, or shape. He further describes form as follows:

> Visible form not only "points" to an invisible, unfathomable mystery; form is the apparition of this mystery, and reveals it while, naturally, at the same time protecting and veiling it. Both natural and artistic form has an exterior, which appears, and an interior depth, both of which, however, are not separable in the form itself. The content (*Gehalt*) does not lie behind the form (*Gestalt*) but within it. Whoever is not capable of seeing and "reading" the form will . . . fail to perceive the content. Whoever is not illumined by the form will see no light in the content either.[26]

This external form that expresses the internal depths of being is not a static existence but a dynamic movement found in the natural rhythm of life. Drawing upon Johann Wolfgang von Goethe's synthetic methodology found in *Die Metamorphose der Pflanzen*, Balthasar illustrates this dynamic movement of form with "the rhythm of the form of plants—from seed to full growth, from bud to fruit." This rhythm demonstrates the harmony of the internal unity with the external diversity of parts, all in continuity with the mysterious life present within the plant.[27] Balthasar also sees

---

26. Balthasar, *GL* I, 151. Balthasar recognizes the contested nature of *Gestalt* in the annals of aesthetic history (Balthasar, *GL* IV, 28–39). See also Simon, "Balthasar and Goethe," 60–76.

27. Balthasar, *GL* I, 444. Cf. Donnelly, *Saving Beauty*, 29–30. Although Balthasar has high regard for Goethe, he "is not claiming that Goethe's 'reverence' or his 'poetic-religious eye' are confessionally Christian. In fact, one of Goethe's most frequently cited sayings proves that his mind was too protean for any received dogma: 'With all the manifold facets of my being, just one way of thinking is not sufficient for me. As a poet and artist I am a polytheist, but a pantheist as a student of nature, and either belief I hold with equal firmness. And if I need a divinity for my personal being, for my moral existence—why, that need too is promptly assuaged'" (Oakes, *Pattern of Redemption*, 97). As such, Balthasar's theological presuppositions to *Gestalt* (i.e., creation, the Incarnation, and the Trinity) keep him from collapsing God's being into the world as Goethe's views logically suggest.

this rhythm of form explicitly in music as he draws upon his own musical insights and that of Christian von Ehrenfels who recovers melodic notions of *Gestalt*.[28] What we must recognize in order to "read a form within the world" are the dynamic movements in the depths of invisible reality that are expressed in and through the tangible forms of the world.[29]

Gestalt, typically associated with the visual, now has an aural component for Balthasar, whereby "hearing is *the* central theological act of perception." The musical character of Balthasar's theological aesthetics is designed to resist the systematization of thought such that "his work is meant to begin a process of communication whose best analogue is that of hearing. For hearing implies movement and movement is the subject and theme of Balthasar's theology."[30] The musical nature of Balthasar's theology, therefore, is not an artificial edifice for expressing his theology. Rather, it is part of the grand theo-symphony under the direction of God's Son through the Spirit where those playing instruments by faith join God's orchestra in making beautiful music.

If hearing is central to the act of theological perception for Balthasar, why is the first volume of his theological aesthetics subtitled: *Schau der Gestalt*, *Seeing* the Form? The answer, for Balthasar, lies in the Greek word *aesthesis* (sense perception). Seeing usually implies a grasping of the other in an attempt to possess or control. Hearing, however, appears to be in less control, submitting to what the other chooses to impart. Beauty, through its self-presentation, is not "in as much control as it might first seem, . . . for beauty . . . draws contemplators out of themselves and into a direct encounter with the phenomenon manifesting itself."[31] Thus, Balthasar weds together seeing *and* hearing under the notion of perception

---

28. Balthasar, *GL* IV, 30–31.

29. Balthasar, *GL* I, 444.

30. Oakes, *Pattern of Redemption*, 137, 139.

31. Ibid., 142–43. See also Balthasar, "Seeing, Hearing, and Reading," in *Spouse of the Word*, 473–90. Balthasar begins with "Seeing the Form" because he privileges God's divine revelation in his theophanic appearances to the Prophets and the Apostles where "the accent, naturally, falls on sight, which is at once, and by way of complement, joined by a hearing which is immediate and not mediated by tradition," producing what Balthasar calls "archetypal faith." This "archetypal faith" is different from "imitative faith" as the tradition of the Gospel is handed down thereby inverting the priority of seeing with hearing. This inversion is not final in that while living between the already and the not yet, there is an eschatological seeing in anticipation of future glory (Balthasar, *GL* I, 308–21).

PANEL ONE: No Room in the Inn

(*Wahrnehmung*), that singular human action of "assent to God's gift of creation and revelation."[32]

The assumption that underlies Balthasar's understanding of perception is an I-Thou relationship, a dynamic, dialogical, personal encounter, that enables communication to take place between persons. Balthasar notes that "hearing remains something intermediary and oscillating between 'I' and 'Thou,' something that streams from the one who speaks to the one who hears."[33] Balthasar also states that the *voice and gaze* of a mother upon her infant child in an I-Thou encounter awakens the child to being and no less to love. This primordial experience opens humanity to the reality of being where the brilliance of the true, the good, and the beautiful, come shining forth in and through *Gestalt*.[34]

Herein lies another crucial element to Balthasar's theological aesthetics—*splendor formae* (the splendor of form). With the use of this phrase, Balthasar follows the Thomistic tradition such that "the beautiful is above all a *form* and the light does not fall on this form from above and from outside, rather it breaks forth from the form's interior. *Species* and *lumen* in beauty are one."[35] By identifying beauty with *Gestalt*, beauty is a transcendental, a part of the "real presence of the depths of the whole of reality" that points "beyond itself to these depths."[36] The splendor of form weaves together two threads found in the tale of beauty—the classical, which emphasizes the intelligibility of form, and the Romantic, which emphasizes the sublime expressed by form. The beauty that breaks forth from within delights perceivers only because of the truth and goodness found in the depths of the same reality, revealing "something infinitely and

---

32. Oakes, *Pattern of Redemption*, 142. Cf. Balthasar, *GL* I, 119–21. By *Wahrnehmung*, Balthasar intends "the strong sense of 'taking to oneself' (*nehmen*) of something true (*Wahres*) which is offering itself. For this particular perception of truth, . . . a 'new light' is expressly required which illumines this particular form, a light which at the same time breaks forth from within the form itself" (120).

33. Balthasar, *Spouse of the Word*, 476.

34. Balthasar, *Love Alone Is Credible*, 76. Cf. O'Donnell, "Hans Urs von Balthasar," 458.

35. Balthasar, *GL* I, 151. Balthasar uses *species* and *lumen* interchangeably with *forma* and *splendor* respectively. Cf. Eco, *Aesthetics of Thomas Aquinas*, 20–48, 80–98.

36. Balthasar, *GL* I, 118. I understand the term "being" to express the traditional notion of *ta onta* as things that actually exist—things that are—such that the investigation of being is an analysis of being in its dynamic totality, including the natural and the supernatural. See chapter two, "The Discovery and Meaning of Being," of Clarke's book, *One and the Many*, for further discussion.

inexhaustibly valuable and fascinating."[37] Therefore, when we perceive this form, we are beckoned to enter into it; yet, we will never be able to do so if we jettison the physical in order to have some neutered spiritual experience because "we are dealing with the beautiful."[38]

Balthasar's intention to integrate the notion of form into theology seeks to overcome the cosmological and anthropological reductions. By recovering the notion of form for theology, the splendor of the internal depths of reality radiates through the external such that the whole is greater than the sum of its parts, producing a unified meaning inconceivable in the parts alone. This expression of the invisible in and through the visible not only reveals but also conceals such that the invisible is not exhausted in the appearing. How do his commitments, though, to the goodness of creation, the Incarnation, and the Trinity inform his understanding of *Gestalt*?

The Gestalt *of Revelation and its Perception*

As we have seen, Balthasar's account of human sense perception presumes an objective reality. There *is* something rather than nothing. Yet, given Balthasar's commitments, "it should be clear from the outset that there can be no question of a univocal transposition and application of categories."[39] If this schema is understood univocally, Christians become pantheists, subsuming God into all creation, or deists, giving flight to the human soul in quest of union with the divine.

Recall the three theological presuppositions at the beginning of this section. According to Balthasar, creation provides the vessel within which God communicates himself as Trinity through himself in the Incarnation. These presuppositions answer theologically the question, "why

---

37. Balthasar, *GL* I, 118. Although beauty with its unique qualities is distinct from its siblings (i.e., the true and the good), it is not separate, for to exclude or isolate beauty from her siblings only causes the true to become "pragmatic and formalistic," concerned only with its verification, and the good to become "utilitarian and hedonistic," concerned only with personal satisfaction (Balthasar, *GL* I, 152).

38. Balthasar, *GL* I, 119. Balthasar insists that the depths of being, communicated through form, are inaccessible and lead to false realities unless we enter into these depths through form. There is a unity between form and the depths of reality that produces a "real presence" within a particular form without exhausting the depths of reality, all the while pointing to something more. Theologies fail to consider the beautiful when they jettison objective revelatory form in favor of a formless mystical union with the divine.

39. Balthasar, *GL* I, 119.

is there something rather than nothing," giving a *theological foundation* to the transcendentals of being. At this point, Balthasar makes a distinction between revelation in creation and revelation in Christ.[40] Revelation in creation manifests God's glory in and through the medium of created forms such that our existence is to be understood as a gift. We owe our existence to someone other than ourselves. Coming to this realization requires aesthetic perception (seeing and hearing), which initiates "us into the deep mystery of all things. This initiation thereby creates awareness in us of the spiritual foundations of life itself; and, ultimately, an awareness of the Creator God who bestows it all . . . as a gift of love."[41]

The glory of God in creation anticipates and foreshadows the manifestation of God's glory in the Incarnation.[42] Jesus Christ, according to Balthasar, is the culmination of the theophanic appearances of God's glory to the Fathers prefigured in the Old Testament. These theophanic appearances (which Balthasar also calls "images") to the likes of Moses, Isaiah, Ezekiel, etc. reveal not only God's glory but also his holiness. These theophanies, overwhelming events in which the living God becomes present, occur throughout Scripture (e.g., Isa 6:5; Ezek 1:28; Dan 10:9; Matt 17:6; Mark 9:6; Acts 9:4–9; Rev 1:17).[43] Yet, as Balthasar insists, there is a "more fundamental order of dependence" found in Christ who "is the goal of the creation of the world, and hence the most fundamental reason for its aesthetic structure lies in him."[44]

Jesus Christ as *Herrlichkeit*, who is the image of the invisible God, brings together these themes that Balthasar articulates in his aesthetic rendering of the Old Testament—glory, holiness, image, and grace. Yet, what seems anticipated, Balthasar notes, is wholly unexpected. God who is invisible makes himself known but not in the way we would expect such that this event cannot simply be subsumed under worldly conceptions. These aesthetic categories are not "annihilated, but rather raised above themselves in an incomprehensibly positive way (*non destruit, sed elevat, extollit, perficit naturam*) in order to contain something which is infinitely greater than themselves."[45] Hence, God's appearing in human form—Jesus

---

40. Balthasar, *GL* I, 429–33.

41. Mongrain, "Von Balthasar's Way from Doxology to Theology," 65–66. See also Balthasar, *Epilogue*, 63–67 and *GL* I, 441–62.

42. Balthasar, *GL* I, 431.

43. Balthasar, *GL* VI, 9–27. Cf. Dupré's section "The Foundation of Scripture," in "Glory of the Lord," 384–412.

44. Waldstein, "Hans Urs von Balthasar's Theological Aesthetics," 16.

45. Balthasar, *GL* I, 609–10.

Christ, the Word made flesh—is the personal manifestation of God's glory, grace, and truth.

What is inconceivable and unexpected, Balthasar argues, is this personal manifestation where the "I" of Christ is in relation not to himself but to the Father. Christ makes a unique claim by asserting that he is the I AM of the Old Testament, affirming his divinity as the Son *of God*. Christ also expresses his unique relationship to God as *Son* of God whereby he lives in loving obedience to the Father. This dialogical I-Thou relationship is characterized by lordliness and holiness in the bond of love.[46] Moreover, it is not only the basis for all other I-Thou relationships but is the essence of God himself, which presumes that there is distinction of persons within the Godhead.[47] That being the case, what appears in the hypostatic union of Christ is "the becoming visible and experienceable of the God who is himself triune,"[48] whereby the *Gestalt Christi* manifests the *Gestalt Gottes* in the glory of the triune God, finding unity in God's love.[49]

How can we perceive the inconceivable, the unexpected glory of God's triune love radiating in and through the *Gestalt Christi*? By all accounts, we are unable to perceive the glory of God's triune love in Christ on our own merits. Yet, what we cannot see with our mind's eye we can only see with the *eyes of faith* in response to God's objective revelation.[50] Faith, though, should not be perceived in these instances as static but as a movement. It is a response of the whole person to God's dramatic and redemptive movements, which he "effects in man (even in his unwillingness and recalcitrance, due to sin), . . . through his Christian *eros* . . . [by] the divine Spirit [who] en-thuses and in-spires man to collaboration."[51]

---

46. For Balthasar, love "is not just any love, but precisely the love of Christ, the love of the new and eternal Covenant: Love as 'heartfelt compassion,' as 'kind, receptive openness,' 'an attitude of lowliness,' 'a meekness that does not defend itself,' 'long-suffering patience,' and thus the winning over, the enduring of one's unendurable brothers, and forgiving them because God has forgiven—in short the sort of 'virtue' that has already received its defining character from the 'perfect bond'" (*Love Alone Is Credible*, 128–29).

47. Balthasar, *GL* VII, 115–61, 439.

48. Balthasar, *GL* I, 432. See also Murphy, *Christ the Form of Beauty*, 145. Balthasar gives an aesthetic rendering to the hypostatic union when he says that "the mandated task is divine, its execution human and the proportion of perfect 'attunement' prevailing between them is both human and divine" (*GL* I, 469).

49. Balthasar's theological personalism has several streams of influence (i.e., Karl Barth, Rudolf Allers, Karl Jaspers, and Martin Buber) that have yet to be fruitfully explored. Such research is needed in light of its seminal role in his theological aesthetics.

50. See Balthasar, *GL* I, 441, 456–57.

51. Balthasar, *GL* I, 121.

Therefore, when the eternal God made himself known in the Incarnation, he disclosed his glory in such a way that through the eyes of faith we "are caught up in the love of the God we cannot see."[52]

Jesus Christ the Beautiful

The glory of the love of the triune God shines most brightly in the *Gestalt Christi* because Christ is not a limitation of the eternal God but a revelation of the archetype of all forms (*Übergestalt*) where "Christ has adopted a form from the world and completes/perfects it by extending it to the ultimate archetype, God's triune nature."[53] Jesus Christ, as *Übergestalt*, is what brings meaning and harmony "to which all particular aspects have to be referred if they are to be understood."[54] By this, Balthasar means that Christ is the center (*Mitte*) of the form of revelation. It does not mean that there are other things needed to complete this form as if more could be added to Christ. Rather, the reality of the church has no meaning or purpose by itself (e.g., as a religious institution or political organization), otherwise it compromises its integrity. The church, on the other hand, reflects the splendor of Christ who institutes and sustains the church, bringing meaning and life to her.[55]

If Christ is his own measure, then he measures himself by demonstrating the *attunement* between one aspect of himself with another. This, Balthasar maintains, is exemplified in the concordance between Christ's mission and existence. This concordance or attunement "may be traced back to the fact that he does not do his own will, but that of the Father,

---

52. Nichols, *Word Has Been Abroad*, 24.

53. Balthasar, *GL* I, 432. For Balthasar, God freely reveals himself through the created order and most fully in the human form (*Gestalt*) of his Son as the Word made flesh. Yet, God is not constituted by his creation (See Balthasar, "Theology and Aesthetic," 64–65). Christ is not an instance of some "general class" of *Gestalt* under which Balthasar subsumes the Incarnation. Rather, he employs an amalgam of concepts to explicate God's divine revelation in Christ.

54. Balthasar, *GL* I, 463.

55. Balthasar, in light of this particular understanding of Christ, argues that Christ is also the Lord of history in that all history is salvation history in the sense that history only has meaning in relation to Jesus Christ, the concrete universal (See Balthasar, *Theology of History*, 79–107). There is no attempt on Balthasar's part to divide the Christ of history from the Christ of faith (*GL* I, 466–67). He endeavors to combine the two, often chastising historic critics who dissect and distort the *Gestalt Christi* with their methodology, which renders them blind to perceiving the *Gestalt* of revelation ("Theology and Aesthetic," 95 and *GL* I, 466).

that he has not therefore given himself this work but rather accepted it in obedience."[56] His obedience, Balthasar asserts, is an epiphany of divine inner-trinitarian obedience where "God can command absolutely and obey absolutely and, as the Spirit of love, can be the unity of both."[57] There is an inseparable bond between Christ's mission (*missio*) in time and his eternal procession (*processio*), exhibiting perfect harmony, concordance, and attunement—a fittingness of Christ's being and actions.

The center of this attunement between Christ's mission and existence is Christ's death and resurrection. How can there be anything beautiful, though, amidst the pain and suffering of Christ on the cross, particularly when Isa 53:2 declares that Christ has "no beauty or majesty to attract us to him, nothing in his appearance that we should desire him?" Balthasar feels the tension of this passage and understands the *Ungestalt* of the cross as further concealment of the *Gestalt Christi* in light of Christ's previous claims to be the *Übergestalt*. Yet, God in his concealment reveals his love most fully in the *Ungestalt Christi* thereby manifesting the splendor of God's triune love in the most repugnant form humanly imaginable.[58] Balthasar remarks that such understanding requires the perception of faith: "At the centre of the form [*Gestalt Christi*], there stands the 'non-form' (*Ungestalt*) of the Cross; beholding this in faith the believer can decipher the 'super-form' (*Übergestalt*) of the trinitarian love that here becomes visible."[59]

This is the key, Balthasar argues, to understanding the problem of Isaiah 53. Christ becomes broken and fragmented because of the scourge of sin in order to reveal the true character of God's beauty, namely his eschatological promise. The *Gestalt Christi*, Balthasar suggests, integrates the sufferings of the cross into the beauty of the trinitarian love of God such that the broken form of Christ brings meaning and hope to a "radically

---

56. Balthasar, *GL* I, 469. Christ's attunement between his person and mission in obedience to the Father is the basis for the Christian's attunement (*Gestimmtsein*) to God, "which is a concordance (*Übereinstimmung*) with the rhythm of God himself and therefore an assent (*Zustimmung*) not only to God's Being, but to his free act of willing which is always being breathed by God upon man" (*GL* I, 251). Note Balthasar's play on words here with the German word *Stimmung*, meaning disposition, mood, or pitch, bringing together both the aesthetic and the theological.

57. Balthasar, *GL* I, 479.

58. Balthasar, *GL* I, 457.

59. Balthasar, *TD* II, 26.

sinful existence" by connecting these broken forms to an eschatological reality beyond itself in order to "transvalue them by redemptive suffering."⁶⁰

Balthasar claims that the purpose of the veiling and unveiling of the *Gestalt Christi* on the cross is to "cross out" the *Gestalt Christi* as disfigured and deformed, for God has given shape to the chaos of destruction and sin through reconciliation. He has demonstrated his power over death through death itself to bring about redemption. God has done the unexpected and inconceivable by communicating his trinitarian love in and through the hideous form of the cross, the most unsightly thing humanly imaginable. By doing so, the *Gestalt Christi* radiates the splendor of God's glory as Christ is perfectly in tune with the Father's will by obeying the Father and fulfilling his mission to the world. Through the *Gestaltungskraft* (shaping power) of the Holy Spirit, Christ's beauty enraptures and beckons perceiving subjects by drawing them out of themselves and into God's drama of redemption. It is the beginning of this journey, this theo-drama, to which we now turn.

Beauty's Demand for Action! The Interrelatedness of Aesthetics and Ethics

At the center of Balthasar's theological aesthetics, we find the beginnings of the theo-drama when God in his loving holiness freely takes action against humanity's rebellion by giving his only Son as a substitute for their just punishment. Such actions require a response, as Balthasar insists because God's self-revelation is not intended for disinterested contemplation. Rather, God's actions in and upon the world require human action, gaining understanding by performing our part. Yet, human action also requires understanding such that we know whom we serve and what part we are to perform. Consequently, through the eyes of faith "death turns into life, and this is something that also takes place in our hearts so that, drawn into the action, [we] can look toward the center in which all things are transformed" for "we have been appointed to play our part" in God's drama of redemption.⁶¹

---

60. Balthasar, *GL* I, 460. See also Balthasar, *TD* II, 26–28.

61. Balthasar, *TD* I, 16. This section will not give a full rendering of Balthasar's theological dramatics, which is beyond the scope of this project, but is written to demonstrate the interconnectedness of his aesthetics and dramatics to give further credence for the importance of theological aesthetics for ethics, bridging theology and life.

Theophanic Appearances and the Creation of Dramatic Space

Balthasar begins his biblical theology of the *gloria Dei* by asking how revelation occurs as God communicates with human persons, noting that humanity's reception occurs by God's grace. This communication between God and humanity, though, does not take place as if God and humanity are equals. Instead, these encounters with God, Balthasar maintains, "can occur only by virtue of a primary sense of being overawed by the undialogical presupposition of the dialogue that has started, namely, the divinity or glory of God." In other words, God through his glory has revealed something about himself *before* he has said anything, making it clear that God, in his ever-greater dissimilarity, must be perceived as he is before his words are heard. Such is the glory of God "without words."[62]

Balthasar turns to explicating numerous biblical theophanies, bringing to light various themes of biblical aesthetics like glory, image, and grace. In his exposition, Balthasar observes that everyone who perceives God's self-revelation does so outside of himself or herself, understanding God only in this encounter. When humanity is confronted, then, with the truth of God's glory, "only then does the contradiction between light and darkness, holiness and sin, come into full view, and *the drama is begun* which . . . is to lead to the reconciliation and redemption of the world."[63] Within this divine-human encounter, God graciously and freely opens up this dramatic space, making himself accessible to humanity.

Life in the Dramatic Space of God

The divine-human encounter, Balthasar notes, is *not* one that pits divine freedom against human freedom where God's omnipotent freedom clashes with humanity's autonomous ability to choose his own destiny. Such notions lead many to advocate divine determinism, which denies human freedom; Pelagianism, which limits God's freedom in order to preserve human freedom; or some compatibilist notion in between. Balthasar

---

62. Balthasar, *GL* VI, 11–12. This snippet of Balthasar's introduction to his biblical theology establishes the fact that there is a measure of understanding necessary before perceiving subjects can respond to God's self-revelation. God, as Balthasar says, gives that measure of understanding in his grace. Yet, what is this understanding? The truth of the matter is that God is God and we are not, for no one can perform his or her part in God's theo-drama without knowing this fact first. "If this shock," of being overawed by God's divine glory, "did not take place, then the whole conversation would rest on a foundation of untruth" (11).

63. Ibid., 13, 16. Emphasis added.

undermines this dichotomy by reframing the discussion with a dramatic metaphor. He remarks: "a successful theatrical production always depends on the harmonious cooperation of three freedoms, which are *not* however equal: for the director must serve the script and the actor must serve both."[64]

When God freely encounters humanity with his glory and humanity still lives, it is impossible for humanity to retain some sort of disinterested reflection as if we can dismiss our antagonism against a holy God. Within this dramatic moment, God gives life "making space for him in God's own realm" where "a covenant relationship becomes possible, . . . a holiness within the space of God's own holiness."[65] This covenant gives life to those who live within it, to those who obey its stipulations, for "you shall be holy because I am holy" (Lev 20:26; 1 Pet 1:16). Therefore, God's merciful covenant brings his beauty and requirement for action together. Yet, how are we to live within this dramatic covenant where God's holiness confronts our sin?

Living the Drama: Beauty Demands Action

This divine-human encounter with God's glory does not draw us into a lonely existence separate from others but rather into the dramatic, communal life of God where we participate in that life, growing in our understanding of God, ourselves, and the world. Balthasar concludes that "Christian action is therefore a being taken up into God's action through grace, being taken up into God's love so that one can love with him. It is only here that (Christian) *knowledge about* God becomes possible."[66]

Balthasar provides a Christological basis for our participation in God's life, rooting the church's existence in the risen Christ where the visible church takes on a particular shape, rooted in the eschatological reality

---

64. Oakes, *Pattern of Redemption*, 217–18.

65. Balthasar, *GL* VI, 13, 149. Balthasar is referring to the Old Testament covenant, yet the New Covenant established in Christ also brings life in that Christ gives form to the fragments of God's glory revealed in the Old Covenant. Commenting on the relationship between the Old and New Testaments, Balthasar remarks: "It is, of course, only on the *theological* level—i.e., with the eyes of faith—that it is possible to see this whole relationship in its objective correctness, and not with the eyes of the historian or psychologist of religion who abstracts from faith" (*GL* VI, 480; see also his extended discussion in the section "Grace and Covenant," *GL* VI, 144–214 as well as "Argumentum Ex Prophetia," 402–14).

66. Balthasar, *Love Alone Is Credible*, 116. See Balthasar, "Theology and Aesthetic, 67.

of the resurrection and unlike the world.[67] Furthermore, Christ's mission, in accordance with the Father's goodwill and pleasure (Eph 1:1–11), gives shape to the church's mission and thus forms the Christian's mission, all "in service of God's comprehensive plan."[68] So, when the church participates fittingly in God's mission, she reflects the splendor of God's triune love to the world, which is the hope of glory. And, as the church lives out Christ's mission of reconciliation, justice, mercy, and peace, her light radiates God's triune love like a city on a hill (Matt 5:14).

God's triune act of sending Christ as a substitute is the supreme act of self-giving. Hence, Christians too must give of themselves if they are to adhere to the covenant of Christ and participate in Christ's self-giving. By participating and abiding in Christ's self-giving, Balthasar argues, Christians bear the fruit of Christ in the power of the Spirit (John 15:5), "which was previously unknown to him."[69] This fruitfulness is not only to be returned to God but shared with our neighbors, which is possible, only when Christians have experienced this dramatic, divine encounter where one attempts to love God and neighbor in tune with the way Christ loved. This horizontal love of neighbor in Christ is derived from the triune love of God that descends to humanity and comes into being through the Spirit such that "the believer who believes and loves not merely in word but also in deed becomes the glorification of the glorious grace of God."[70]

Balthasar's theological aesthetics ultimately rests on the splendor of God's triune love that radiates through the *Gestalt Christi* and enraptures perceiving subjects whereby God's beauty demands action—*a theological aesthetics of Christian living*. Our performance of Christ's mission in the dramatic theater of God's glory is "the glorification of the glorious grace of God," from which Balthasar infers three things. First, our efforts to glorify God cannot merely be the worship that comes from our lips; rather "we must praise him through our existence, inasmuch as this is an existence

---

67. Balthasar, *GL* VII, 543.

68. Balthasar, *Love Alone Is Credible*, 126. Balthasar further notes that the church "is the moon, not the sun: the reflection, not the glory itself. Put more precisely, she is the response of glorification, and to this extent she is drawn into the glorious Word to which she responds, and into the splendor of the light without which she would not shine. What she reflects back in the night is the light of hope for the world" (Balthasar, *GL* VII, 543).

69. Balthasar, *GL* VII, 418, 420. See Balthasar's extended discussion in the section entitled "Giving Back the Fruit to God," *GL* VII, 415–31.

70. Balthasar, *GL* VII, 443–44. See Balthasar's extended discussion on loving our neighbors in the section entitled "The Brother for Whom Christ Died," *GL* VII, 432–84.

that is in him and therefore what it truly ought to be: an existence in the love that hands itself over."[71] Second, our existence must be seen in light of hope found in God's eschatological glory such that our lives emulate the proleptic proclamations found in several of the doxologies of the New Testament (e.g., Eph 1:3-14; Rev 7:12). Third, our outward expression of praise to God is the result of an intrinsic relationship to God's glory. God's activity in us through Christ in the Spirit produces a life of "faith, love, and hope, [which] are the divine life that is lived in us, a life that comes from divine glory and enables us to live the Christian life (δυναμούμενοι κατὰ τὸ κράτος τῆς δόξης αὐτοῦ, Col 1:11)."[72]

Balthasar, through his theological aesthetics, seeks to address Christian theology's defunct view of reality by rendering a theological account of beauty that attends to the objectivity of God's glory and the subjectivity of human perception. He desires to maintain an analogical relationship between God and his creation. God communicates himself to his creatures by using various created forms while remaining distinct from his creation. The incarnate Son—the Word made flesh—is the fullest expression of God's self revelation that communicates his divine glory, thereby identifying Christ as *Herrlichkeit* and *Übergestalt*. These terms signify the uniqueness of the *Gestalt Christi* as God communicates to his creatures the unexpected self-giving love of the triune God through the person and work of Christ. What, then, might be the significance of Balthasar's theological aesthetics for contemporary theology? In short, what might it mean to do theology "after Balthasar"?[73]

The Significance of Balthasar's Theological Aesthetics: A Critical Appropriation

Commenting on the state of theology after the onset of modernity, Balthasar characterizes those theological systems that subscribed merely to the true as focused on "correct propositions" while those that subscribed merely to the good as focused on what is "most useful and healthy" for human beings. This, however, has not always been the case, for "when the saints

---

71. Balthasar, *GL* VII, 397.

72. Ibid., 399.

73. See Bychkov and Fodor, eds., *Theological Aesthetics after von Balthasar*. Although this work does not advocate a particular way forward, it does begin to lay the groundwork through its critical and constructive essays for doing theology "after Balthasar."

interpreted their existence in the light of God's glory, they were always the guardians of the beautiful."⁷⁴ A full-orbed understanding of reality, he insists, leads to the tethering of aesthetics and ethics in light of truth. Herein lies one of the important contributions of Balthasar's theological aesthetics—the dissolution of the partition between scholar and saint.

Christian Theology and the Life of the Christian

Many relational theists, like Jürgen Moltmann, recognize this tension between scholar and saint as theology becomes ossified and praxis becomes legalistic such that theologians and churches are irrelevant and obsolete. Moltmann, like most relational theists, attempts to resolve this crisis by turning to the "way of orthopraxy," the way of "*verum facere*," by attending to the relational.⁷⁵ This relationality, says Moltmann, is found in "non-identity, [the] self-emptying for the sake of others and solidarity with others. It cannot be established in isolation, but only revealed in contact with others." Thus, the "Christian life is a form of practice which consists in following the crucified Christ, and it changes both man himself and the circumstances in which he lives. To this extent, a theology of the cross is a practical theory."⁷⁶

Balthasar concurs with Moltmann's critique of the church where fossilization, petrifaction, rigidity, and legalism persist. He also agrees with aspects of Moltmann's solution in that he does not attempt to resolve this crisis by capitulating to the presumed dichotomy between theology and praxis. Rather, the cross of Christ as an act of non-identity, "as 'God' in

---

74. Balthasar, *GL* IV, 38–39.

75. Moltmann, *Crucified God*, 8, 11.

76. Ibid., 17, 25. Moltmann, although he does little to develop the connection between God's beauty and God's glory or say much about what God's beauty entails, *does* note "a radical shift in our understanding of the glory of God" in that "God reveals his strength in the weak, his honor, in lowliness and his splendor in the cross of Christ." As such, God's glory "is not the splendor of otherworldly superior power but the beauty of love which empties itself without losing itself and forgives without giving itself away" (*Theology and Joy*, 60). His intention is to join aesthetics and ethics by emphasizing the need for joy in the Christian life: "We must note that these are inseparable both in our awareness of God and in the life of faith" such that "the beautiful in God is what makes us rejoice in him" (63). In this briefest of comments on God's beauty, Moltmann makes several notable remarks, namely his affirmation of an objective beauty in God, our subjective response, and the interconnectedness of aesthetics and ethics. One has to wonder, though, why these insights do not reverberate into his subsequent writings nearly a decade later. Perhaps, his understanding of the God-world relation inhibits him from doing so.

his opposite: godlessness and abandonment by God" is lived out for the sake of others.[77] It is at this point, though, that Balthasar departs from Moltmann and other relational theists who believe that God's identity is not only revealed in and through but *is*, ontologically speaking, his non-identity. As a result, the Wholly-Otherness of God is compromised, destroying the analogical relationship between God and the world, blurring, if not erasing, the Creator-creature distinction. Furthermore, relational theism becomes inattentive to beauty as it focuses on the good and the way of orthopraxy.

Relational theists are not alone in neglecting beauty as many contemporary theologians avoid the rhetoric of beauty because of its supposed affinities with pleasure, satisfaction, or escapism, keeping the tragic realities of human existence at bay. Balthasar, on the other hand, argues for a christocentric understanding of beauty that *includes* the tragic realities of human existence. His approach dispels these platitudes in order to explicate the holy triune love of God and its eschatological promise through Christ's assumption of the *Ungestalt* of the cross for the world and his return as the *Herrlichkeit* and the *Übergestalt* in the resurrection. In this, the shaping power (*Gestaltungskraft*) of the Holy Spirit prevails in the very chaos of sin. The nocturnal sides of human existence are not avoided or ignored but are victoriously overcome because God's beauty encompasses the tragic realities of human existence in a way that does not constrict God to human actions nor distance God beyond them.

God reveals his beauty definitively in the death and resurrection of Christ. Yet, the scourge of sin prevents our natural abilities from perceiving his glory that radiates in and through the *Gestalt Christi*. In order to see the hope of glory hidden in the *Ungestalt* of the cross, we need theological perception—the eyes of faith. Perceiving God's beauty is not an act of violence that attempts to grasp, control, or manipulate the form; rather, this perception of faith is one that responds to God's beauty who freely appears in and through the *Gestalt Christi*. Such a response maintains the integrity of God's beauty, taking God's self-showing on its own terms rather than our own. God's beauty gives rise, then, to "the most prodigious drama, which indeed it already contains within itself." Thus, "whoever is moved in faith must go out on the stage,"[78] for God's enrapturing beauty *puts us in our place* within his drama of redemption and dissolves the bifurcation

---

77. Moltmann, *Crucified God*, 27.
78. Balthasar, *GL* II, 12.

between theology and life.[79] Christian theology becomes a "spiritual activity, aware not only of a rational and ethical but of an aesthetic responsibility to the relative proportions of the various parts of revelation."[80] Hence, Balthasar's effort to dissolve the bifurcation between scholar and saint by contending for a full orbed understanding of reality that includes the true, the good, and the beautiful is one his most significant contributions.

Balthasar's Christocentrism

Jesus Christ is central to how Balthasar brings theology and the Christian life together. In fact, Balthasar agrees with Barth regarding the christological necessity for theological discourse: "Such a starting point is quite legitimate—indeed if we want to take the Bible seriously, it is absolutely essential." Yet, as Balthasar asserts, "it is a big step from there to the *narrowing* of everything to that one point," for Barth "ends up talking about Christ so much as *the* true human being that it makes it seem as if all other human beings are mere epiphenomena."[81] Balthasar levels this critique in an effort to preserve the value of the created order and the truth, goodness, and beauty found therein because Barth's christological reductionism seems to limit understanding to the act of revelation itself. Barth, according to Balthasar, sees creation merely as a *presupposition* to the Incarnation such that "he does not give [creation] its proper due."[82]

---

79. Kevin Mongrain offers an apt summary of how Balthasar relates theology and the Christian life: "Failing to do so [reintegrate beauty into theology] would mean failing to understand and attain the existential disposition and spiritual posture required for knowing God in the only way God can possibly be known, namely, as self-giving love offered as gift of creation and, ultimately, in the gift of the Incarnation. Attaining this understanding requires a love for creation and a willingness to participate in the Incarnation and the Paschal Mystery with the whole of one's being—heart, will, and mind. Von Balthasar views this understanding as doxology, and he is convinced that it and it alone is the only path to true theology" (Mongrain, "Von Balthasar's Way from Doxology to Theology," 59–60).

80. Balthasar, *Word Made Flesh*, 121.

81. Balthasar, *KB*, 242–43. For a defense of Barth's christocentrism and adherence to the analogy of faith rather than the analogy of being, see Johnson, *Karl Barth and the Analogia Entis*, 201–30.

82. Balthasar, *KB*, 242. Balthasar offers other examples like Barth's inadequate ecclesiology: "Too much in Barth gives the impression that nothing much really happens in his theology of event and history, because everything has already happened in eternity: for example, . . . he transposes time [in such a way that] sin is ever-past and justification ever-future, and rejects all talk of growth, progress—even of a possible lapse and loss of grace and faith. In short, Barth rejects all discussion of anything in

PANEL ONE: No Room in the Inn

Because of this christocentrism, Balthasar identifies Jesus Christ as *Übergestalt* and *Herrlichkeit*—the measure of all things. He understands created being to be dependent upon Christ because, as the Scriptures attest, all things came into being through Christ (John 1:3) and hold together in Christ (Col 1:16–17). This opens the created order to metaphysical investigation where there are many *logoi spermatikoi* that exhibit the *created* character of earthly truth, goodness, and beauty. In this way, Balthasar asserts, "the order of creation cannot be deduced as a whole from the order of revelation, no more than it can be deduced from grace." In fact, ""we are permitted—*even obligated*—to look at the order of nature from Adam to Christ and from created reason to covenant faith."[83] Thus, the most comprehensive metaphysical reflections on being "hint at an ultimate meaning beyond and yet also somehow *in* the totality of being."[84] To what, though, does the *created* character of earthly truth, goodness, and beauty point?

As previously mentioned, Balthasar maintains that "the meaning and movement of God's revelation in creation is his will finally to reveal himself in the Incarnation of Christ" such that "this first 'natural' revelation ... will seem to be like a preparation, foundation and onset of God's intimate revelation of his Word opening up the deepest regions of his being."[85] To discern God's self-revelation in his Word, Balthasar recognizes the Hebrew Scriptures as essential, for the glory manifested in the Old Testament is anticipatory of the New. Christ as "the radiance of God's glory and the exact representation of God's being holds all things together by the power of his word" (Heb 1:3) and perfects the fragments of God's glory revealed in the Old Testament. That being the case, the life of Christ from birth to death contributes to his understanding of the *Gestalt Christi* to which all creation points, demonstrating the dynamic rhythm of God's life.

Balthasar grounds these dynamic movements ontologically in what I call the divine eternal kenosis of the Godhead such that "the immanent Trinity must be understood to be that eternal, absolute self-surrender whereby God is seen to be, in himself, absolute love; this in turn explains his free self-giving to the world as love, without suggesting that God 'needed' the world process and the Cross in order to become himself."[86] This

---

the realm of the relative and temporal that would make for a real and vibrant history of man with his redeeming Lord and God" (*KB*, 371).

83. Ibid., 280, 310. Emphasis added. Are we truly *obligated*, though, to begin with nature as such and then proceed to Christ?

84. Balthasar, *Epilogue*, 22.

85. Balthasar, *KB*, 302.

86. Balthasar, *TD* IV, 323.

primal intra-trinitarian kenosis is the total self-giving of the Father where "the Father strips himself, without remainder, of his Godhead and hands it over to the Son." Yet, the Father does not exist prior to this kenosis; rather, the Father just "*is* this movement of self-giving that holds nothing back." Consequently, the total divestiture of the Father into the Son and the Son's reciprocation "involves the positing of an absolute, infinite 'distance' that can contain and embrace all the other distances that are possible within the world of finitude, including the distance of sin."[87] The Son's reciprocation is an uninhibited, self-surrender characterized by thanksgiving and joy, not unlike the Father. The Spirit proceeds from the Father and the Son such that he is the common bond of love between them, bridging this infinite difference.[88] These eternal movements of *divine eternal kenosis* serve as the "primal *kenosis* [that] makes possible all other kenotic movements of God into the world," including creation and the Incarnation, culminating in the ultimate kenotic event—Christ's death and descent into hell.[89]

Re-form-ing Beauty

Balthasar's theological aesthetics, with its focus on the centrality of Christ as *Herrlichkeit* and *Übergestalt*, takes significant steps toward reforming contemporary conceptions of beauty that aid in integrating beauty back into contemporary theological discourse. He exposes the false dichotomy between theology and the Christian life as he tethers theological aesthetics with ethics that leads to a performative aspect of truth. Yet, Balthasar's understanding of sin and prevenient grace, which are based on a divine

---

87. Balthasar *TD* IV, 323. In this context, Balthasar offers biblical support for his position by appealing to John 14:26 and 16:13–15, indicating the intra-trinitarian love between the persons of the Trinity. In other contexts, he cites Phil 2:6, appealing specifically to the notion of kenosis (*TD* II, 268). It remains to be seen, though, whether his interpretation of these passages is viable. I will discuss these matters in chapter four.

88. Balthasar *TD* IV, 324. Balthasar's articulation of God's divine eternal kenosis that posits an infinite distance within the Godhead serves as the basis for the *possibility*, not only of other kenotic events within the economy including the Incarnation, but also of "every other separation—be it never so dark and bitter" (325). For Balthasar, this includes divine suffering such that "the possibility of such experience and suffering—up to and including its christological and trinitarian implications—is grounded in God (324). Yet, Balthasar subscribes to divine impassibility "that excludes from God all intramundane experience and suffering." Balthasar acknowledges that "to think in such a way is to walk on a knife's edge" (324). In chapter four, I will examine Balthasar's notion of divine impassibility to see if he remains unscathed by this knife's edge, all in an effort to thicken the doctrine of impassibility in light of God's beauty.

89. Ibid., 331. See also *TD* IV, 317–61 and Balthasar, *Mysterium Paschale*, 23–36.

eternal kenosis, seem to blur the lines between justification and sanctification and undermine the efficacy of *Herrlichkeit* and *Übergestalt*.

Balthasar follows traditional Catholic dogma, noting that though our "turn toward God can have various levels, it always occurs *praeveniente gratia*" as Vatican I affirms: "For the most merciful Lord stirs up and helps with his grace those who are wandering astray, so that they may be able to come to a knowledge of the Truth."[90] To be sure, Balthasar does acknowledge the deleterious effects of sin; yet, it seems that sin has only brought spiritual sickness to humanity, merely distorting rather than destroying humanity's relationship with God. As Balthasar remarks, "this can only mean that even in unbelief and worship of idols man is continually dealing with the real God . . . because God is already formally implied in every creaturely act of thought because of our natural relationship to him as a creature."[91] It is this "natural relationship" to God "as creature," according to Balthasar, that grounds humanity's relationship with God rather than God's reconciling acts in Jesus Christ. What, though, does Balthasar's *creative-redemptive* approach imply about the created nature of humanity, particularly humanity's capacity for God?

Balthasar rightly maintains, following Henri de Lubac, that creation is a gratuitous, undeserved existence, consisting of both the natural and the supernatural. In accordance with Vatican I, he maintains a sharp distinction, though, between creation and covenant, in that creation's "elevation to being adopted by God is a second and loftier work that should not be explained in terms of the first level but from its own intrinsic character." As such, within the realm of creation, "the relative significance of nature is quite sufficiently protected . . . [as] a realm of provisional meaning that is not directly derivable from grace but rather serves as the presupposition to grace."[92] The crucial question for Balthasar is how much of humanity's *capax Dei* should be assigned to nature and how much to grace. Keeping in mind God's creative-redemptive movement, revelation in creation is intended to serve as the preparation for the particular revelation of God's Word. Coordinately, humanity's inherent capacity for God is a gratuitous gift of God's creative action that is the preparation for the "higher capacity" of faith. Hence, Balthasar sees nature and grace operating in harmony

---

90. Balthasar, *KB*, 323. See also "Grace and Sin" in Balthasar, *KB*, 364–80.
91. Ibid., 319.
92. Ibid., 296, 300.

to open "a way from nature to grace" where "there can be many levels, phases, foreshadowings and starting points."[93]

Since Balthasar predicates humanity's *capax Dei* on the basis of God's act in creation as *distinct* from God's reconciling act in Jesus Christ, he seems to blur the lines between justification and sanctification sufficiently enough to wonder whether he advocates a synergistic understanding of redemption that undermines God's freedom and electing purpose in Christ, begging the question as to whether God's covenant of grace is necessary for humanity to have a relationship with Christ at all.[94] Moreover, by rooting human ontology first in the created order, Balthasar appears to posit a continuous, unbroken relationship between God and humanity, for even "a negative relationship to the God of grace is still a relationship, even a very real relationship, to him!"[95] But, such a claim seems to minimize the depth, depravation, and destructive character of the human condition, of human sin. The extent of the human condition is revealed only in light of Christ's human nature that "shows us the . . . hopelessness or our illusions . . .," for it is only "the human nature of Jesus [that] spares and forbids us our own. Thus it is our justification," as Barth argues.[96]

Such notions seem to question the efficacy of the christological terms *Herrlichkeit* and *Übergestalt*, particularly when Balthasar declares God's glory to radiate in and through the *Gestalt Christi* in such a way that overawes and enraptures perceiving subjects into God's theo-drama.[97] Is Christ not supposed to be the measure of all measures such that Christ's humanity is definitive for understanding our humanity rather than simply perfecting it or completing it? Moreover, Balthasar seeks to establish an analogous point of contact for these christological terms, irrespective of God's reconciling act in Christ, within the provisional realm of graced nature by positing a metaphysical glory conceived as "nothing other than the totality of [the individual instances of earthly] beauty."[98] Yet, without the redemption of our human capacities of perception, it seems impossible to discern between true delight and our sinful proclivities to possess and indulge in those things that please us. Any sort of effort to connect

---

93. Ibid., 310–11.
94. See Jüngel, *Justification*, 15–50, Wright, *Justification*, 79–110, and McGrath, *Iustitia Dei*, 1–54.
95. Balthasar, *KB*, 288.
96. Barth, *CD* 3/2, 47. Cf. Jüngel, *Justification*, 161–62.
97. Balthasar, *GL* I, 121.
98. Balthasar, *GL*, V, 614.

PANEL ONE: No Room in the Inn

these earthly instances of beauty with the divine glory communicated through these christological terms seems likely only in retrospect of God's reconciling action in Christ by the power of the Spirit.

If we follow, though, Barth's axiom regarding the relationship between creation and covenant whereby "creation is the external basis of the covenant while the covenant is the internal basis of creation,"[99] a covenantal and communicative understanding of the God-world relation, which includes privileges and responsibilities, ensues. In doing so, we can preserve God's freedom and humanity's *relative* freedom as God graciously works and wills *through* the created order. Such notions advance a monergistic soteriology, stressing the destructive nature of sin, God's initiative, and humanity's response. We can participate fittingly in God's covenant, dramatic as it is, by reasoned faith and faithful reason, "making *covenantal* contact," as Kevin Vanhoozer notes, such that "we know God as Lord and ourselves as servants."[100]

Furthermore, the natural human faculties of reason, imagination, perception, etc. are part of the created order that become *deformed* at the Fall, causing us to misperceive reality in illogical and fantastical ways. What is needed is *reform* by the One who *transforms* our minds so that we are able to discern what God's will is—that which is true, good, and beautiful (Rom 12:1-2). Our createdness affirms the reliability of human cognition, although our finite, situated perspectives only see in part such that "forming beliefs, giving warrants, making inferences, analyzing critically does not take place in a vacuum but in fiduciary frameworks." Our fallenness guarantees distortion, deformation, and subversion, causing our human faculties to function improperly thereby necessitating redemption. We are in need of personal, more specifically, intellectual virtues such that knowledge of God "is less a matter of following correct procedures . . . than becoming the right sort of person," a person who follows after God's heart in the manner of Christ (1 Kgs 14:8; Phil 2:1-18).[101] It is within this

---

99. Barth, *CD*, 3/1, §41.

100. Vanhoozer, *Drama of Doctrine*, 301.

101. Ibid., 301-5. Vanhoozer posits a "confessing epistemology" by following the theological framework of Creation-Fall-Redemption-Consummation, forming a "three-stranded epistemological cord," namely reliabilism, fallibilism, and intellectual virtue that draws upon "the merits of three philosophical theories of knowledge." He qualifies them, though, with Scripture in that "we know only dimly. While the maps [Scripture] are trustworthy and reliable, our use of them is not. Knowers are ever on the verge of finding themselves in a Faustian drama, where the lust for absolute knowledge results in deals struck with the devil. Humans lack the knowledge of angels; our knowledge remains partial, our virtue incomplete" (304).

framework, so it seems, that God's glory remains efficacious such that *Herrlichkeit* and *Übergestalt* become the theological loci of a trinitarian understanding of God's beauty.

If we register these concerns with Balthasar's theological aesthetics, what are the implications? Daniel Gallagher contends that there is an "infinite distance separating sensible and supersensible beauty" because of "the ambivalent way in which we experience the beautiful in the sensible world," implying that beauty needs to be put in her place behind the other transcendentals.[102] To be sure, Gallagher's critiques regarding the noetic effects of sin must be heeded if theological aesthetics is to contribute to a thicker understanding of reality, all the more to emphasize God's reconciling act in Christ by the power of the Spirit. The true and the good are not immune from such concerns either, although in different ways. Rather, theological aesthetics must account for beauty's "elusiveness, its complexity, and ambiguities" so that such tensions do not lead to the discarding of beauty from theological discourse.[103] If God's beauty is an aspect of his being, what are the ramifications for articulating God's divine communicative actions? In other words, how can we employ the merits of Balthasar's christocentrism encapsulated in the terms *Herrlichkeit* and *Übergestalt* in light of these gentle criticisms?

Theology "after Balthasar"

Balthasar's theological aesthetics emphasizes the indispensable notion of the Creator-creature distinction, the importance of the *Gestalt Christi*, the interrelation of aesthetics and ethics, and the personal nature of the triune God. The Creator-creature distinction is the fundamental assumption that formalizes the fact that God is God and we are not. When this distinction is contested, a Feuerbachian slip occurs, humanity becomes the measure

---

102. Gallagher, "Analogy of Beauty and the Limits of Theological Aesthetics." Gallagher offers several pertinent critiques regarding a kind of theological aesthetics that posits an "unbridled optimism." To mitigate this critique, we must remember that beauty does not come to the King's ball without her escorts—truth and goodness. Articulating a theology of beauty reliant on God's self-revelation should also diminish much of these concerns; yet, his cautionary note is apropos in that "the effects of original sin have debilitated man's capacity to apprehend beauty as an analogous concept connecting the sensible to the supersensible."

103. O'Conner, "Theological Aesthetics and Revelatory Tension," 415. See also Sherry, *Spirit and Beauty*, 43–49 where he makes note of these same difficulties and concerns.

Panel One: No Room in the Inn

of all things, and God's glory is domesticated in the process. *How*, then, does this Wholly Other God communicate himself to his creation?

Balthasar commends to us, in response to this question, the significance of *Gestalt* primarily based on the Word taking on human flesh in the form of a servant—the *Gestalt Christi*. The "how" or manner in which God communicates himself becomes important and not merely the content or the "what" of God's self-revelation, inextricably linking form *and* content. Numerous implications ensue from this conclusion. For example, biblical genre becomes essential to discerning the meaning of a biblical text; the manner in which we do theology (i.e., the intellectual virtues) says volumes about our understanding of God rather than merely the content; and, present human existence, as devilish as it may seem at times, is not to be discarded in an excessively ascetic lifestyle in favor of some otherworldly disembodied reality. Rather, human existence, with its tragic and idyllic moments, should be lived with joy in relationship with others, all to the glory of God.

Balthasar's tethering together of aesthetics and ethics demonstrates the continuity of the knowledge of God rather than its atomization. God's self-appearing is not merely for contemplation, scrutiny, or analysis. Instead, his self-showing requires action. Such connections emphasize the theoretical *and* the performative element of the knowledge of God rather than merely its cognitive counterpart. Christ's mission of reconciliation, hope, mercy, compassion, justice, and peace gives shape to the church's mission and thus forms the Christian's mission, all in accordance with the Father's good pleasure (Eph 1:1–11). As such, when the church participates fittingly in God's drama of redemption, she reflects the splendor of God's triune love to the world, which is the hope of glory.

Balthasar's theological personalism is another fundamental presupposition to his theological aesthetics and his dramatic metaphor because he takes seriously God's self-revelation as he shows himself to be, namely self-related in his Triunity. His theological personalism is humble in its attempts to conceptualize God's being. Graham Cole's remarks, as a self-avowed biblical personalist, are indicative of Balthasar's position: "It has a modest aim, namely to look at life steadily, if not whole, utilizing the category of person as Actor and the distinction between the creator and creation, to do so" such that "moral, aesthetic, intellectual and physical experience are interrogated from this perspective, the construction of such a metaphysic have a provisional character" that acknowledges "the eschatological tension" of only knowing in part.[104]

---

104. Cole, "Towards a New Metaphysic of the Exodus," 80.

Theology that is attuned to these particulars outlined above will not only be relevant to the Christian life but will also radiate the glory of God's triune love in the church and to the world.[105] Yet, we must adequately account for our finite and fallen human capacities for perceiving both divine and earthly beauty, for we are in desperate need of Christ's redeeming work. Our finite human faculties are never disinterested. We always see from some limited perspective. Our fallenness distorts what we think, say, and do, often inducing conflict and tension with others. There is no need for skepticism, though, as we pursue the knowledge of God, for God has spoken and speaks, giving us enough of himself "to know where we are and what we have to do." What is needed is "epistemic humility and patience" that does "not degenerate into epistemic sloth."[106]

The eschatological component of beauty also suggests that what little we do perceive "is the dynamic vision of the seeds and promise of renewal and consummation in God of our fallen and fragmented world," for "there is tension between what is and what should be, and between what is and will be, a tension that is reflected in our experience of beauty as revelatory and our understanding of that experience."[107] This notion enables us to situate our present understanding of God's beauty not only in light of God's divine glory but also in light of what is to come so that we may act fittingly within God's drama of redemption.

These particulars for doing theology after Balthasar can be encapsulated methodologically into what I am calling a *redemptive-creative* emphasis. This approach stresses the redemptive work of the cosmic Christ by looking *protologically* back through Christ's redemptive suffering and glorious resurrection whereby he redeems creature and creation while also looking forward *eschatologically* towards the hope of glory. In doing so, we acknowledge the Creator-creature distinction, the goodness of creation, and the depth of sin's effects on creature and creation such that "theology

---

105. Francesca Murphy provides a loose framework for doing theology "after Balthasar" that integrates God's beauty back into theological discourse: "If beauty is double-sided, its representation will stand outside, facing us, and yet draw us into itself. Hence, a theology that is based in beauty will be objective whilst including participating subjects. It will be objective without being objectivist" (*Christ the Form of Beauty*, 34). Dan Treier and company also offer sage advice for moving forward: "If the doctrines of creation, incarnation and sacrament are to have authority for Christian approaches to aesthetics, then we must attend to the reality of the Fall; the dynamics of the life, death, and resurrection of Jesus; and the workings of the Spirit in the life of the church" (*Beauty of God*, 10–11). Any way forward will surely include these elements.

106. Vanhoozer, *Drama of Doctrine*, 304.

107. O'Connor, "Theological Aesthetics and Revelatory Tension," 416.

PANEL ONE: No Room in the Inn

[needs to] fashion a set of ontological categories about created being which are oriented towards 'the new,' towards that which the creation becomes by virtue of the regenerative action of God in Christ through the power of the Spirit," as John Webster aptly notes.[108]

We are able to posit a notion of God's beauty that preserves the efficacy of God's glory captured by Balthasar's identification of Christ as *Herrlichkeit* and *Übergestalt* whereby we live within the dramatic life of God. In doing so, we participate in God's beauty such that our affections are properly ordered through prayer in our worship of God, our *fruitio Dei* is declared in our witness, and we are able to see, in part, without illusion, demonstrating the wisdom of God. We turn now to chapter three where we will exposit a relevant biblical motif—the Suffering Servant—that fleshes out these christological terms in order to expound theologically in chapter four upon divine ontology, namely God's beauty-in-act.

---

108. Webster, "Eschatology, Ontology, and Human Action," unpub. mss.; quoted in Vanhoozer, *Remythologizing Theology*, 175–76n151. We will explicate this redemptive-creative notion further at the beginning of chapter four.

The Hinge

3

Following a Biblical Trajectory

HANS URS VON BALTHASAR, IN MANY WAYS, HAS BEGUN THE TASK OF reforming and reintegrating beauty into contemporary theological discourse, declaring that "beauty is the word that shall be our first"[1] as we discussed in chapter two. Yet, he notes the beleaguered status of beauty that ensues from the metaphysical reductionism found in the *esse univocum* of Duns Scotus (Being as a Concept) and Meister Eckhart (Being as God). To counteract these reductionisms, in part, Balthasar attempts to retrieve a notion of *Gestalt* for theology—that dynamic unity of parts which "the mind sees [as] an organized whole, with all the articulation of detail necessary for the comprehension of the basic idea manifest in its fullness."[2] To facilitate this retrieval, Balthasar identifies Jesus Christ as *Übergestalt* because Christ is *Herrlichkeit* as the one who brings together the heavenly and the earthly. He understands Christ's beauty—the archetype of all earthly beauty—as the concordance between his mission and existence that enraptures God's people into his drama of redemption. This, he surmises, demonstrates the interconnectedness between aesthetics and ethics, as well as all the transcendentals of being, thereby contributing to the dissolution of the divide between theology and life.

Balthasar, though, does seem to undermine these christological terms and their intended outcomes as he blurs the lines between justification and sanctification by predicating human ontology on God's act of creation rather than God's electing purpose to reconcile the world in and through Christ. Consequently, humanity maintains its relationship to God on the basis of the created order, even if it is a negative relationship. Such notions tend to minimize the effects of sin on humanity and the created

1. Balthasar, *GL* I, 18.
2. Balthasar, "Theology and Aesthetic," 63.

93

The Hinge

order, leaving open the possibility for human self-justification. Hence, Balthasar's desire to retain the viability of the created order, provisional as it may be, distinct from God's electing purpose and reconciling act in Christ seems to undermine the efficacy of God's glory because Christ as the Lord of Glory only *fulfills* or *perfects* the created order rather than *trans*forming or *re*forming it from the destruction of sin.

If we advocate, as we suggested in chapter two, a reversal of Balthasar's creative-redemptive motif by privileging God's electing purpose and reconciling act in Christ (not only of human persons but also for the whole of creation), life is understood as a gift and human persons find their identity, hopeless as it may be, in the One who is life and gives his life on our behalf. Christ is our justification and not we ourselves. Moreover, human actions are not mere epiphenomena, for not only do we live and move and have our being in Christ but all things hold together in him (Acts 17:8; Col 1:17). Hence, Jesus Christ is Lord of covenant and creation, preserving the efficacy of God's glory and allowing us to employ *Herrlichkeit* and *Übergestalt* constructively as the theological loci of a trinitarian understanding of God's beauty. How, then, might we proceed?

Balthasar declares that the "Bible is full of statements about God's glory, and the passages and vistas are far more numerous than most believers realize: glory is a fundamental statement that leavens all of Scripture."[3] As such, we could move forward in any number of ways. Some, like William Dyrness, have surveyed the biblical canon, tracing the semantic word groups and their associated passages "that are most often employed in an aesthetic sense (the visibly pleasing or luminous)" in order to depict a biblical notion of God's beauty.[4] Dyrness argues that the Hebraic Scriptures understand beauty as that which shares "in the ordered meaning of God's creation," when applied to an "object (or an event) is simply its being what it is meant to be."[5] Dyrness establishes this thesis by examining seven different word groups, careful to read them within their context, in order to ascertain the semantic range of meanings by their usage while recogniz-

---

3. Balthasar, *GL* IV, 11. Francesca Murphy notes that "those who read the Scriptures in light of von Balthasar's work need not be tied to his sometimes too a priori schema, in its entirety. They could learn from him how to compose from Scripture a synthetically beautiful picture. Such synthesis would be imaginative; that is, bounded by the forms of the biblical stories; and second, metaphysical, that is, exalted by the splendor and truth of those stories" (*Christ the Form of Beauty*, 182). Such is the nature of expositing a biblical trajectory for understanding God's beauty.

4. Dyrness, "Aesthetics in the Old Testament: Beauty in Context," 422.

5. Ibid.

ing the tentative nature of "word studies" as noted by James Barr in his *Semantics of Biblical Language*. Yet, as helpful as his brief semantic study is, Dyrness provides minimal canonical context that leaves his important study bereft of how it fits within the scope of God's drama of redemption.[6]

Others, like Edmund Clowney, have attempted to identify particular themes within the redemptive-historical narrative of Scripture associated with beauty. Clowney situates his discussion of beauty within the redemptive-historical narrative of Scripture by beginning with the beauty found within the created order prior to the Fall, the consequent effects thereof regarding beauty and our perceptions, and the forthcoming new order brought about by God's gracious redemption. His study of the text coalesces into three overarching themes: 1. beauty related to Israelite worship reflecting the majesty of God's presence, 2. the beauty of design and craftsmanship reflecting God's wisdom, and 3. the beauty of delight reflecting the loveliness of God's grace. Clowney connects these themes to the New Testament by showing how they each point to their fulfillment in Christ.[7] He also speaks to the important subjective aspects of beauty, noting how God's people in fellowship with him enjoy "the beauty of divine fullness."[8] Despite these strengths, Clowney's account lacks a theological center, most notably a trinitarian one, as his essay bears no witness to the Holy Spirit and his relationship to God's beauty.

Balthasar, our main conversation partner, follows a theological trajectory by focusing on the theophanic appearances of God beginning in the Old Testament that culminates with Jesus Christ in the New.[9] In fact, the characteristics of biblical theophanic accounts resonate throughout his theological aesthetics (e.g., divine initiation, impartation of holiness, rev-

---

6. Similar concerns are still pressing in his later work, *Visual Faith: Art, Theology, and Worship in Dialogue*, due in part to his efforts to craft a biblical aesthetics without examining New Testament themes. His development of a theological perspective of art rightly notes the need to reflect further on "what is called the economic Trinity," yet his understanding of God's beauty remains disconnected from such convictions. For a fuller treatment of all aesthetic terms in both Testaments see Jo Ann Davidson's PhD diss., "Toward a Theology of Beauty," although her rendering of God's beauty lacks form as any discussion of the Trinity is notably absent.

7. Clowney, "Living Art: Christian Experience and the Arts," 235–53.

8. Ibid., 248.

9. Balthasar's theological development of God's beauty that converges on God's theophanic appearances beginning in the Old Testament and culminating in the New reflects his concurrence with Gerhard von Rad's assertion that "the descriptions of theophanies are undoubtedly the most central subject of an OT aesthetic, for they reveal more clearly than all else how the special experience of God undergone by Israel became normative for the special features in the experience of beauty" (*Old Testament Theology*, 366–67).

elation and concealment, theophanic speech, etc.), concluding that "only the entire biblical revelation mediates in a total form what God wanted to communicate to us of his glory."[10] Thus, Balthasar renders a notion of God's beauty rooted in Christ's death and resurrection and the Holy Spirit's shaping power. There is much to commend in Balthasar's theological account of God's beauty; yet, as we have seen in chapter two, Balthasar seems to undermine the efficacy of God's glory and the two key christological terms central to his theological aesthetics.

Each of these offers a significant contribution to the biblical mosaic regarding God's beauty and is necessary to a fuller description. To be sure, we can gain knowledge of God from all aspects of his self-revelation since he spoke long ago to our forefathers, Abraham, Isaac, and Jacob, as well as through the prophets (Heb 1:1). It is through God's Son, though, that we gain a fuller understanding of who God is because Jesus Christ is the exact representation of God's being, of his beauty. Christ is the center of God's actions, ordering and clarifying all other accounts such that we gain a fuller understanding of the parts in light of the whole of God's drama of redemption. By this, I do not intend to imply that these other contributions, such as God's beauty in creation, are not important components to understanding God's beauty. Rather, as *components*, they find their meaning only in God's definitive self-revelation in Jesus Christ who is the "radiance of God's glory" and the "exact representation of God's being" (Heb 1:3).[11] By beginning with the Suffering Servant motif and connecting it to the death and resurrection of Jesus Christ, the contours of a trinitarian account of God's beauty emerge, declaring the deep wisdom of God.

This chapter further develops Balthasar's christological terms, in light of our gentle critiques in chapter two, by elucidating a relevant biblical motif rooted in the thematic patterning of the Suffering Servant in the Old Testament. This pattern forms the framework for elucidating God's suffering glory as we deal with the nocturnal sides of life in order to avoid an aestheticism that conceives of God's beauty by turning "away from biblical revelation to invent some sterile conceptual understanding

---

10. Balthasar, *GL* VI, 416; See Niehaus, "Theology of Theophany," 1247–49 for a fuller discussion.

11. Begbie, "Created Beauty," 25–31, offers six characteristics of a theological account of created beauty that is ordered to the beauty of the triune God. He says little, though, about the particulars of a trinitarian account of beauty, which is ultimately the concern of this project. See also Patrick Sherry's *Spirit and Beauty*, 77–99 regarding the relationship between the Holy Spirit, beauty, and creation.

of [his] beauty."[12] We look specifically to God's servant Jeremiah because one of the crucial concerns surrounding God's reconciling act in Christ on the cross, particularly for relational theists, is his "cry of dereliction." Is Christ's cry of forsakenness to the Father one of abandonment, of lament, some combination, or simply a misunderstanding? While each of the various suffering servants in the Old Testament make unique contributions to this thematic pattern, Jeremiah's message to the Israelites, laments to Yahweh, and embodiment of God's wisdom offer insights into the debate surrounding Christ's "cry of dereliction." To flesh out the wisdom of the Suffering Servant motif, we examine the New Testament perspective on Jesus Christ as the fulfillment of this particular pattern, noting both the continuity and discontinuity. Finally, we affix these motifs with a theological interpretation of Col 1–2:5 where Paul joins four important concepts for understanding God's beauty—$\mu\upsilon\sigma\tau\acute{\eta}\rho\iota\text{o}\nu$, $\delta\acute{o}\xi\alpha$, $\sigma o\phi\acute{\iota}\alpha$, and $\pi\acute{\alpha}\theta\eta\mu\alpha$. This trajectory suggests God's beauty to be communicative of his glory rather than merely an "appropriate parenthesis" as Barth surmised—an important step before conceptually expanding upon God's beauty-in-act. Let us look now at the thematic patterning of the Suffering Servant in the Old Testament.

The Thematic Patterning of the Suffering Servant

The Suffering Servant motif in the Old Testament is a well known theme that has drawn the interests of numerous scholars from across the theological spectrum, both in Judaism and Christianity.[13] The seminal passages commonly associated with this theme are Bernhard Duhm's so-called "Servant Songs" of Isaiah contained within Isa 40–55. Debate among biblical scholars continues over the identity of the Servant of Yahweh along two broad trajectories, the collective identity of Israel (whether historical, ideal, or the remnant) or the particular identity of an individual (e.g., an anonymous contemporary of Isaiah, Isaiah himself, Zerubbabel, Ezekiel, Uzziah, Cyrus, a messianic figure, Jesus Christ, etc.).[14] These debates are tangential to this proposal in that they uniquely contribute to the overall

---

12. Mongrain, "Von Balthasar's Way from Doxology to Theology," 61.

13. The literature discussing the Suffering Servant is legion. See the extensive bibliographies at the end of North, *Suffering Servant in Deutero-Isaiah* and Janowski and Stuhlmacher, *Suffering Servant*.

14. Christopher North assesses that there are four general theories: *the* servant is an anonymous contemporary of Isaiah, the prophet Isaiah himself, the corporate identity of Israel, or a Davidic messianic figure most likely pointing to Jesus Christ (North, *The Suffering Servant in Deutero-Isaiah*, 3–5).

The Hinge

motif of the Suffering Servant in the Old Testament while illuminating only aspects of it. What is important to our task is the *thematic pattern* that is sketched by these various Suffering Servants of Yahweh, all of which point to Jesus Christ who is its continuous and discontinuous fulfillment. What, then, are the general characteristics of a suffering Servant of Yahweh?

The Servant of Yahweh

The Servant of Yahweh (עֶבֶד־יהוה) is a prominent phrase in the Old Testament that usually designates an individual but sometimes the nation of Israel as God's chosen representative, instrument, or agent called to perform a specific task. The Servant of Yahweh is often tasked as a leader or messenger who intercedes on behalf of another based on the unique master/servant relationship, often communicating or appealing to Yahweh's covenantal promises (e.g., Gen 24:14; Exod 32:13; Deut 9:27). This relationship, though, is not one of presumption but of dependence on God, the divine master. Each servant has a unique part to play within God's drama of redemption.[15]

Two of the foremost figures in Israel's history frequently identified as Servants of Yahweh are Moses and King David. Moses, as a leader of God's people, is known as God's faithful servant who communicates directly with God, face-to-face, such that he deserves the utmost respect (Num 12:6–8). He is tasked by God as his servant to lead the Israelites out of Egyptian captivity to the Promised Land, declaring God's promises and provisions as mediator of the Sinai covenant (1 Kgs 8:53, 56; 2 Kgs 18:12; 21:8), promulgating the Law, and issuing specific directions for entering the Promised Land (Josh 1:7, 13, 15). At the conclusion of his life, he is eulogized as "the Servant of Yahweh" (Deut 34:5), encapsulating his unique role within God's drama of redemption. Similarly, King David serves as the mediator of the Davidic covenant and is charged to deliver Israel from her enemies, establishing his kingdom rule (2 Sam 3:18). Because of God's promises and faithfulness to the line of David, God demonstrates his long-suffering toward his people despite their obstinate disobedience (1 Kgs 11:34; 2 Kgs 8:19). Such faithfulness and long-suffering by God on account of his covenant with David extends beyond David's kingship as the prophets attest (Isa 37:35; Jer 33:21–22, 26; Ezek 34:23–24; 37:24–26).[16]

---

15. Carpenter, "עבד."
16. Blenkinsopp, *Isaiah 40–55*, 118–20.

The prophets of Israel are also designated as the Servants of Yahweh, both individually and collectively. As a group, the prophets serve as God's divine messengers sent to declare "the word of the Lord" to his people, imploring them to maintain their fidelity to God's covenantal ideals, warning them of impending judgment, and exhorting them to remember God's covenantal faithfulness (Isa 1:10–31; Jer 2:4–37; Ezek 3:16–21). God's prophets are privy to parts of his divine plan (Amos 3:7) and are given divine authority such that those who disregard their proclamations incur God's divine anger and wrath (2 Kgs 9:7; 17:23). Individually, prophets, as Servants of Yahweh, experience God's call, receive a specific message from God, and proclaim that message through words, signs, and symbols to address the contemporary situation of God's people and then to the nations (e.g., Isa 6; Jer 1; Ezek 2; Amos 7:15; Hos 9:8). Their prophetic missions often result in vitriolic opposition, familial abandonment, ridicule, and even death.[17]

What, though, is significant about this characteristic of suffering? To be sure, not all Servants of Yahweh endure the same degree of suffering. Some, like Moses, experience the ire of God as they intercede on behalf of God's people for their disobedience (Exod 32:11–14, 30–34). Others, like Elijah, entreat Yahweh to take their life so that they will not have to face suffering any longer, yet experience refreshment from God (1 Kgs 19:4). Still others, like Jeremiah, lament their existence as they undergo constant ridicule and persecution, seeing no fruit of their labors (Jer 11:18–20). And some, like Zechariah (1 Chr 24:20–21) and Uriah (Jer 26:20–23), suffer death as they discharge their prophetic office. To that end, "suffering and death can be the price to pay for a prophetic mission," which "can [also] have a positive, salvific effect on others" whereby "a prophet can substitute for others by taking on himself the consequences of their wrongdoing." This notion of vicarious suffering by the prophet that has a redemptive effect for others ". . . is *unprecedented*."[18] Here is the looming question: why is the Suffering Servant a relevant biblical motif for discerning a trinitarian understanding of God's beauty?

---

17. Schultz, "Servant, Slave," 1183–97.

18. Blenkinsopp, *Isaiah 40–55*, 119. Emphasis added. Blenkinsopp aptly notes that Isa 53, with its own unique contributions to this idea of "substitution," is not the first or only one to espouse this notion. In fact, he asserts that this idea of "atoning for the sins of [God's] people" is latent, for example, in Abraham's attempts to petition Yahweh to spare the cities of Sodom and Gomorrah (Gen 18:22–33) and Moses's offer of his life for the Israelites' transgressions of the golden calf (Exod 32:30–34).

The Hinge

A Relevant Biblical Motif

Recall from chapter one the contemporary understanding of beauty that dismisses it from a variety of disciplines, in part, because beauty's ascription to the ornamental and innocuous pleasant signifies an escape from the pain and suffering of reality. These assumptions render beauty innocuous, limiting our understanding of the real to the true and/or the good or to some cynical and suspicious postmodern aestheticism. Our efforts to retrieve an understanding of God's beauty must account for these realities; otherwise, God's beauty becomes a figment of our imaginations unrelated to the banes of human existence, succumbing to the accusations made by relational theists.

The way forward, as we intimated in chapter one and developed in chapter two, looks to where God has revealed himself most fully, namely his Son, Jesus Christ, who is the radiance of God's glory and the exact representation of his being as attested to in Holy Scripture (John 1:1–14; Col 1:15–20; Heb 1:1–4). This is why in chapter two we critically appropriated Balthasar's notion of Christ as *Übergestalt* and *Herrlichkeit*—the distinct speaking and doing form (*Gestalt*) of God's beauty. This christocentric understanding of beauty *includes* the tragic realities of human existence and dispels these ethereal platitudes by looking to Christ's assumption of the *Ungestalt* on the cross and his return as *Herrlichkeit* and *Übergestalt* in the resurrection. In this, the shaping power of the Holy Spirit prevails in the very chaos of sin, victoriously overcoming the nocturnal sides of human existence. Examining the New Testament accounts in isolation from the Old, though, limits our understanding, raising the question of how we relate the two Testaments.

Balthasar depicts the relationship between the Old and New Testament as more than promise and fulfillment. He envisions the history of Israel not only as preparatory of the coming Messiah (i.e., *praeparatio evangelica*) but also prophetic: "If it is true that the historical-critical method has destroyed the old form of the *argumentum ex prophetia*, which understood sayings of the old covenant as having been spoken with direct reference to Christ, . . . the elimination of this all too naïve concept left space for something much more important and splendid, viz. for the prophetical character of the whole history of Israel."[19]

Israel serves, then, not only as a sign that has its fulfillment in Christ but also as a pointer to the Lamb who takes away the sin of the world.

---

19. Balthasar, *GL* VI, 402.

Balthasar contends that "the forms of the Old Testament, taken together, form something like an arrow pointing out the direction; [and] its sharp, unambiguous head is the Servant of Yahweh."[20] Yet, Israel blunts "this arrow-head in the evasions of the post-exilic theology of glory" by refusing to acknowledge her divine mission as the Servant of Yahweh.[21] In doing so, there is "the discrepancy between the form and what fills it out." Therefore, I concur with Balthasar in "that which brings fulfillment can be understood only together with *what* it fulfills."[22] This implies that the Suffering Servant motif exhibits a thematic patterning that points to a subsequent fulfillment; yet, this fulfillment in Christ, as we come to learn in the New Testament, only makes sense in light of the Old Testament pattern.[23]

That being the case, it seems that the Suffering Servant of Isaiah is the natural place to develop this relevant biblical motif for discerning God's beauty. To be sure, an examination of the particulars would reveal commonalties with all the other Suffering Servants of Yahweh in the Old Testament while emphasizing certain aspects particular to the Isaian account. For example, the Suffering Servant of Isaiah is set aside before birth for a divine mission (Isa 49:1), receives divine knowledge and instruction (Isa 50:4), is tasked to deliver that message first to Israel and then to the nations (Isa 49:6), feels inadequate and ill-equipped to perform the assigned task (Isa 49:4), and experiences suffering in his fulfillment of it (Isa 53:3–12).[24] These are common features of the Suffering Servant motif, yet the Suffering Servant in Isaiah emphasizes a particular aspect of the overall motif not necessarily emphasized in the others. Although the Isaian account highlights the vicarious suffering of the Servant similar to other accounts, "the sins of the people represented by the speaker and the sufferings of the Servant" are "redirected from its due target to the Servant . . . *by a positive act of God.*"[25] This positive act of God is unique to the Isaian account and alludes to one way God deals with his people. Thus, through the centuries,

---

20. Ibid., 411.
21. Ibid.
22. Ibid., 412.
23. Ibid. Balthasar underscores the typological relationship between the Old and New Testaments, insisting that "every attempt to interpret the form, message and subsequent impact of Christ in the world necessarily fails unless it is able to assess it all precisely in its closeness to and its distance from the old covenant (*GL* VI, 403). See also Goppelt, *TYPOS*.
24. Blenkinsopp, *Isaiah 40–55*, 119.
25. Ibid., 120. Emphasis added. Cf. Spieckermann, "Conception and Prehistory," 1–15 and Janowski, "He Bore Our Sins," 48–74.

The Hinge

Christian biblical interpretation has rightly connected these themes with Christ's death on the cross, although not without controversy.[26]

The Problem of Isaiah 53

Some contend, because of Yahweh's initiative to redirect the suffering to the Servant (Isa 53:6) according to his good pleasure (Isa 53:10), that God's justice is capricious at best and sadistic at worst. In support of this claim, Immanuel Kant's objection that transgressions and guilt are not transferable from one person to another is often mentioned.[27] Yet, these theological difficulties, as important as they are for discerning the *effects* of Christ's vicarious sufferings on our behalf (e.g., penal substitution, satisfaction, etc.), are not the primary concern of this proposal. Rather, the *act* of vicarious suffering and what it reveals about the nature of God is more of our concern. Nevertheless, Isa 53, particularly Isa 53:2b, presents a problem for this proposal as it relates to explicating God's beauty-in-act.

Isaiah depicts the Suffering Servant as having no form/beauty (לֹא־תֹאַר) and no splendor (וְלֹא הָדָר) so much so that we should turn our eyes away from him (וְנִרְאֵהוּ), for nothing in his appearance is desirable or attractive to us (וְלֹא־מַרְאֶה וְנֶחְמְדֵהוּ). On a *prima facie* reading of this text, the Suffering Servant of Yahweh is deformed, ugly, and unattractive, which begs the question of how we can associate beauty with Jesus Christ if he is in fact the fulfillment of this passage. Commenting on Isa 53, Jerome presents the dilemma this way: "If he did not have beauty or glory, but his form was base and lacking ... how then can it be said in the psalms, 'Gird your side with your sword, O might one, with your beauty and fairness' [Ps 45:62]?"[28] Isa 53 seems problematic to associate beauty with Jesus

---

26. The essays, contained within the aforementioned books edited by Janowski/Stuhlmacher and Bellinger/Farmer, provide a superb introduction to the various issues from various viewpoints surrounding the Christian interpretation of Isa 53 and its implications for Christian theology.

27. See Kant, *Religion within the Boundaries of Mere Reason*, 88–93. Others question whether Jesus of Nazareth sees himself as fulfilling the mission of the Suffering Servant or even whether he had Isa 53 in mind (Morna D. Hooker's work, *Jesus and the Servant*, is paradigmatic). In response, I am in substantial agreement with Parsons essay on the matter, "Isaiah 53 in Acts 8," 104–19 and Thrall's essay, "The Suffering Servant and the Mission of Jesus," 281–88, where she concludes, "since Jesus affirms that his death is foretold in Scripture it is difficult to deny the possibility that he saw himself as destined to carry out the mission of the Suffering Servant" (286).

28. Elliot, ed., *Isaiah 40–66*, 162.

Following a Biblical Trajectory

Christ, not to mention including Christ's suffering in our account of God's beauty. How might we address this problem?

Following Duhm's designations, this passage is found within the fourth Servant Song where Isaiah offers an oblique picture of the righteous Servant of Yahweh who brings peace through his suffering. This description by Isaiah is intended to bring comfort to the Israelites who are in exile.[29] Yet, this is a perplexing passage in that what onlookers perceive about the Servant of Yahweh does not fit with his subsequent actions. In fact, it seems as if the Servant's "fate is described from two antithetical standpoints" as Klaus Baltzer notes, where "on the one hand an account of the Servant's fate is given, seen from the outside (vv. 2–3 and 7–9)" while on the other "his life and sufferings are interpreted under the aspect of what he did for the community (vv. 4–6 and 10)."[30] Isaiah summarizes this contrast at the beginning of the this final Servant Song (Isa 52:13–15), noting how the Servant of Yahweh will be exalted (גָּבַהּ) despite those who are appalled (שָׁמֵם) by his appearance. How can this be? As such, Isaiah is dismayed by the unbelief of God's people (Isa 53:1) as he explicates this contrast in greater detail (Isa 53:2–12).

Isaiah 53:2 describes the Servant's life as he sprouts up (עָלָה) like a tender shoot (יוֹנֵק), like a root (שֹׁרֶשׁ) out of the dry ground, echoing the messianic prophecy "in the line of Jesse" found in Isaiah 11:1–10. Is this what we should expect, though, from the royal line David? Are not these saplings cut off and burned? Would not the strong cedars of Lebanon where there is plenty of water (Isa 41:18) be a better depiction of this royal line rather than the withered plants found in the parched and barren land of the desert where life struggles for survival (Jer 2:6)? Besides, how can the Messiah, the one who will redeem Israel from her oppressors, be one who is undesirable and without the honor due him? Indeed, this is a troubling and perplexing passage, particularly for those in exile.

Yet, in light of the broader context, what is this passage trying to say about this Suffering Servant whom Yahweh will glorify? It seems that the purpose of the text is to reveal how "the appearance of the servant was such that man, judging from the wrong perspective, would completely misjudge him."[31] Looking to Christ, John Calvin remarks similarly: "The Prophet shews by what means the kingdom of Christ must be set up and

---

29. Goldingay, *God's Prophet, God's Servant*, 139–40.
30. Baltzer, *Deutero-Isaiah*, 404.
31. Young, *Book of Isaiah*, 3:342.

The Hinge

established, that we may not judge of it by human conceptions."[32] In other words, the appearance and actions of this Suffering Servant as well as Yahweh's actions of exaltation are *counterintuitive* to those looking in from the outside. How can we find beauty, then, in what is so appalling without glorifying suffering?

Augustine, in seeing Jesus Christ as the fulfillment of Isa 53, provides some helpful insight: "What is it we love in Christ—his crucified limbs, his pierced side, or his love? When we hear that he suffered for us, what do we love? Love is loved. He loved us, that we might in turn love Him; and that we might return His love He has given us His Spirit."[33] Three things are evident in Augustine's response: (1) The beauty of the cross is not the suffering, brutality, or cruelty but the *act* of self-giving love revealed through suffering; (2) Christ's suffering is for our benefit; and, (3) such beauty perceived in and through the cross by faith is understood only in light of the whole of God's drama of redemption. This is the counterintuitive nature of *God's suffering glory* such that God's beauty-in-act radiates in weakness (2 Cor 12:9).

This explanation draws our attention to the unexpected in God's communicative actions, particularly in Christ, in that God often uses the foolish things of this world to humiliate the wise and the weak things to shame the strong (1 Cor 1:27). So, why not draw further upon the Suffering Servant in Isaiah to fashion a biblical trajectory for discerning God's beauty-in-act? Such a project is worthy of consideration and would provide a thicker account. Are there, though, additional themes emphasized in the other Suffering Servant accounts that may elucidate different aspects of Christ's death and resurrection germane to our project? The prophet Jeremiah overlaps with several pertinent themes from the Isaian account. The prominent theme of embodied wisdom found in the laments of Jeremiah, however, may in fact illuminate Christ's "cry of dereliction" on the cross differently than relational theists who see Christ's cry as a point of debarkation for rooting suffering eternally in the Godhead. Let us examine these themes in Jeremiah in order to begin sketching the contours of our biblical trajectory.

---

32. Calvin, *Commentary on the Book of the Prophet Isaiah*, 113–14.
33. Augustine, *Expositions of the Psalms*, 235.

The Old Testament Wisdom of the Suffering Servant in Jeremiah

Jeremiah, as the son of Hilkiah, possesses a priestly pedigree from the Levitcal city of Anathoth in the land of Benjamin just a few miles from Jerusalem (Jer 1:1). He becomes a prophet (נָבִיא)—a Servant of Yahweh (עֶבֶד־יהוה)—at God's calling, similar to the call-patterns of previous prophets like Isaiah (Isa 6) and Moses (Exod 4) where a dialogue between the prophet and God ensues in which the prophet bemoans his inadequacies and God reassures him of his presence and provision (Jer 1:5–10). As the עֶבֶד־יהוה, Jeremiah not only proclaims Yahweh's message but also lives it out as he stands amidst the tension of God's judgment and covenantal renewal. He is one of Yahweh's Suffering Servants who seeks to call the people of God back to their covenantal ideals, embracing the peace, wisdom, righteousness, and love of God.[34]

Jeremiah ministers during the reign of Josiah and his sons in the final years of Judah's existence as a nation (Jer 1:1–3). These are turbulent days filled with international and national calamities as the powerful Assyrian and Egyptian empires decline and the Babylonian empire rises to prominence, all the while Judah struggles to maintain her independence and seeks to restore her boundaries and influence to Davidic levels.[35] Yet, Judah becomes the harlot, not unlike the story of Hosea and Gomer, as their infelicitous worship, crooked justice, and oppression corrupt Yahweh's covenantal ideal, leading to death, destruction, and exile (Jer 3:1–24; 5:1–5; 10:17–22; 11:3–4; 13:18–20; 23:1–2).[36]

Using the rhetorical device of the lawsuit pattern, Jeremiah indicts Judah for failing to fulfill her covenantal obligations while God, because of his חֶסֶד, remains faithful (Jer 3:12; 13:14; 15:16).[37] In doing so, Jeremiah declares the wisdom of God by imploring the people of Judah to repent and live obedient lives according to the Torah by loving the Lord God wholly,

---

34. Lundbom, *Jeremiah*, 107–20. For further discussion, see Brueggemann, "Book of Jeremiah," 130–45.

35. For further details regarding the soci-political background of Jeremiah, see 2 Kings 21–25 and 2 Chronicles 33–36 as well as any number of commentaries such as McKane, *A Critical and Exegetical Commentary on Jeremiah* and Thompson, *Book of Jeremiah*. See also Malamat, "Last Kings of Judah," 137–56 and "Twilight of Judah," 123–45.

36. See Thompson, *Book of Jeremiah*, 81–85 on relating Jeremiah and Hosea.

37. McConville, "Theology of Jeremiah," 755–67. See also Huffmon, "Covenant Lawsuit in the Prophets," 285–95.

The Hinge

fleeing from idolatry, seeking justice, and walking humbly in God's ways (Jer 2). These appeals echo the blessings and curses that Moses delivers to Israelites generations ago, providing continuity amidst the discontinuity of disobedience (Jer 11:26–32).[38] His message to God's people, though, brings him suffering as he laments to God over Judah's impending doom and the hardship of discharging his prophetic office.

The Message of Jeremiah and His Laments to Yahweh

Jeremiah's message to the people of Judah, although laced with hope, wisdom, and promise (Jer 24:7), is one of death, destruction, and despair because of their importunate apostasy (Jer 2–3). If the people of God do not repent, they must suffer the wrath of God (Jer 4–6) as he brings about the pangs of famine, war, and exile. Jeremiah's vivid declarations of judgment graphically depict tragic ruin as "destruction is heaped upon destruction" (Jer 4:20), leaving "the earth formless and empty" and the "heavens without light" (Jer 4:23); all because Judah no longer fears Yahweh (Jer 4:18). Consequently, Jeremiah endures considerable anguish as he laments over Judah's impending doom (i.e., Jer 11:18–23; 12:1–6; 15:10–21; 17:14–18; 18:18–23; 20:7–13; 20:14–18) and suffers loneliness in his celibacy (Jer 16:2–4), rejection by his own family (Jer 11:21–23), physical torment at the hands of temple leaders (Jer 20:2), imprisonment (Jer 38:1–13), accusations of treason, sedition, and desertion (Jer 26; 37:11–16), and exile in Egypt (Jer 41:16—44:30). Through his lament and suffering, Jeremiah serves as a mediator between Yahweh and Judah, struggling to understand God's ways.[39]

Jeremiah's individual laments or confessions to Yahweh are a part of a broader compendium of laments in the Old Testament that express Israel's sincere, dialogical responses to the travails of life. Walter Brueggemann remarks that the genre of lament is generally characterized by an "address, complaint, petition, motivation, vow of offering, [and] assurance of being heard" with the intent being not "to deny nor to dull the extremity, but to

---

38. See Holladay's "Background of Jeremiah's Self-Understanding," 153–64 and Seitz, "Prophet Moses and the Canonical Shape of Jeremiah," 3–27 for exploring the parallels between Moses and Jeremiah. See also Scalise, "Logic of Covenant and Lament in Jeremiah," 395–401 and VanGemeren, "Prophets, the Freedom of God, and Hermeneutics," 79–99.

39. See Miller, "Trouble and Woe," 41–45 and Westermann, "Role of the Lament," 34–35.

shape it so that it may be received in the context of faith."[40] Claus Westermann also notes that the genre of lament "is set within the context of the account of deliverance which became the basis of Israel's relationship with God;" and, "is thus related to the saving acts of God," thereby "appeal[ing] to God's compassion."[41] He further categorizes laments into "the lament of the dead" and "the lament of affliction" where the former "looks backward . . . bewail[ing] the death of another" while the latter "looks forward . . . reach[ing] out for life." As such, laments of affliction are prayers addressed to God, "giving voice to suffering" as the afflicted present their "sufferings before the one who alleviates suffering, heals wounds and dries tears."[42]

Jeremiah's laments exhibit several of these general characteristics as he directs his complaints, frustrations, and accusations to Yahweh. On two occasions, Jeremiah contests the parity of God's justice as he questions why his own family plots to murder him, since he is like "an innocent lamb led to the slaughter" (Jer 11:18-23), and why the wicked prosper, demanding they be appropriately punished (Jer 12:1–6). In another instance, he cries to Yahweh for deliverance from his tormentors as they mock his unfulfilled prophecies (Jer 17:14–18). After all, is it not Yahweh who deceived him into discharging the responsibilities of the prophetic office (Jer 20:7–8, 10)? His circumstances continue to grow bleaker and bleaker to the point that he curses the day he was born and laments his sorry existence (Jer 20:14–18).[43] So, where is Yahweh's deliverance? Is God not supposed to alleviate his pain and vindicate these injustices, particularly for his servant?

This apparent lack of inaction can be disheartening. It is for Jeremiah who rarely receives a response from God; and when he does, it is not what he expects. When Jeremiah questions God's divine justice, God responds by questioning his faith and intestinal fortitude (Jer 12:1–6). On another occasion, Jeremiah's lament has a sharp accusatory tone, demanding to know why he is suffering when in fact he has been faithful to God's calling (Jer 15:10–18). God replies to Jeremiah's accusations by calling him to repentance (Jer 15:19–21). Yet, in an even more perplexing account, when Jeremiah bemoans his existence and demands God to exercise his justice

---

40. Brueggemann, "From Hurt to Joy, From Death to Life," 6.
41. Westermann, "Role of the Lament," 21, 24.
42. Ibid., 22, 31–32.
43. Bright, "Prophet's Lament and Its Answer," 59–74.

against his tormentors, God is deafly silent (Jer 20:7–18).[44] How, then, is lament functioning in these instances?

Without question, Jeremiah's laments give voice to his horrendous suffering, allowing him to verbalize and honestly face the painful realities of his existence. His conversations with Yahweh are real and authentic. Yet, despite his incessant complaints, he continues to discharge the duties of his prophetic office faithfully as he delivers God's message to the people. He, in fact, affirms his calling and commitment on several occasions, for Yahweh's word is in his heart like a fire and he is weary of holding it back. Indeed, he cannot (Jer 20:9, 11–13). How, though, is he able to do this amidst his agony? It appears that as a Servant of Yahweh he has *the privilege of presence*—the privilege of being in Yahweh's presence and the presence of Yahweh in his life, no matter how unexplainable circumstances may be at times. Jeremiah has the privilege of bringing his supplications, in all their brutal honesty, before Yahweh; and, as his servant, Yahweh is with him wherever he goes (Jer 1:8). As such, his lament shapes his faith as he seeks to understand the ways of God.

The Embodiment of God's Wisdom

Jeremiah metaphorically portrays his embodiment of Yahweh's wisdom as he remarks, in the midst of one of his laments, that the word of the Lord is such a delight that he eats it (Jer 15:16), not unlike the prophet Ezekiel who eats the scroll containing his prophetic message (Ezek 2:8—3:3). Jeremiah further demonstrates this notion through his lament and suffering as he "*shatters* old worlds (brings them to an end) and *forms* and evokes new worlds (causes them to be)" with "poetic passion and stunning imagination," for Jeremiah "enters into the pathos of God."[45] As Terence Fretheim notes, "God calls the prophet to take the word received and embody that word from the moment of the call onward. The prophet, in effect, is called to function as an ongoing theophany." Thus, "we see . . . a more extended appearance of the Word of God in human form" where "the story of God is lived out in the story of the prophet."[46] One part of the story, illustrating

---

44. Balentine, "Jeremiah, Prophet of Prayer," 339–40.

45. Brueggemann, "Book of Jeremiah," 134–35. See also Fretheim's chapter, "Prophet, Theophany, and the Suffering of God," in *Suffering of God*, 149–66 and Heschel, *Prophets*, 130–77.

46. Fretheim, *Suffering of God*, 151–52.

Following a Biblical Trajectory

this point, is King Zedekiah's and Judah's rejection of Jeremiah's prophecy as they cast him into a muddy and dungy cistern.

King Zedekiah implores Jeremiah to petition Yahweh for discernment regarding the impending destruction of Jerusalem at the hands of the Babylonians (Jer 37:1–3). Yahweh speaks to Jeremiah, instructing him to tell King Zedekiah and the people that Pharaoh, who has come to their aid, will return to Egypt, allowing the Babylonians to seize and destroy the city of Jerusalem (Jer 37:6–10). After having been falsely accused of treason and put in prison, King Zedekiah pardons him and inquires if there is any word from the Lord (Jer 37:13–21). Jeremiah tells him what Yahweh has said, yet the king does not listen. Jeremiah proceeds to declare the word of the Lord to the people, foretelling of their impending doom (Jer 38:1–3). His message enrages city officials as they accuse him of encouraging desertion and call for his death. Zedekiah does not stand in their way, and Jeremiah is thrown into a cistern (בּוֹר) where he sinks (טָבַע) down into the mud (Jer 38:4–6).

The actuality of Jeremiah's imprisonment in the depths of the cistern not only serves as a tangible manifestation of Jeremiah's laments to Yahweh but also may in fact personify Yahweh's laments over Judah's descent into perdition. Jeremiah, at the beginning of his ministry, implores the people of Judah to fear the Lord and heed his commands, insisting that if they turn from their errant ways Yahweh will restore to them life and covenantal blessing (Jer 2).[47] Yet, the people of Judah reject the living water of Yahweh (מַיִם חַיִּים) and dig their own cisterns, which are in need of water (Jer 2:13). So, as Jeremiah literally descends into the shadowy depths of his personal cistern in Jer 38:4–6, he incarnates his laments of death and despair as he sinks deeper into the dark abyss. Similarly, Jeremiah's descent into the cistern and being mired in the mud represents Judah's apostasy and movement away from God's wisdom, bringing to mind Yahweh's laments over Judah's perpetual backsliding (e.g., Jer 8:5–7).[48]

Jeremiah is not some tragic figure, though, akin to Shakespeare's King Lear. Rather, he is an instrument of God who conveys, in all that he is and does, what is fitting for life within God's drama of redemption. He serves as a mediator between God and his people, displaying God's wrath and holiness while bringing comfort and hope through his suffering in

---

47. See Sirach 24 and Baruch 3:9—4:4 for the idea of wisdom associated with the Torah where one obtains life and covenantal blessing through obedience to its teachings.

48. See Smith, "Jeremiah IX 9—A Divine Lament," 97–99 for a succinct account of divine laments in Jeremiah.

light of the coming covenantal restoration. Yet, Jeremiah's embodiment of God's wisdom and subsequent entry into God's pathos "does not mean Jeremiah slides over to God's side of the equation," for Jeremiah can no longer bear the tension between God's covenantal holiness and the people's apostasy nor see how to resolve this tension (Jer 12:5; 15:18).[49] As such, we come to realize through Jeremiah's life, and particularly his lamentations, God's longsuffering love and his patient compassion amidst his holiness and justice (Jer 3:12; 13:14; 15:16). Therefore, "it is as if Jeremiah himself becomes, in the very life and ministry he has to take on as a prophet, an embodiment of God's final grace to his people, even as they endure the judgment he has brought on them. In this respect he strongly resembles the figure of the Suffering Servant."[50]

The Contribution of the Prophet Jeremiah

Jeremiah's contributions to the thematic pattern of the Suffering Servant offer interesting insights for our proposal while prompting several questions. If the nature of lament, as previously described, is to petition God for a reprieve from suffering, the logic of lament "expects God to act justly by vindicating the innocent sufferer."[51] The supplicant's despondent cry in desperation is "an act of faithfulness, . . . premised on the reliability and accessibility of God, on a vision of the way the world is supposed to be and is not."[52] Yahweh is not bound to act, though, in accordance with the supplicant's demands or petitions. Rather, he is free to respond in a manner and timing according to his good pleasure, in a manner fitting his divine nature. Such responses may be inexplicable as is the case with Jeremiah, for his ways are not our ways. Nevertheless, "we can say that the lament as such is a *movement toward* God" that brings the supplicant into Yahweh's presence.[53]

Through lament, Jeremiah finds himself in Yahweh's presence, although his petitions are not answered in a manner that he expects. He is *faithfully obedient* to his calling, executing the commands of Yahweh as he is instructed. Such obedience in the face of suffering and adversity

49. Brueggemann, "Book of Jeremiah," 134.
50. McConville, "Theology of Jeremiah," 760. See also O'Connor, "Lamenting Back to Life," 34–47.
51. Scalise, "Logic of Covenant and Lament in Jeremiah," 399.
52. Brueggemann, "From Hurt to Joy, From Death to Life," 8.
53. Westermann, "Role of Lament," 32. Emphasis added.

demonstrates a deep wisdom on the part of Jeremiah, a wisdom that is counterintuitive to the world's wisdom. By all accounts, Jeremiah should have forsaken his calling. He should have joined the family business. No one would have faulted him for doing so. In fact, his family, friends, and contemporaries probably would have lauded him for such actions. Yet, the wisdom he possesses seen in and through his laments is not the conventional wisdom of the world but lies in the "fear of the Lord" (Prov 9:10), for "the speaker is aware that his destiny is in God's hand. He is helpless and does not doubt that Yahweh can and may transform the situation."[54] This notion is consistently manifested in Jeremiah's life as one who embodies the wisdom of Yahweh.

Jeremiah's laments to Yahweh, as previously mentioned, are part of the broader compendium of laments within the Old Testament. Biblical scholars have examined Jeremiah's confessions as they relate, particularly, to the Psalms of Lament, noting various redactions and similarities of form and source.[55] One Lament Psalm of interest to our proposal is Ps 22. William Holladay goes so far as to suggest that Ps 22 is an integral part of Jeremiah's self-understanding.[56] Perhaps, Ps 22 echoes in his mind. The clearest connection comes when Jeremiah laments the ridicule he receives for his prophetic message (Jer 20:7), for (כֻּלֹּה לֹעֵג לִי) (everyone mocks me), similar to Ps 22:8 when the Psalmist complains that (כָּל־רֹאַי יַלְעִגוּ לִי) (all who see me mock me). Further ties are suggestive in the poetic imagery of Jeremiah when Yahweh appoints him as a prophet before birth (Jer 1:5), not unlike the Psalmist's commitment to Yahweh from his birth (Ps 22:9–10).

The extent to which Jeremiah has Ps 22 in mind is indeterminable. The point is to fortify Jeremiah's laments within the broader genre of lament as an appropriate response to his agony. In doing so, "the doctrine of the incarnation could take on new meaning,"[57] as Westermann notes, particularly for Christ's "cry of derelection" when he too invokes the tradition of lament (Mark 15:34; Ps 22:1).[58] Christ has "taken up the lament

---

54. Brueggemann, "From Hurt to Joy, From Death to Life," 8.

55. See the following Baumgardner, *Die Klagegedichte des Jeremia* and Carrol, *From Chaos to Covenant*.

56. Holladay, "Background of Jeremiah's Self-Understanding," 153–64.

57. Westermann, "Role of Lament," 38.

58. There is, of course, disagreement regarding what exactly Christ meant or even if Christ utters the opening strophe of Psalm 22 (see Reumann, "Psalm 22 at the Cross," 39–58). What seems certain, though, is "that the cross is also the exaltation of Jesus—but it is an exaltation that takes full seriously the depths of despair, lament, and dying involved" (52).

The Hinge

of those of his people who suffer, that he too [has] entered into suffering. Hence, his suffering is a part of the history of those who have suffered, who have found their language in the psalms of lament."[59] This association is germane to our proposal in that relational theists like Jürgen Moltmann contend that Christ's "cry of dereliction" is the point of debarkation for surmising that Christ dies a "death of complete abandonment by God."[60] Yet, if the genre of lament is in view here, whether Christ is appealing to the first strophe of Ps 22 or the entire psalm, does Christ's lament not convey a movement *toward* God rather than complete separation? To be sure, Christian theology *must* give voice to and address the blight of human suffering present today as Moltmann and other relational theists rightly demand. The question is *how* we are to hold together "the full reality of human suffering and the indivisible bond of love between the Father and the Son in a single subject."[61]

The wisdom discerned through the laments by the Suffering Servant Jeremiah leads to several well-rehearsed theological questions. If Jeremiah embodies God's divine wisdom, to what extent does God suffer? Does God share in our human sufferings as a fellow sufferer, limiting and making himself vulnerable for the sake of genuine human interaction? Or is his suffering simply an anthropomorphism designed to communicate a particular truth? What is the nature of God's love as a fellow sufferer? And, what are the implications of Jeremiah's embodied performances of God's Word for participation in God's dramatic covenant of grace?

These questions, while only suggestive, strike at the heart of the concerns espoused by relational theists who seek to safeguard God's love and compassion as the "sharing of experience" in order to depict God as one who cares for and is involved with his creation.[62] Yet, we have only traced

---

59. Westermann, "Role of Lament," 34. Cf. Miller, "Trouble and Woe," 45 and Brueggemann, "From Hurt to Joy, From Death to Life," 18–19.

60. Moltmann, *Crucified God*, 276. In another context, Moltmann makes God's passion his axiomatic starting point: "If we are to understand the suffering of Christ as the suffering of the passionate God—it would seem more consistent if we ceased to make the axiom of God's apathy our starting point, and started instead from the axiom of God's passion" (*Trinity and the Kingdom*, 22; cf. Moltmann, "The Passion of Christ," 19–28).

61. Yocum, "Cry of Dereliction?," 79.

62. Fiddes, *Creative Suffering of God*, 16. Cf. Moltmann, *Trinity and the Kingdom*, 38. Clark Pinnock claims that "God risked suffering when he decided to love and be loved by the creature. A lover's existence is inescapably affected by the other, especially when the loved one acts in ways that grieve and disappoint" ("Systematic Theology," 119). Such notions of God's love lead relational theists to ask "how could the

the thematic pattern of the Suffering Servant and the wisdom therein through the laments of Jeremiah and are in need of filling it out by turning to the Christ-form attested to in the New Testament. In doing so, we will be in a better position to address, in part, some of these concerns and questions.

New Testament Attestations: Fleshing Out the Wisdom of the Suffering Servant

Balthasar identifies Israel's disobedient post-exilic existence as a "formless" existence, lacking many historical markers indicative of Israel's being a nation (e.g., land, the temple, etc.), thereby obscuring the glory of God. Yet, when God took on flesh he became "much more fleshly" and "was to penetrate the flesh much more deeply than Israel could ever dream of."[63] In doing so, Christ fulfills what Israel could not as the Servant of Yahweh and reveals Israel's purpose to "point" beyond itself to the One who is the self-giving of the Father. In that way, "the God who becomes man would ... have to be understood in terms of the history of God's relationship with his people—a history which ultimately reaches the point where God, as the God of judgment, suffers for his people."[64] Let us briefly examine how Christ "fleshes out" the Suffering Servant of the Old Testament.

Jesus Christ and the Suffering Servant Motif

Elucidating Jesus' *prophetic mission*, the New Testament has numerous intimations linking Jesus' ministry to the prophetic ministries of the Old Testament prophets of which Jeremiah is often cited. For example, just as God sent Jeremiah to pronounce judgments against Jerusalem, Jesus also warns the Israelites of the impending doom due to their obstinate behavior, lamenting what is to come (Jer 7:25; Matt 23:39—24:1). Jeremiah admonishes God's people regarding numerous injustices and the shedding of innocent blood if they do not amend their ways and accept God's wisdom (Jer 7:6), only later to find out that it is his life that is in danger (Jer 26:15). Similarly, Jesus chastises the Pharisees for their hypocritical behavior and incites them to finish what their forefathers started when they shed the

---

immutable, impassible God become incarnate and suffer in Christ," concluding that this "God could not" (LaCugna, *God for Us*, 300).

63. Balthasar, *GL* VI, 411.
64. Westermann, "Role of Lament," 38.

innocent blood of the prophets, all the while knowing that he will be the one they will crucify (Matt 23:29–37; Luke 11:37–54). Jeremiah even remarks that he is "like a gentle lamb led to the slaughter," regarding the conspiracy against him (Jer 11:19), not unlike Jesus who Luke identifies as the Suffering Servant (Luke 13:31–35; Acts 8:32).[65] What becomes evident, then, from these connections is that Jesus not only identifies himself with the prophets of the Old Testament, particularly as the Servant of Yahweh, but also declares himself to be the fulfillment ($\pi\lambda\eta\rho\delta\omega$) of the collective testimony to which they point (Luke 4:14–21).

Entwined with Jesus' fulfillment of his prophetic mission is a *priestly dimension*. Prophet and priest, though distinct in Israel's history, have overlapping roles. Like prophets, priests seek to embody God's wisdom by foretelling and forthtelling of Yahweh's covenantal instructions. Unlike, prophets, priests enter into Yahweh's presence to intercede on behalf of the people, appealing to Yahweh's covenantal faithfulness. Jeremiah's proclamations to the people of Judah, imploring them to adhere to the Torah, speak of the importance of duty and obligation to the covenant because obedience to God's statutes brings life. Yet, we also see God's wisdom manifested in Jeremiah's laments and sufferings as he intercedes on behalf of Judah while struggling to understand God's ways. His intercession and struggle give us "insights, however hard or exalted, into the human condition—insights originating in the exercise of the human intellect in observation and experience but becoming ultimately the canonical word of God himself."[66] Thus, through his lament and suffering, Jeremiah serves as mediator and intercessor between Yahweh and Judah not only embodying the wisdom of God but also interceding on Judah's behalf by appealing to God's steadfast love. Similar to being the fulfillment of the prophetic tradition, Jesus is the great high priest who is the *one* mediator between God and humanity (1 Tim 2:5; Heb 2:11–18; 5:1–10). He intercedes on behalf of his people (John 17) and continues to do so after his ascension (Rom 8:34). Jesus lives a perfect, sinless life of obedience even to the point of death, offering himself as a sacrifice (1 Pet 1:19), a fragrant offering to God (Eph 5:2), for "the Son of Man did not come to be served but to serve and to give his life as a ransom for many" (Mark 10:45). Hence, Jesus Christ, the great high priest, can be considered *the* Suffering Servant of God.[67]

---

65. Winke, "Jeremiah Model for Jesus in the Temple," 155–72.

66. Wilson, "Wisdom," 1276–85. See also Nickelsburg, "Reading the Hebrew Scriptures," 238–50.

67. See Cullmann, *Christology*, 51–82 and Guthrie, *New Testament Theology*, 258–68.

If Jesus Christ is our one Mediator and the Suffering Servant of God, what do these names say about his identity? Somewhat counterintuitively, the writer of Hebrews acknowledges the *kingly status* of Christ saying that the Father "has crowned him with glory and honor," putting all things under his rule (Heb 2:5–8). Yet, the author notes that we do not see the totality of Christ's reign at the moment, but what we do see, at times, is the glory of Christ (Heb 2:8). Where, though, is Christ's glory most prominently revealed—in his miracles, in his teachings, in creation? The author of Hebrews declares that Christ's glory is revealed categorically in his death and suffering and by implication his resurrection and ascension (Heb 2:9; cf. Rom 6:4; 1 Pet 1:21), conquering death "by making peace through his bloodshed on the cross" (Col 1:20). Thus, Jesus is the Christ through whom God has definitively spoken to us, appointed him heir over all things, and created the world such that Jesus Christ is the radiance of his glory and the exact representation of his being (Heb 1:1–3).

That being the case, Christ's death and resurrection become necessary for discerning God's beauty because it is fitting (πρέπω) that God, in bringing his people to glory, should perfect (τελειόω) the author of their salvation through suffering (πάθημα) (Heb 2:10; cf. John 12:27–28; 17). Similarly, we can make an argument for discerning God's beauty through Christ's death and resurrection by looking to the fourth Gospel (John 12:27–28; 17). Recall Christ's instructions to his disciples shortly after Peter's confession that Jesus is the Son of the living God. Christ admonishes them *not* to make his divinity public (Matt 16:20; cf. Matt 17:9). Why? The time had not yet come. Although throughout Christ's life and ministry we see glimpses of his glory through his miracles, when is the appropriate, fitting, or right time (ὥρα) for God to reveal his glory publicly? Jesus says, in his high priestly prayer, "Father, the hour has come. Glorify your Son so that he may glorify you." And now, "Father, glorify me in your presence with the glory that I had with you before the beginning of the world" (John 17:2, 5). That hour (ὥρα) is none other than the appointed hour of his death and resurrection (John 13:1).

What is it, though, about the nature of God that he should bring about peace through pain? What is so beautiful about that? Is God sadistic for accomplishing his purposes in this manner? The writer of Hebrews suggests that Jesus suffered these things so that by God's grace he might taste or partake (γεύομαι) of death for everyone (Heb 2:9). Does this mean, then, that God's act in Christ's death was done out of sympathy? Herein lies the crux of the matter for understanding God's beauty: *why is it*

The Hinge

"fitting" for God to glorify his Son through his death and resurrection? Looking to the Apostle Paul, we turn now to his address to the people of Phrygia in the letter to the Colossians in order to glimpse the beauty of God's deep wisdom in the Suffering Servant of Christ, setting a biblical trajectory for conceptually expanding upon God's beauty in the act of Christ's redemptive-creative suffering that suggests an answer in chapter four as to why it is fitting for God to glorify his Son in his death and resurrection.

A Theological Interpretation of Colossians 1—2:5

The focus of our theological exposition of Col 1–2:5 centers on Paul's use of the term μυστήριον clustered in verses 1:26, 1:27, and 2:2. By focusing on this cluster, lines connecting Christ's glory, wisdom, and redemptive-creative suffering begin to emerge, elucidating the contours of God's beauty. Considering the Pauline corpus, then, μυστήριον refers predominately to something which is hidden in the past and now revealed, namely "the saving purpose of God effected in Christ, summed up in the gospel itself," and at times may refer "to some element of God's saving purposes (e.g., Rom 11:25–26; 1 Cor 15:51), rather than to the whole."[68] Such veiling and unveiling is predicated on God's freedom (Eph 3:9).

One of the few Gospel references to μυστήριον also makes this point when Jesus explains his use of parables to his disciples in order to reveal τὰ μυστήρια τῆς βασιλείας τῶν οὐρανῶν, namely that he is the Messiah (Matt 13:11–17). As such, Paul's use of μυστήριον is intimately tied to the *kerygma* and particularly the wisdom of God (1 Cor 2:6–9). If God's wisdom is veiled, how are we able to understand it? Paul declares that God reveals his μυστήριον through the Spirit and is undiscoverable by human wisdom (1 Cor 2:10–16). Thus, Paul uses μυστήριον "for θεοῦ σοφίαν ἐν μυστηρίῳ τὴν ἀποκεκρυμμένην. The μυστήριον is God's pre-temporal counsel which is hidden from the world but revealed to the spiritual. This has been eschatologically fulfilled in the cross of the κύριον τῆς δόξης, and it carries with it the glorification of believers."[69]

Paul's three particular usages of μυστήριον in Colossians 1–2:5 reflect many of these same characteristics but also exhibit several important distinctions that fill out its christological content further. First, in Colossians

---

68. Carson, "Mystery and Fulfillment," 415. See also Bockmuehl, *Revelation and Mystery* and Bornkamm, "μυστήριον," 820.

69. Bornkamm, "μυστήριον," 820. See also Carson, "Mystery and Fulfillment," 415–19 and Bockmuehl, *Revelation and Mystery*, 124–26, 178–93.

1:25, Paul explicates τὸν λόγον τοῦ θεοῦ, a common phrase for the gospel, by describing the content or message of his proclamation as μυστήριον (Col 1:26). In doing so, he uses a familiar "once hidden, but now has been disclosed" formula (τὸ ἀποκεκρυμμένην . . . νῦν δὲ ἐφανερώθη; Rom 16:25–26; 1 Cor 2:7–10; Eph 1:9; 3:5) where the emphatic νῦν accentuates a decisive moment within God's drama of redemption. What was previously veiled by God is now unveiled by him in the life, death, and resurrection of Christ thereby forming not only the christological basis for μυστήριον but also giving it an eschatological dimension as well.

Second, Paul's use of μυστήριον in 1:27 suggests, by the context and its genitival construction, that it possesses a magnificent or glorious quality that points to the bestowal of a lavish inheritance found only in Christ, "in whom are hidden all the treasures of wisdom and knowledge" (Col 1:3).[70] Moreover, Paul's use of δόξα, in this instance, seems to echo the Hebrew notion of כָּבוֹד that the Israelites associated with God's great acts (Exod 14:17; Ps 96:3) and his presence (Exod 40:34; Ps 26:8). Perhaps, then, Paul "emphasizes that this wonderful mystery partook of the character of God himself" such that "the presence of this 'personal' *doxa* of God in Christ means the presence of salvation."[71]

Paul affirms this notion in the subsequent relative clause, ὅ ἐστιν Χριστὸς ἐν ὑμῖν, ἡ ἐλπὶς τῆς δόξης, which further explicates the referent τοῦ μυστηρίου τούτου. This specific description of mystery, ἐστιν Χριστὸς ἐν ὑμῖν, "is a shift in focus from the goal (reconciliation of Jew and Gentiles) to the means ('Christ')" that stresses the personalization of μυστήριον in light of the previous pericope, 1:15-20, where Christ is the personification of divine Wisdom creating and holding the cosmos together.[72] Furthermore, Epaphras had proclaimed the mystery of Christ to them whereby

70. The concatenative genitives in this construction, τὸ πλοῦτος τῆς δόξης τοῦ μυστηρίου τούτου, seem to be attributive in nature such that δόξης acts as an adjective rendering τὸ πλοῦτος τῆς δόξης as "glorious riches" and is a distinct quality "of this mystery" thereby giving it an emphatic connotation (Wallace, *Greek Grammar*, 86–88).

71. O'Brien, *Colossians, Philemon*, 86; Aalen, "Glory," 44–48.

72. Dunn, *Epistles to the Colossians and to Philemon*, 122. Paul's conventional phrase for expressing the means by which we attain reconciliation is in Christ (see Gal 3:14, 26, 28; Eph 2:13, 15–16, 21–22). Dunn remarks that "strictly speaking the divine presence indwelling individual humanity should be expressed in terms of the Spirit of God; hence the more typical Pauline balance between 'us in Christ' (see on 1:2) and 'the Spirit in us' (e.g., Rom 8:9, 11, 15–16, 23, 26). But given the overlap between Wisdom and Spirit as ways of speaking of divine immanence, a degree of interchange between 'in Christ' and 'Spirit in' formulation is no problem" (122–23). Cf. Moo, *The Epistle to the Romans*, 491.

The Hinge

they responded in faith to the message, receiving Jesus Christ as Lord (Col 1:7; 2:6). As such, "they had his life within them. They therefore had a sure hope that they would share in the fullness of glory yet to be displayed,"[73] namely ἡ ἐλπὶς τῆς δόξης, for "'Christ in you' is 'the hope' of that 'glory' because retransformation into the divine image and glory is a lifelong process already underway in the person of faith (see also Col 1:11; 3:4, 10)" in the power of the Holy Spirit.[74]

Finally, Paul exhorts his readers to pursue wisdom—the performance knowledge necessary to living fitting lives in the manner of Christ (1:9-10), for this is the goal (τέλειος) that Paul desires the Colossians and those at Laodicea to attain and the reason why he labors/struggles (κοπιάω/ἀγών) for them (1:28—2:1). In doing so, Paul gives further detail as to what that "complete" picture will look like in Christ, for his exhortations and encouragement must penetrate their hearts (καρδία)—the core of their being "not only [where] emotions were rooted, but also thought and decision ("heart"; see, e.g., Rom 1:21, 24; 8:27; 9:2; 2 Cor 9:7)"—in order to attain unity and harmony as a community of faith (Col 2:2).[75] The overarching goal that Paul desires his readers to pursue, which will only be attained fully in the *eschaton*, is found in the phrase εἰς ἐπίγνωσιν τοῦ μυστηρίου τοῦ θεοῦ, communicating the object of their knowledge (τοῦ μυστηρίου) and the source of that knowledge (τοῦ θεοῦ).[76] This knowledge is only of Christ (Χριστοῦ) who is the preeminent One (1:15) in whom are hidden all the treasures of wisdom and knowledge (2:3).[77] Thus, by

---

73. O'Brien, *Colossians, Philemon*, 87.

74. Dunn, *Epistles to the Colossians and to Philemon*, 123.

75. Ibid., 130. There is some dispute as to the meaning of phrase συμβιβασθέντες ἐν ἀγάπῃ. Some understand the aorist passive participle of the verb συμβιβάζω to mean "instruct" (O'Brien, *Colossians, Philemon*, 93) while others contend that it means "bring together, unite, or reconciled" (Lohse, *Colossians and Philemon*, 81). It seems that the latter is preferable in this instance given the subsequent dative construction ἐν ἀγάπῃ often associated with unity (Rom 14:15; 1 Cor. 16:14; Phil 2:1-2; see Dunn, *Epistles to the Colossians and to Philemon*, 130) as well as the parallel passage in Col 2:19 where "bonded" is unavoidable (See Lohse, *Colossians and Philemon*, 80-81).

76. Harris suggests that "this fourth and final aim (telic) is not introduced by καίν, which suggests that Paul is here redefining his aim or stating it comprehensively" (*Colossians and Philemon*, 81).

77. The idea communicated in ἀπόκρυφος, in contrast to 1:26 where Paul uses the perfect passive participle (ἀποκεκρυμμένον) to convey the sense of something hidden in the past and now (νῦν δὲ) dramatically revealed, expresses that all the treasures of wisdom and knowledge, *without exception*, exist (εἰμί) in Christ. As such, "to search for other sources of knowledge apart from him is a useless enterprise." Thus, "Paul is encouraging the readers to look to Christ as the only 'place' where the treasures of

awkwardly inserting the genitive Χριστοῦ, Paul draws our attention back to Christ who is the alpha and omega of God's wisdom in that "Christ has become to Christians all that the Wisdom of God was, according to the Wisdom Literature, and more still" (1:15–20).[78]

If Christ, then, is the focal point of God's μυστήριον, which he discloses in his freedom, Paul's inclusion of the christological hymn in 1:15–20 becomes a key text for ascertaining God's identity as well as our life in Christ.[79] What is this wisdom of God that is inconceivable by human reasoning? What is this glorious quality that Paul speaks of regarding God's mystery? And, how is this hope of glory attained?

At the outset of this passage, Paul associates Christ with the Hebrew Wisdom literature, delineating Christ's priestly mission as the agent, sustaining power, and the goal of creation to which we previously discussed. He identifies Christ in this manner because he is the εἰκὼν τοῦ θεοῦ τοῦ ἀοράτου.[80] Christ is not only the mediator of creation, but is also the mediator of redemption, reconciling all things, including creation, unto himself through himself (1:20). Christ's actions, as the ἀρχή, πρωτότοκος ἐκ νεκρῶν demonstrate that he is the preeminent One not only of creation but also of redemption (1:19) whereby Christ is the Lord of Glory. That being the case, "Paul's presentation of our Lord's work of redemption as the restoration of the goodness of creation *casts the glow of redemption over the entire section*,"[81] thereby emphasizing the *redemptive-creative* actions of Christ.

---

wisdom and knowledge are to be found" (O'Brien, *Colossians, Philemon*, 95).

78. Moule, *Epistles of Paul the Apostle to the Colossians and to Philemon*, 86.

79. There is some debate as to whether this passage is a Christological hymn or early Christian confession due to its highly stylized grammatical structure and literary resonance. In other epistles, Paul uses rhetoric that parallels similar language found in ancient hymns that praised God and Christ. Some of the Old Testament Scriptures that resemble these hymns include Isaiah 44:24–28 and Psalm 103:2–5. It is possible that Paul used a similar hymn in Colossians 1:15–20 (See Gordley's excellent work, *The Colossian Hymn in Context*). On the other hand, some scholars tend to think that the same passage might be a form of a primitive Christian confession of faith (See Bruce, *Ephesians and Colossians*, 171).

80. Paul identifies Jesus as εἰκὼν τοῦ θεοῦ τοῦ ἀοράτου (1:15), which is "of primary importance . . . for understanding God's actions in the world" and "of who Jesus is in relationship to God" (Thompson, *Colossians and Philemon*, 28). In doing so, Paul clearly delineates Christ's deity as the one in whom all of God's fullness dwells (Col 1:19; Ps 24:1; Jer 23:24). Moreover, this phrase echoes the creation narrative, bringing to mind the creation of Adam and Eve in the image of God (Gen 1:27) and alluding to Christ's redemptive work to restore God's image in humanity (28).

81. Deterding, *Colossians*, 64. Emphasis added.

The Hinge

How, though, does Christ accomplish this redemption of all things? As a new act of creation, Christ brings about reconciliation through the counterintuitive notion of making peace through the blood of his cross (1:20).[82] Christ's redemptive-creative work secures the hope of glory in order to present us as holy and blameless before the Father (1:22). If Christ is the image of the invisible God, God's glory must be understood in light of his μυστήριον, accounting for the glory found in the wisdom of Christ's redemptive work and in its eschatological promise. We attain God's glory, then, by receiving, in faith, his spiritual wisdom that leads to our Spirit-filled participation in the redemptive-creative works of the Lord of Glory such that we grow in our understanding of God as we walk humbly in his ways from glory to glory (1:9–12). We see the importance not only of the Spirit's role in communicating God's wisdom to us, but also the *performative* element in obtaining the knowledge of God. Thus, our participation "in Christ" is appropriately suited to his works such that Paul rejoices in his sufferings (Col 1:24; 2 Tim 3:12; 2 Cor 1:6–7).[83]

This biblical trajectory connecting the wisdom found in the Suffering Servant motif with the redemptive-creative and eschatological implications of μυστήριον provide a biblical basis for fleshing out Balthasar's understanding of Jesus Christ as *Übergestalt* and *Herrlichkeit*. Moreover, this pattern forms the framework for elucidating God's suffering glory as we deal with the nocturnal sides of life in order to avoid an aestheticism that conceives of God's beauty as ornamental, nostalgic, and innocuous, signifying the beautiful as an escape from the pain and bane of our existence. Before conceptually expanding, though, upon this biblical trajectory to elucidate a trinitarian understanding of God's beauty, we need to discuss the relationship between God's glory and his beauty.

---

82. As to why Christ's blood needed to be shed, see Heb 9:13–14 and Lev 17:11, for "it is the blood, which represents life that brings atonement." See also John 15:13 elucidating the impetus behind God's actions in Christ's death on the cross—his self-giving love, for "greater love has no one than this, that one lay down his life for his friends."

83. See Treier's second chapter, "Wisdom: Knowing God and Living Virtuously in Communion," in *Virtue and the Voice of God*, 31–66, where he details "the Christology and the pneumatology essential for Christian wisdom" to which this exposition substantially agrees (57). What is missing, though, which can be inferred in places, is the *beauty* of "knowing God and living virtuously in communion" with him.

Discerning the Relationship between God's Glory and His Beauty

Reformed theology often remarks that "all truth is God's truth," following John Calvin when he says, "If we regard the Spirit of God as the sole fountain of truth, we shall neither reject the truth itself, nor despise it wherever it shall appear, unless we wish to dishonor the Spirit of God."[84] And, by implication, God "is not only the source of all truth and all goodness, but also the source of all beauty," as Karl Barth contends.[85] If God is the source of all truth, goodness, and beauty, what is the relationship between earthly beauty and God's beauty; and, where does God's glory fit into this discussion?

The crucial issue regarding this relationship turns on how one explicates the God-world relationship. For example, those who subscribe to the dualistic, platonic worldview contend that earthly beauty participates (i.e., through reflection) in an infinite, ideal beauty such that the ideal is attained by jettisoning and devaluing material existence while the soul seeks unity with the Infinite. Those who subscribe to a hierarchical, neo-platonic worldview, commonly called the "The Great Chain of Being," maintain that the world emanates from God's being such that earthly beauty, as the last and least perfect emanation, seeks its ethereal return back to its eternal Source. Others who subscribe to say a process model see the world as organic to God whereby the world's dynamism constitutes his being such that his beauty is in his becoming.[86] Each of these models is deficient in their construal of the God-world relation because they either reject the goodness of creation (i.e., Platonism), blur the line between Creator and creature (i.e., Neo-Platonism), or reject the distinction all together (i.e., Process Metaphysics). Consequently, many still affirm the medieval synthesis of the analogy of being promulgated by Aquinas that contends for an analogous God-world relationship.[87]

Balthasar argues for such a conclusion that emphasizes the ever-greater dissimilarity of the analogy of being. The God-world relation, according

---

84. Calvin, *Institutes*, 2.2.15.

85. Barth, *CD* 2/1, 664.

86. John Cooper's excellent work, *Panentheism* for a well-informed and thorough survey of each of these models of the God-world relationship. See also Farley's *Faith and Beauty*, 15–30 for the implications of these models for discerning God's beauty.

87. See Sherry, *Spirit and Beauty*, 53–76 and Harries, *Art and the Beauty of God*, 31–46, where both survey the landscape of those explicating the God-world relationship in terms of beauty.

The Hinge

to Balthasar, is established first in the order of creation rather than in God's reconciling act in Christ. This presupposes a prior correspondence at the level of being and establishes the possibility of any correspondence at the level of faith. The *analogia entis*, however, becomes concrete and real only within the *analogia fidei*, which for Balthasar unveils itself ultimately as the *analogia amoris*. Thus, his theological approach has a *creative-redemptive* emphasis that examines "the order of nature from Adam to Christ and from created reason to covenant faith, *within* the prevailing order of revelation and faith" as we discussed in chapter two.[88] Balthasar desires to establish an analogous point of contact within the created world as well as a metaphysical sense of glory, where this glory "is nothing other than the totality of [the individual instances of] beauty," in order to recover a biblical understanding of God's glory.[89] That being the case, Balthasar correctly emphasizes the ever-greater alterity of the analogous relationship between God and the world in an effort to preserve God's freedom and Wholly Otherness. Yet, his implicit ascription of the image of God to *both* creation and humanity seems to blur the relationship between God and cosmos thereby further undermining the efficacy of God's glory.[90] How might we discern, then, the relationship between God's beauty and earthly beauty in light of God's glory?

Recall from chapter two that Balthasar considers God's glory as "his 'wholly-otherness,' which he can communicate only in such a way that, even as it is communicated, it remains his and only his." In other words, "this glory (*Herrlichkeit*) of God's—his sublimeness (*Hehrsein*) and lordliness (*Herrsein*), which are sovereignly active both in himself and in his self-disclosure—is . . . precisely what constitutes the distinctive property of God, that which for all eternity distinguishes him from all that is not

---

88. Balthasar, *KB*, 302.

89. Balthasar, *GL* V, 614. For a succinct essay on how Balthasar relates earthly beauty and divine glory see Balthasar, "Weltliche Schönheit und göttliche Herrlichkeit," 513–17.

90. Although Balthasar does not explicitly develop the notion of creation as image, it is an underlying supposition requisite to his argument, which draws nature and grace closer together than anticipated (See "The Image," *GL* VI, 87–143). He seems to affirm this notion of creation as image after reflecting back on his work in May of 1988: "In the trinitarian dogma, God is one, good, true, and beautiful because he is essentially Love, and Love supposes the one, the other and their unity. And if it is necessary to suppose the Other, the Word, the Son, in God, then the *otherness of creation is not a fall, a disgrace, but an image of God*, even as it is not God" (Balthasar, *My Work in Retrospect*, 118; emphasis added).

God."[91] Balthasar correctly emphasizes the sublimity and lordliness of God's glory that is distinctly his. Yet, is God's sublime glory, "unrepresentable to the senses and the imagination" such that it "is extolled as formless, untamable, indeterminate and uncontrollable, . . . a formless divine presence, devoid of love or goodness, and thus potentially oppressive?"[92]

On the contrary, we see in 2 Pet 1:16–21 that ὑπὸ τῆς μεγαλοπρεποῦς δόξης, a voice says "This is my beloved Son in whom I delight (εὐδοκέω). Listen to him!" (Matt 17:5).[93] Sublime Glory speaks! In doing so, a communicative relationship between God and the world emerges such that "God's glory is His overflowing self-communicating joy" that "speaks and conquers, persuades and convinces" that demands a response.[94] God's sublime glory is not formless but finds its beautiful expression in the Son in whom the Father delights. *God's beauty, then, is the form of his sublime glory that attracts us, persuades us, convinces us, and draws us unto himself, demanding a response.* Jesus Christ, as incarnate Beauty, is the distinct speaking and doing form of God's glory where "the beauty of Jesus Christ is not just any beauty. It is the beauty God. Or, more concretely, it is the beauty of what God is and does in Him" by the power of the Spirit.[95] As such, Christ is "the becoming visible and experienceable of the God who is himself triune" whereby the *Gestalt Christi* manifests the *Gestalt Gottes*

91. Balthasar, *GL* VI, 10.

92. Begbie, "Created Beauty," 23–24. Radical Orthodoxy faults Kant for the contemporary divorce between beauty and the sublime such that the experience of the sublime is such an overwhelming ineffable event, taking us to the limits of our finitude, that we feel wonder and awe, even terror (See Bauerschmidt, "Aesthetics: The Theological Sublime," 201–19). David B. Hart contends that the crucial metaphysical assumption behind this disjunction between the sublime and the beautiful is that "the unrepresentable . . . is somehow truer than the representable (which necessarily dissembles it), more original, and qualitatively *other* (*Beauty of the Infinite*, 52).

93. Peter is referring to his experience of Christ's transfiguration where Christ took on the form of his heavenly glory. Although Christ's transfiguration is important to ascertaining the communicative relationship between God's glory and his beauty, it is his death and resurrection where God's beauty is revealed in its fullest such that even Christ says to Peter, James, and John to remain quiet about this vision until *after* the resurrection (Matt 17:1–13). We also see the Father's pleasure expressed indirectly to the Son when Christ performs miracles as the fulfillment of prophecy (Luke 4:1–13; cf. Isa 42:1).

94. Barth, *CD* 2/1, 653. See Vanhoozer, *Remythologizing Theology*, 181–240 where he expounds upon the notion of divine communicative action and its implications for the doctrine of God by examining biblical accounts of God's dialogical action and interaction with humanity. See also Schwöbel, "Theological Ontology of Communicative Relations," 43–67.

95. Barth, *CD* 2/1, 665.

as the radiant glory of the triune love of God.[96] He is *incarnate Beauty* in whom the Father delights. Yet, what is it about the incarnate Son that pleases the Father; and, how does God's beauty attract and draw us unto himself? We best heed the command of Sublime Glory and listen to the Son who is the Lord of Glory (*Herrlichkeit*) and the measure of all things (*Übergestalt*) as we conceptually expand upon God's beauty-in-act, for he is Incarnate Beauty.[97]

---

96. Balthasar, *GL* I, 432. It is important to note at this point, along with Balthasar and Barth, that *one cannot discern God's beauty apart from God's glorious triune life* (Barth, *CD* 2/1, 658–60; cf. Balthasar, *GL* I, 52–56).

97. Although Augustine does not use the phrase incarnate Beauty, he directly identifies God's beauty with the Son: "He is 'beautiful' as God, *the Word with God*; ... He then is 'beautiful' in Heaven, beautiful on earth; beautiful in the womb; beautiful in His parents' hands: beautiful in His miracles; beautiful under the scourge: beautiful when inviting life; beautiful also when not regarding death: beautiful in 'laying down His life;' beautiful in 'taking it again:' beautiful on the Cross; beautiful in the *Sepulchre*; beautiful in Heaven" (*Expositions on the Book of Psalms*, 230).

PANEL TWO

God's Beauty-in-Act

The Impassible Suffers as Incarnate Beauty

WE BEGAN OUR JOURNEY, IN PART ONE, EXAMINING THE FIRST PANEL of the diptych structure of our argument by asking whether the cross of Christ is a dilemma for classical theism. Relational theists contend that the cross is a dilemma that creates a metaphysical gap between who God is *ad extra* in Christ and who he is *in se*. They indict classical theism for smuggling in Greek philosophy—chiefly the doctrine of impassibility—through Augustine, Anselm, and Aquinas that construes God as unaffected and unconcerned about his creation. In doing so, the Gospel is rendered impotent as Christianity faces a crisis of identity and relevance in the modern world, unable to address the suffering of our day and the widening gulf between theology and life.

Relational theism's depictions of classical theism as well as their solution to the supposed dilemma reveal that perfect being theology appears to be the culprit rather than traditional classical theism, as seen in the introduction. Regarding their depiction of classical theism, it seems that relational theists read the Christian tradition through the lenses of a Cartesian variety of perfect being theology. Yet, their critiques of *contemporary* renderings of classical theism may not be too far afield, since these renderings appear to have imbibed aspects of perfect being theology. Regarding their solution to the supposed dilemma, relational theists appear to exchange a Cartesian model for a panentheistic or process model. God is still a maximally perfect being, just a maximally and perfectly related one. As such, perfect being theology succumbs to Feuerbach's critique where our conceptions of God mirror our own positive qualities, except without limit, turning theology into anthropology. Moreover, contemporary conceptions of perfect being theology tend to mimic the precision of modern science and analytic philosophy, both of which inherently *restrict* reality to

Panel Two: God's Beauty-in-Act

the true and/or the good while ignoring other aspects (i.e., God's beauty) that may address, in part, some of the concerns of relational theism.

Retrieving an understanding of God's beauty for theological discourse, though, is an arduous task. As we saw in chapter one, contemporary theology perceives beauty as a deformed and beleaguered notion, giving little credence to it as a deep symbol able to articulate the metaphysical reality of this world, much less God's divine reality. Although there are dangers and pitfalls to avoid, can we afford not to speak of God's beauty, as Karl Barth suggested? Greater danger, in my estimation, lies in the *omission* of God's beauty from theological discourse and the ascription of the imagination to the non-real because such actions diminish Christian worship, witness, and wisdom. Incorporating beauty into theological discourse, then, must avoid sentimental, nostalgic, and hedonistic motifs. Such rhetoric presumes a subjectivist ideal where beauty loses its ability to convey meaning beyond the realm of personal taste, relegating beauty to the ornamental and innocuous pleasant. Thus, any notion of God's beauty apt for theological discourse must privilege God's divine triune discourse attested to in Holy Scripture while guided by the Christian tradition.

We turned to converse with Hans Urs von Balthasar's theological aesthetics in chapter two in order to appropriate critically his emphasis on Jesus Christ as *Herrlichkeit* and *Übergestalt*. We also highlighted Balthasar's christocentrism that alludes to Christ's singularity, God's divine freedom and trinitarian nature, and the inherent connections between creation and redemption. Yet, Balthasar blunts the force of these christological terms, *Herrlichkeit* and *Übergestalt*, by blurring the lines between justification and sanctification because he roots humanity's relationship with God in the created order (i.e., creative-redemptive). As such, he seems to minimize the destructive nature of sin, opening the door for a synergistic soteriology predicated on a grace (i.e., prevenient) that stirs or helps rather than transforms and reforms. If we advocate, though, a redemptive-creative motif that privileges God's elective purpose and his reconciling actions in Christ, a covenantal and communicative understanding of the God-world relation that includes privileges and responsibilities ensues. In doing so, we can preserve God's freedom and humanity's *relative* freedom as God graciously works and wills *through* the created order. God's glory remains efficacious, rendering *Herrlichkeit* and *Übergestalt* as two properly theological terms for retrieving a notion of God's beauty.

In chapter three, the hinge that connects parts one and two, we developed a relevant biblical motif through the thematic patterning of the Suffering Servant in Jeremiah. We observed Jeremiah's obedience to deliver

Yahweh's message to the people of Judah while enduring senseless suffering. Such obedience in the face of adversity demonstrated a deep wisdom, a counterintuitive wisdom, embodied in Jeremiah's laments as he cried out to Yahweh in agony while continuing to faithfully fulfill his calling. Having traced this thematic patterning in Jeremiah, we fleshed it out by explicating the Christ-form in the New Testament, noting the prophetic mission, priestly dimension, and kingly status of Christ's fulfillment of what Israel could not do as the Servant of Yahweh. We concluded our biblical trajectory with a focused theological exposition of Col 1–2:5 where Paul joins four important concepts for understanding God's beauty— μυστήριον, δόξα, σοφία, and πάθημα. This trajectory suggested a communicative God-world relationship whereby God's beauty is the form of his sublime glory that attracts, persuades, convinces, and draws us unto himself, demanding a response.

We turn our attention, now, to the second panel of the diptych structure of this proposal where we conceptually expand upon God's beauty-in-act through the notion of incarnate Beauty, which allows us to explicate its objective, subjective, and relational components. In doing so, we begin to address the deleterious effects of perfect being theology (both static and dynamic forms) that anesthetizes God's beauty and stifles the imagination, hindering Christian worship, witness, and wisdom. We end with a brief case study of Balthasar's position on divine impassibility, critiquing his notion of divine eternal kenosis while intimating what we can learn of God's impassibility in light of his beauty. We are prepared, then, to move to our fifth and final chapter where we ascertain how God's beauty transforms our imaginations (2 Cor 3:18) so that we are able to participate creatively and fittingly in the dramatic movements of his triune life while flourishing in an unjust world.

Incarnate Beauty: The Redemptive-Creative Suffering of Christ in the Spirit

Balthasar, out of concern to establish a metaphysical point of contact within the created order, insists on emphasizing the created character of earthly truth, goodness, and beauty *prior* to articulating the ever-greater dissimilarity of God's beauty. Yet, how can he establish, say, the truth of the matter, within the created realm without kneeling at the Eucharistic altar? It seems to me that there will always be competing notions of truth, goodness, and beauty unless we do so; and even then, our finitude and

Panel Two: God's Beauty-in-Act

fallenness still inhibit *absolute* clarity. The clarity and cogency of truth, goodness, and beauty is found only when we acknowledge Christ's *redemption* of the created order, including our human faculties, for the pure in heart will see God (Matt 5:8). By accentuating a redemptive-creative motif, we are able to incorporate both a protological and an eschatological perspective in light of our present condition, all the while affirming the goodness of creation.

A redemptive-creative motif can affirm with Balthasar the preeminent place of Christ for exegeting the Godhead, for Christ is that "inner vitality in which the transcendentals are identified with his identity" such that "all God's traits, insofar as they are features of the only true and one God, are aspects of the God who steps forth and interprets himself in Christ: the God who is only God as Father, Son, and Holy Spirit."[1] As such, it is impossible to separate the life of the three persons from God's essence while God's essence is common to all three persons, for "it is their eternal life itself in its procession."[2] With Balthasar, we can affirm that God's *esse* is his *essentia* (i.e., divine simplicity) such that God *is* true, good, and beautiful. Yet, these conclusions cannot be deduced by the philosopher who does not know of God's gratuitous acts in Christ. It is the one who kneels at the altar in faith and seeks understanding from the apse of the cathedral who sees with the wisdom of God.

A redemptive-creative emphasis also acknowledges the goodness of creation, for creation is a graced existence such that it does not have to be; yet creation too is in bondage to sin as it decays and returns to that which it came—nothingness (Rom 8:18–25). Although Balthasar acknowledges the pervasiveness of sin, he seems to mitigate its effects on the world and humanity when it comes to perceiving earthly beauty. This is our *present* condition, one that necessitates redemption if we are to live within God's reality rather than one of our own making (Rom 1:22–25). By looking *protologically* back through Christ's redemptive suffering and glorious resurrection, we see the fittingness of the created order such that it declares the glory of God (Ps 19). Yet, it is precisely because of our need for Christ's redemption that we must look forward *eschatologically* towards the hope of glory, for we continue to walk among the ruins of this earthly city in anticipation of the *civitas Dei*.

Therefore, our emphasis on Christ's redemptive-creative suffering for discerning God's beauty orients our speech eschatologically in light of

---

1. Balthasar, *Epilogue*, 92–93; Balthasar, *KB*, 328.
2. Balthasar, *Epilogue*, 92–93.

The Impossible Suffers as Incarnate Beauty

Christ's resurrection by looking protologically through Christ's redemptive-creative acts, rooted in God's electing purpose, all the while acknowledging our present condition. We affirm with John Webster that "created being and history are thus not that in terms of which the resurrection of Jesus is to be placed, but rather the opposite." The created order is to be defined in light of the risen Christ because the world was not only created through him but also holds together in him as the pre-eminent One such that "created being is being in this divine act of *transfiguration*, being in the miracle to which Paul points with such wonder: ἰδοὺ γέγονεν καινά (2 Cor 5:17)."[3] What, then, does the redemptive-creative suffering of the risen Christ in the Spirit indicate about God's beauty?

Love that Lies in Obedience

Paul intercedes for the people in the Lycus Valley just prior to reciting the christological hymn (Col 1:15–20), praying that they will live a life that is fitting, worthy, and pleasing unto the Lord such that their actions manifest the fruit of Christ's redemptive-creative actions. Such a life is predicated on a *prior life* that pleased the Father, namely the life, death, and resurrection of Christ (Col 1:9–14) who as the Son of God became a Servant (Phil 2:5–13).[4] In doing so, "Jesus' life is . . . characterized by a deep paradox: he puts forth his absolute 'I' which is the prerogative of God's glory in absolute poverty and vulnerability that is, in an absolute lack of lordly glory." Yet, this supposed paradox between what Balthasar calls the "claim" and "poverty" of Christ is dissolved "only if one sees it as an expression of the unique obedience and love with which Jesus looks up to his Father."[5] We see this dissolution in Christ's high priestly prayer to the Father in John 17 where, "lifting up his eyes to heaven," he asks the Father δόξασον σου τὸν υἱόν, ἵνα ὁ υἱὸς δοξάσῃ σέ (John 17:1).

Peering into this intratrinitarian dialogue between the Father and Son reveals the personal love of the Son for the Father manifested in his obedience and rooted in the eternal, mutual, and unified love between the

---

3. Webster, "Resurrection and Scripture," 141–42. Emphasis added.

4. Kettler, "Vicarious Beauty of Christ," 14–24 correctly extends the beauty of Christ beyond the cross arguing that "a theology of the vicarious humanity, not just death, of Christ provides a fresh way to ground theological aesthetics in the reconciling life of Christ" such that "the vicarious humanity of Christ . . . avoids isolating the death of Christ from his life and resurrection" (14, 18).

5. Waldstein, "Hans Urs von Balthasar's Theological Aesthetics," 21. See also Balthasar, *GL* VII, 115–61.

Panel Two: God's Beauty-in-Act

Father and the Son (John 17:5, 10, 21, 24, 26). The Father glorifies the Son and is pleased with him because "the Son has 'accomplished' his work of love in the work of obedience" to the very end (τελειόω), even death on a cross.[6] In this way, the Son has glorified the Father and is now asking the Father to glorify him with the glory that he had with the Father *before* the world was (17:4–5). What we see in Christ's obedience to the Father and the Father's glorification of the Son is "the radiance of their eternal love."[7] *God's beauty, therefore, is the attunement or fittingness of the incarnate Son's actions in the Spirit to the Father's will that radiates the splendor of God's triune love.* In other words, it is fitting for the Father to glorify the Son because the Son does all that the Father plans for him to do. He leaves nothing undone. The Son's obedience to the Father is not one of duty or compulsion but one of love, self-giving love that takes him to the point of death (Phil 2:8), for the Son does not desire to do his own will but the will of the Father (Matt 26:39; John 4:34; 6:38). The Father delights in the Son because of his perfect obedience, illuminating the beauty of God's holiness and wisdom.[8] Who, though, illumines God's beauty so that the world may believe and know of this glorious triune love (John 17:21, 23)?

Is it the work of the Son? Is it the work of the Father? It is the work of the Spirit who is the bond of love between the Father and the Son. As the bond of love, he reveals himself "as that which is absolutely living, creative, independently . . . as the eternal fruit in God and the endless fruitfulness in the world. The 'Spirit' is this result of the mutual love, apparently an end but in truth the creative new beginning," as Balthasar so aptly remarks.[9] The Spirit is the fruit of the love that lies between the Son and the Father such that he is the mutual, personal love—the *communio*—between the Father and the Son (1 John 4:7–16).[10] When, though, does the Father send the Spirit into the world so that the Spirit will glorify the Son? What must take place *before* this occurs?

---

6. Balthasar, *GL* VII, 249.

7. Ibid.

8. Jonathan Edwards speaks aptly of the beauty of God's holiness in his work, *A Treatise Concerning Religious Affections*, 258–59. Yet, by linking the spiritual beauty of Christ's holiness to the human soul as the most proper image of Christ's beauty, I wonder if, by implication, he renders to us a docetic Christ. More, though, needs to be said to substantiate this claim.

9. Balthasar, *GL* VII, 251. Emphasis added.

10. Augustine, in *De trinitate*, 4.20.28, 5.5.6, 5.11.12, describes the Holy Spirit in similar terms, arguing that he is the "bond of love" between the Father and the Son and as "Gift" (4.20.27–29).

The Impassible Suffers as Incarnate Beauty

Jesus indicates that the sending of the Spirit as a comforter and counselor, who will convince (ἐλέγχω) the world, will not occur until he is glorified (John 7:39) and ascends to the Father (John 16:5–11). The Spirit glorifies Christ by unveiling Jesus' speech and actions seen and heard by the disciples within the inner depths of their being. This process is the glorification of the Son by the Spirit, "which is nothing other than the bringing to light of the love that lies in obedience."[11] The Holy Spirit is the Beautifier—the one who communicates God's beauty to the world such that Christ is glorified through the work of the Spirit in the church (John 16:5–15). As the fruitfulness of the love between the Father and Son, this fruit does not appear on its own accord. Rather it is given by the Father through the Son as a free gift such that "the Spirit . . . gives the interpretation of Christ (and in him, the Father) through the Church to 'the world.'"[12] In other words, the church, as the fruit of the Spirit's arrival at Pentecost, glorifies Christ's loving obedience to the Father (John 17:9–10). What, then, might it mean to identify the Holy Spirit as the Beautifier?

Following Edwards, Patrick Sherry claims, as we discussed in chapter one, that the Spirit *is* divine beauty, yet is this what we mean by beautifier?[13] The Spirit's name is appropriately the *Holy* Spirit who is the Spirit of the Father and the Son, possessing a mission proper to himself (John 15:26).[14]

---

11. By emphasizing the coming of the Spirit by the Father at the behest of the Son, I do not intend to imply that the Spirit was not operative prior to this moment as if he is only now showing up on the stage of God's drama of redemption. Rather, the Spirit of God was operative throughout the Old Testament (creation: Gen 1:2; construction of the tabernacle: Exod 31:3; prophetic tradition: Num 11:29, etc.). He was also at work in the life and ministry of Christ (birth: Luke 1:14–17; baptism: Luke 2:39–53; ministry: Luke 4:14–19). Christ is the "Bearer of the Spirit" as well as the "Bestower of the Spirit" as Graham Cole aptly notes in his work, *He Who Gives Life*, 149–208.

12. Balthasar, *GL* VII, 252–53. See also Cole's chapter, "The Spirit, the Church, and the Hope of Glory," in *He Who Gives Life*, 209–58. For the role of the Spirit as beautifier see Edwards, *Discourse on the Trinity*, 123 and 130 as well as *Treatise Concerning Religious Affections*, 201, 257.

13. Sherry, "The Beauty of God the Holy Spirit," 5–13 argues that the Holy Spirit should be the source of beauty as the Beautifier, intimating at times the Spirit's separate operation from the Son. By doing so, the work of the Spirit loses its christological control, allowing for "works of the Spirit" to be conflated with the human spirit. He is correct to call our attention to the neglect of the doctrine of the Spirit, particularly regarding God's beauty such that a proper account entails a trinitarian account and not merely a christological one.

14. See Coffey, "Proper Mission of the Holy Spirit," 227–50 where he argues that the Spirit is the Love of the Father *for* the Son that preserves a proper mission of the Holy Spirit while attempting to account for the supposed western and eastern misgivings. I believe a similar argument can be made for *per filium*.

PANEL TWO: God's Beauty-in-Act

Jesus tells his disciples that he must go away so that another may come who will comfort them and lead them into truth, that one is the Spirit (John 14:16). The Spirit speaks *not on his own initiative* but only what he hears, bearing witness to Christ and what is to come (John 16:13). The Spirit is not some rogue member of the Trinity, communicating and acting on his own accord. Rather, his actions are *fitting* to what he hears from the Father and the Son thereby manifesting his obedience, not unlike the loving obedience of the incarnate Son to the Father's will in the power of the Holy Spirit (John 14:10). The Holy Spirit, therefore, acts distinctively as a communicative agent because of his mission to beautify both the church and the world.

We can conclude, then, that there is not only an attunement, concordance, or fittingness between Christ's mission and his existence as Balthasar concludes but also between the Spirit's mission and his existence that radiates the glory of God's triune love. Balthasar says that "the central concern of a theological aesthetics must be the correspondence between obedience and love."[15] By doing so, God's beauty is not merely understood christologically as "the image of God's glory," like some may charge.[16] Instead, a trinitarian account of God's beauty emerges because Christ "nowhere *controls* his own glorification, that is to say, the relationship between his obedience to the Father and his own glory, but once for all entrusts himself, in what concerns his glorification, in prayer to the Father, from whom the Spirit goes forth into the Church and world to accomplish conviction, vindication, and glorification."[17] Therefore, the Son is the *expression* of while the Spirit is the *impression* of God's beauty.[18] God's beauty is indiscernible apart from his glorious love radiating in his triune life. What, though, is this love that radiates from God's triune being?

---

15. Balthasar, *GL* VII, 261–62. Although Balthasar does not make this connection with the Spirit, which may be why some believe he has scantly dealt with the Third Person of the Trinity, it seems that he would approve so long as the Spirit does not proceed from the Father alone.

16. Sherry, "Beauty of God the Holy Spirit," 12.

17. Balthasar, *GL* VII, 262.

18. Balthasar, *GL* II, 348. We can agree with Paul Evdokimov, an Eastern Orthodox theologian, who aptly surmises a trinitarian account of divine beauty: "The Father pronounces his Word and the Spirit shows him forth; the Spirit is *the Light of the Word*" such that "the Beauty of the Son is the Image of the Father—Source of Beauty, revealed by the Spirit of Beauty" (*Art of the Icon*, 7, 24).

No Greater Love: The Fittingness of the Atonement

Jesus, talking with his disciples about being in him and the joy that comes from obedience, declares that there is no greater love than this, "that one lay down (τίθημι) his life for his friends" (John 15:13). In making this statement, Jesus not only intimates as to the kind of selfless, sacrificial love that he requires of his followers (Luke 9:23) but alludes to his impending death on the cross—the quintessential example of self-giving love. It is the kind of love that binds together all of the virtues that we are "to put on" as new creatures in Christ (Col 3:12-14). Thus, "this love is not just any love, but precisely the love of Christ, the love of the new and eternal Covenant: Love as 'heartfelt compassion,' as 'kind, receptive openness,' 'an attitude of lowliness,' 'a meekness that does not defend itself,' 'long-suffering patience,' and thus the winning over, the enduring of one's unendurable brothers, and forgiving them because God has forgiven" as Balthasar so aptly remarks.[19]

God's love does not mean, then, "the willingness to share feelings;" rather, it "is exercising the option to communicate" such that God communicates his love supremely by sending us his Son as an atoning sacrifice for our sins (1 John 4:9-10).[20] That being the case, Jesus' death on the cross and resurrection are "God's final exegesis, who here proves himself once for all as love."[21] It is only in light of *this kind of love*, God's self-giving love, that we can begin to understand why it is fitting for God to glorify his Son on the cross and, in some sense, be able to speak about the beauty of the cross, for therein lies the deep wisdom of God. How is it, though, that we can speak of the atonement as fitting?

---

19. Balthasar, *Love Alone Is Credible*, 128–29. There are many facets to understanding God's love, which he reveals to us through his communicative acts attested to in Scripture (e.g., self-giving, compassionate, selfless, patient, long-suffering, covenantal, liberating, holy, sovereign, etc.). See Grogan, "Biblical Theology of the Love of God," 47–66 and Ayres, "Augustine, Christology, and God as Love," 67–93 that speak to this simple-complex reality that "God is love."

20. Plantinga, "Deep Wisdom," 155.

21. Balthasar, "God Is His Own Exegete," 284. God's love is at the heart of the so-called "relational turn" where relational theists contend that a truly loving God is a suffering God who shares in our experiences. Paul Fiddes remarks: "To love is to be in relationship where what the loved one does alters one's own experience" (*Creative Suffering of God*, 50). Such notions, though, seem to understand God's love on the basis of human experience where, as Sallie McFague notes, God's love is "the most intimate and important kind of *human* love" (*Models of God*, 126; emphasis added). In doing so, God's voice, what he says about himself, drowns in the cacophony of babbling humanity. See Hart, "How Do We Define the Nature of God's Love?," 94–113.

Panel Two: God's Beauty-in-Act

Balthasar pronounces that Anselm's *Cur Deus homo* is "the acme of Christian aesthetics" because he "contemplates the highest inner accord (*rectitudo*) of the divine revelation in creation and redemption." Anselm, according to Balthasar, "discerns its truth from the harmony, from the faultless proportions, from the way in which it must be so (*necessitas*), something dependent on the utmost freedom and manifesting the utmost freedom, and this vision reveals to him absolute beauty: God's beauty in the freely fashioned form of the world."[22] Anselm's understanding of the atonement, which centers on God's honor (understood too as glory), expounds upon this fittingness within the triune God and the necessity of humanity to submit willingly to God's ways in order to bestow the honor which is due to him. When humanity, though, determines what is right in its own eyes and becomes a measure unto itself, humanity "dishonors God" and disturbs "the order and beauty of the universe" because humanity fails to submit to God's good governance, as Anselm contends.[23] How, though, is God's honor rectified?

God, according to Anselm, has established within his Kingdom order the necessity for giving recompense or punishment such that to do otherwise violates "the beauty of order, and God would appear to be failing in his governance."[24] Because humanity has stained God's honor, it is incumbent upon humanity to make recompense for the honor and glory it has sought to take from God, "and this is the satisfaction which every sinner is obliged to give to God."[25] Humanity, then, is responsible for satisfying God's justice for its sin; yet, because of humanity's sinful condition, only God can do so—hence, the necessity of *cur Deus homo*. Jesus Christ, the God-man, is the one and only person who can make recompense. What could be more fitting than when the Father, out of his free love, says "to a

---

22. Balthasar, *GL* II, 211. It may be said, what of God's freedom if he must do the fitting thing. Yet, if God has determined himself to be who he is, can God act against his nature? This seems to me to be the crux of what Anselm and Balthasar, for that matter, mean by *necessitas* whereby if God has freely determined himself to be a certain way, there is a theo-logic or grammar or a fittingness to his actions. Otherwise, God would not be who he has declared himself to be.

23. Anselm, *Cur Deus homo*, I.15.

24. Ibid., I.15. Cf. I.11–12, 19. It is not fitting, according to Anselm, "to forgive a sin out of mercy alone, without any restitution," for "to forgive a sin in this way is nothing other than to refrain from inflicting punishment. And if no satisfaction is given, the way to regulate sin correctly is none other than to punish it. If, therefore, it is not punished, it is forgiven without its having been regulated." Such "is not fitting for God to allow anything in his kingdom to slip by unregulated" (I. 12).

25. Ibid., I.11.

The Impossible Suffers as Incarnate Beauty

sinner condemned to eternal torments and lacking any means of redeeming himself, 'Take my only-begotten Son and give him on your behalf,' and that the Son himself should say, 'Take me and redeem yourself.'"[26] How does the cross of Christ, though, fit within the whole of God's drama of redemption?

Recall our previous discussions regarding God's μυστήριον as "God's pre-temporal counsel which is hidden from the world but revealed to the spiritual."[27] There exists a tension in God's self-revelation such that even the disciples did not fully understand Christ's mission until after the resurrection and the coming of the Spirit (John 15:26–27). Yet, as we learned, this veiling and unveiling associated with God's μυστήριον is the wisdom of God, for his ways are not our ways (Isa 55:8). God has done the unexpected and inconceivable by communicating his trinitarian love in and through the hideous form of the cross, the most unsightly thing imaginable. Thus, as we contemplate the exterior form of the cross, it is clearly detestable; yet, as we look in and through the cross with the eyes of faith God's wisdom manifests the splendor of his triune love.

This is the key to deciphering the problem of Isa 53 that we discussed in chapter three. Christ becomes *Ungestalt* because of the scourge of sin, for "it is only through being fragmented that the beautiful really reveals the meaning of the eschatological promise it contains."[28] The *Gestalt Christi*, Balthasar maintains, integrates the sufferings of the cross into the beauty of the trinitarian love of God by giving meaning and hope to our sinfully plagued existence. The broken and fragmented form of Christ on the cross signifies not only his bearing of our sin but also is related beyond itself to God's divine reality. As such, "the form of the Redeemer, and this form, in turn, takes the modalities of fallen existence upon itself so as to transvalue them by redemptive suffering."[29] The *Gestalt Christi* radiates the

---

26. Ibid., II.20; cf. II.6–9. David Hogg authors a compelling work entitled, *Anselm of Canterbury*, where he articulates Anselm's theology of beauty, not simply in *Cur Deus homo* but also in his other major works, particularly *Proslogion* (I am grateful to Adam Johnson for bringing this work to my attention). See also Olsen, "Balthasar and the Rehabilitation of Anselm's Doctrine of the Atonement," 49–61. Cf. Crisp, "On the Fittingness of the Virgin Birth," 197–221, arguing for the fittingness of the virgin birth of Christ, along Anselmian lines, contra those who contend that the virgin birth is not necessary for the Incarnation, and Brown, "Beauty of Hell," 329–56, where he argues for hell's existence based on Anselm's notion of fittingness.

27. Bornkamm, "μυστήριον," 820.

28. Balthasar, *GL* I, 460.

29. Ibid. Cf. Balthasar, *TD* II, 26–28. Regarding the problem of Isaiah 53 and the ugliness of Christ on the cross, Barth says that "if the beauty of Christ is sought in a

splendor of God's glory as Christ is perfectly in tune with the Father's will by obeying the Father and fulfilling his mission to the world—*the beauty of holiness*.

To reiterate, the glorification of the Son at the moment of his death and resurrection is not the lauding of the grotesque, for "there is no beauty in the cross by itself," which is why Christ's resurrection is essential to discerning God's beauty.[30] The resurrection demonstrates that death is swallowed up (καταπίνω) by life (2 Cor 5:4), swallowed up in victory (1 Cor 15:54; Isa 25:8)! Thus, "in the fullness of life, Jesus possesses death in himself as something he has gone through and overcome through the self-giving of love."[31] This is the beauty of Christ that enraptures perceiving subjects by drawing them out of themselves through the *Gestaltungskraft* of the Holy Spirit and into God's drama of redemption.

Resurrection Reality: The Redemptive-Creative New Beginning

Our previous investigations regarding God's μυστήριον also reveal an eschatological component such that God's beauty possesses a "hidden eschatological transfiguration" that points beyond itself through itself.[32] We see the contours of this conclusion in Paul's phrases Χριστὸς ἐν ὑμῖν and ἡ ἐλπις τῆς δόξης (Col 1:27) as Christ's resurrection signifies (Col 1:18, 20). The resurrected Christ is the living One (Rev 1:18) who is full of divine life such that our participation in his life and he in us, by the Spirit, brings life, both now and in the hereafter. There is, in the resurrected Christ, a dramatic movement where Christ lays down his life on his own accord and takes it up again, all at the behest of the Father (John 10:17–18). Webster remarks that "this movement is the actuality of God's livingness as the one 'who was and is and is to come' (Rev 1:8)."[33] In addition, Christ's ascension continues this dramatic movement upwards. Although he is no

---

glorious Christ who is not crucified, the search will always be in vain. Who does not do this? And who finds it at this point? Who of himself does not find the opposite here?" As such, "the glory and beauty of God shines out in this unity and differentiation. In this it persuades, convinces, and conquers. This unity and differentiation is God's *kalon* which itself has the power of a *kalein*" (*CD* 2/1, 665).

30. Kettler, "Vicarious Beauty of Christ," 17. Cf. Viladesau, *Theological Aesthetics*, 191.

31. Balthasar, "Death is Swallowed Up by Life," 49.

32. Balthasar, *GL* III, 341.

33. Webster, "Resurrection and Scripture," 139.

The Impossible Suffers as Incarnate Beauty

longer present physically, his divine glory and majesty is ever-present as the exalted Christ. Thus, as Webster concludes, Christ's ascension, and by implication his absence, is his presence in the Spirit where "this presence of the risen and exalted one is a *communicative* presence. He is present, not simply as an inert or silent *substratum*, but as the king of glory: resplendent, outgoing, and therefore eloquent."[34] What, then, are the implications of Christ's glorious and communicative presence for God's beauty in creation and in us?

Creation has and retains its existence in and through Christ whereby it reaches its eschatological goal in him (Col 1:15–17; Heb 1:3; Eph 1:10). Creation is distinct from its Creator and thus, as Jeremy Begbie contends, it attests to God's beauty in its own uniqueness such that the beauty of creation is not found behind the veil of the sensual or empirical or in some ethereal reality. Rather, "creation's beauty is just that, the beauty of *creation*." Moreover, God is committed to his "good" creation (Gen 1–2) and is thus devoted to its flourishing such that God's creation is full of his beauty as the Creator of the world who is actively involved through his Spirit, "bringing things to their proper end in relation to the Father through the Son."[35]

Creation, though, is in bondage to the death and decay of sin (Gen 3), deforming its existence with corruption and distortion all the while groaning for its transfiguration (Rom 8:20–22). Yet, in light of the risen Christ and the sending of his Spirit, we need not live in despair and without hope because the fragmented beauty of this world finds wholeness and completion in "the beauty of the future that has already been embodied in Christ." Hence, we can "voice creation's praise" by looking eschatologically toward the beauty of the new heaven and earth (Rev 22) that future beauty we will enjoy in the presence of the triune God of which this present reality can only offer "but a miniscule glimpse."[36] The Holy Spirit, as

---

34. Ibid., 140–41.

35. Begbie, "Created Beauty," 25.

36. Ibid., 28. Begbie offers sage advice for discerning God's beauty in creation: "If we do attempt to discern creaturely signs of God's beauty in creation, we should be careful not to do so on the basis of some presumed *necessity* of created beauty to resemble God's beauty or to resemble it in particular ways, but only on the basis of what God has actually warranted us to affirm by virtue of his particular and gracious acts, climaxing in Jesus Christ. The naiveté of assuming we may simply 'read off' God's beauty from creation is most obvious when we are confronted with the creation's corruptions and distortions (however we are to understand these), and when we forget that our perception of creation as reflecting God's beauty depends on the work of the Holy Spirit" (26). See also Sherry, *Spirit and Beauty*, 121–41 and Begbie, *Voicing Creation's Praise*, 169–85.

Panel Two: God's Beauty-in-Act

the Beautifier of creation, is actively involved in creation's transfiguration, anticipating the *shalom* that is to be.

Regarding the transfiguration of humanity, the risen Christ's presence in us (Χριστὸς ἐν ὑμῖν) as the Lord of Glory, comes also through his Spirit (John 14:16–20), having been sealed in Christ with the Holy Spirit of promise who is the guarantee of our future inheritance (Eph 1:13–14), ἡ ἐλπις τῆς δόξης. Calvin describes this union in Christ whereby "the Holy Spirit is the bond by which Christ effectually unites us to himself."[37] Yet, we groan in the midst of our present sufferings for a future glory, hoping for what we do not see and persevering until we do (Rom 8:18–25). As such, "the Spirit's task is to restore glory to fallen creation, . . . to bring us to glory, to create glory within us, and to glorify us together in Christ,"[38] for "if anyone is in Christ, they are a new creation; the old has gone and the new has come" (2 Cor 5:18). The risen Christ is the first fruits (Col 1:18) of this new creation such that the Spirit renovates (ἀνακαινόω) our deformed *imago Dei* as we participate in that life, transforming us from glory to glory (Col 3:10). We eagerly long in hope for the time when we will live in God's city where there will be no more suffering, no more pain—a time when the risen Christ will redeem us, consummating our glorification as we live in the fullness of God's beauty (Rev 21–22).[39] What, though, of the present where we only see glimpses of God's beauty? How can we flourish in a city of ruin?

The Spirit is continuously at work glorifying the Father through the Son, particularly in the church as she manifests God's wisdom. We spoke briefly in the previous section about how the Spirit glorifies the Son "by instituting in the Church, and so making known before the world, the unity of the love between the Father and the Son that was lived out in the distance of the Passion for the sake of the world—for he himself *is* this unity of love."[40] Jesus expects his followers, by the power of the Spirit, to love as he has loved, abiding in him and obeying his commandments (John 15; 1 John 4:7–21). In doing so, we live in a manner worthy of the Lord Jesus Christ that is pleasing unto the Father, manifesting his wisdom, bearing fruit in every good work, and growing in our understanding of him (Col 1:9–10). The church is caught up in the dramatic movements of Christ in

---

37. Calvin, *Institutes*, 3.1.1.

38. Ferguson, *Holy Spirit*, 91, 249.

39. See Sherry, *Spirit and Beauty*, 142–59 and Balthasar "Eternal Life and the Human Condition," 4–23.

40. Balthasar, *GL* VII, 255.

The Impossible Suffers as Incarnate Beauty

the Spirit, laying down her life so that Christ can take it up again by the power of the Spirit and transfigure her into the beautiful bride she has been called to be before the Lord (Col 1:22). Abiding in Christ through the power of the Spirit is the mechanism, then, for a flourishing existence.

The Holy Spirit is also the mediator of communion between the Father and the Son as well as between God and humanity such that the Spirit is the *communio* or the κοινωνία *ad intra* between the Father and the Son that has christological implications *ad extra* in the life of the church.[41] This communion or κοινωνία within the life of the church comes by the Spirit as he empowers believers and distributes spiritual gifts in order to manifest God's glorious triune love to the world (John 15–17). This "new life, which the Spirit brings to God's people is a liberated life, . . . a fruitful life, . . . [and] a sanctified life."[42] This is the *Gestaltungskraft des heilige Geists*—the shaping power of the Spirit that communicates God's beauty (*schönsprechen*) to us by transforming our imaginations and enabling us to envision our part in his drama of redemption. Hence, communion with God and others is the medium for a flourishing existence.

The Communication of God's Beauty to the World

We advocated previously for a communicative God-world relationship based on the notion that God as sublime glory speaks. This notion is particularly implicit in Balthasar's theophanic accounts of God's self-presentation or, as Balthasar says, God's self-showing. In the broadest sense possible, then, divine communication is God giving of himself (i.e., triune life) through himself (i.e., Word and Spirit) *pro nobis* in order to accomplish his purpose in accordance with his good pleasure. Balthasar states it this way: "It begins with a Voice, . . . full of living, unconditional, unquestionable authority" that finds his perfect self-expression in his self-showing (beauty), self-giving (goodness), and self-saying (truth), for "God's splendor *is* his self-surrender, and this . . . *is* his truth."[43] We turn

---

41. Barth also uses *communio*, *vinculum pacis*, and the bond of love to describe this relationship (see *The Holy Spirit and the Christian Life* and *CD* 1/1, 483–87). I affirm the *filioque* clause but perhaps *per filium* (John 15:26) is a better way to promote a *vinculum pacis* among disputants of *filioque*. Nevertheless, the importance of *filioque* or *per filium* is to ensure christological controls such that the Holy Spirit does not become a human spirit devoid of his deity and proper mission to bear witness to the Son.

42. Cole, *He Who Gives Life*, 209–58, especially 224–29.

43. Balthasar, *Epilogue*, 29, 85.

Panel Two: God's Beauty-in-Act

now to articulating *what* God is communicating to us about his divine beauty in light of *who* he is as the triune God.

The Objectivity of God's Beauty

Our investigations into God's beauty reveal an objective component such that beauty is inherent to God himself and not within our subjective faculties of perception. Augustine alludes to this same sort of objectivity, in his *Confessions*, when he ponders, "Do we love anything save what is beautiful? But what then is beautiful? And what is beauty? What is it that allures us and delights us in the things we love? Unless there were grace and beauty *in* them they could not possibly draw us to them."[44] God's beauty is pleasing because it *is* beautiful rather than being beautiful because it pleases. The warrant for this claim is evident in the economic intratrinitarian dialogues when God the Father expresses his pleasure (εὐδοκέω) with God the Son at his baptism and transfiguration (Matt 3:17; 17:5), identifying his beauty particularly within himself and with the Son.[45] Such notions of objectivity are in direct contrast to postmodern conceptions where beauty is a matter of personal taste.

Understanding God's beauty, in and through the incarnate Son, speaks to the necessity of form since the invisible God becomes visible whereby the Son takes on the form (μορφή) of a servant, humbling himself even to the point of death on a cross (Phil 2:6–11).[46] Following Balthasar's emphasis on Christ as the unique speaking and doing form (*Gestalt*) of God, we can conclude that God's beauty is not some ethereal and inaccessible reality sought for in the denunciation of material existence.

---

44. Augustine, *Confessions*, IV.13.20. Emphasis added.

45. As we discussed previously, the Holy Spirit in some sense *is* also beauty. Yet, we understand the Spirit's beauty only on account of the Son's who is God's definitive expression of himself (John 1:14; Col 1:15; Heb 1:3). Nowhere does the Father express his pleasure in the Spirit, only in his Son. We have come to understand God's beauty as the fittingness of the Son's actions to the Father's will that radiates God's triune love. We see the same type of fittingness in the Spirit who, as the *communio* of love, only does what he hears thereby bringing glory to the Son. This is what it means to employ christological controls when speaking of the Spirit. Similarly, there are also pneumatological controls on the incarnate Son in the execution of his divine mission (Matt 4:1). Thus, to speak of God's beauty, we must give a trinitarian account. To neglect one or the other only diminishes our understanding of the whole.

46. Harries aptly stresses the importance of form: "It is the form which distinguishes a painting from a splurge of paint, music from a cacophony of sound, a novel or play from a rambling anecdote. In them all, the details relate to one another and the whole in a way which achieves a satisfying unity" (*Art and the Beauty of God*, 22).

The Impossible Suffers as Incarnate Beauty

Rather, God's beauty, as the form of God's sublime glory, is accessible in and through the form of a humble, obedient, and suffering Servant who is glorified by the Father in the resurrection and by the Spirit in the church.

Although the *Gestalt Christi* does not exhaust the Gestalt *Gottes*, it is the unique, singular expression of God's triune being. The splendor of God's triune love radiates in and through the *Gestalt Christi*, making visible the divine and dynamic, dialogical I-Thou-We relationship that is characterized by lordliness and holiness in the bond of love. The pinnacle of God's splendor comes when the *Gestalt Christi* becomes *Ungestalt* on the cross, traveling into the depths of hell and returning as the *Übergestalt* in the resurrection. Christ is his own measure and the measure of all things as *Übergestalt* and *Herrlichkeit*. What does God's singular expression of his triunity in the *Gestalt Christi* reveal to us about his beauty?

Christ, being the Lord of Glory and the unique form that measures all others, displays God's beauty as *fittingness*, which is exemplified in the concordance between Christ's mission and existence such that he acts in accordance with who he is (John 8:42–47).[47] This concordance or attunement, Balthasar notes, "may be traced back to the fact that he does not do his own will, but that of the Father, that he has not therefore given himself this work but rather accepted it in obedience."[48] Moreover, the Holy Spirit exhibits a similar fittingness in that he does nothing on his own initiative, only doing what he hears by bearing witness to Christ and what is to come.

There is an inseparable bond existing between Christ's and the Spirit's mission in time and their eternal processions, exhibiting perfect harmony, concordance, and attunement—a fittingness of being and action. This divine trinitarian order connects to God's wisdom, for the Son knew how to act in light of his divine mission in every particular situation, including when Jesus delays his arrival in Bethany to aid an ailing Lazarus, who dies, only for Jesus to raise him from the dead (John 11:1–46). There is not a dissonant moment in which Jesus acts unfittingly, for he always acts in accordance with who he is as the Son of God. Such is the beauty of God's wisdom.

---

47. Christ's attunement between his person and mission in obedience to the Father is the basis for the Christian's attunement (*Gestimmtsein*) to God, "which is a concordance (*Übereinstimmung*) with the rhythm of God himself and therefore an assent (*Zustimmung*) not only to God's Being, but to his free act of willing which is always being breathed by God upon man" (*GL* I, 251). Note Balthasar's play on words here with the German word *Stimmung*, meaning disposition, mood, or pitch, bringing together both the aesthetic and the theological.

48. Balthasar, *GL* I, 469.

Panel Two: God's Beauty-in-Act

God the Father sends the Son into the world on the basis of his self-giving love (John 3:16–17). The Son perfectly performs, in the Spirit, his divine mission from the Father, submitting to the Father's will, not his own, and acting on the basis of self-giving love. The fittingness of these actions radiate the *splendor* of this mutual love between the Father and the Son whereby the Holy Spirit, as the fruit of this love, is the mutual, personal love—the *communio*—between the Father and the Son (1 John 4:7–16).[49] Thus, this "light does not fall on this form from above and from outside, rather it breaks forth from the form's interior [whereby] *species* and *lumen* in beauty are one," as Balthasar notes.[50] This splendor radiating outwards from God's triune being is the beauty of his holiness, for "God is Light and in him there is no darkness at all" (1 John 1:5).

Bringing these lines of thought together, we can discern God's beauty on the basis of these intratrinitarian dialogues. In doing so, a trinitarian understanding of God's beauty emerges such that the incarnate Son is the expression of and the Holy Spirit is the impression of God's beauty. There is an I-Thou-We relationship—a dynamic, dialogical, personal encounter that enables communication to take place between persons characterized by lordliness and holiness in the *communio* of love. This theological personalism is not only the basis for all other I-Thou relationships but is the essence of God himself.[51] The incarnate Son, as the *expression* of God's beauty, makes God's beauty perceptible, for he is the *form* or image of the invisible God. The Holy Spirit, as the *impression* of God's beauty, communicates and affects the *splendor* of God's beauty in the cosmos and the church through his *Gestaltungskraft*.

God's beauty is real and not to be relegated to the realm of the ornamental and innocuous pleasant whereby humanity seeks such beauty in order to escape from its painful existence. On the contrary, God's beauty becomes *deformius* on the cross in order to bring about *transformatio* in the resurrection, for "it is only through being fragmented that the beautiful really reveals the meaning of the eschatological promise it contains."[52] God's beauty brings hope as we look to that future glory—the hope of glory—when we shall *see* God face-to-face. Yet, how can we see or better said, *perceive*, God's beauty? We turn now to explicating this subjective encounter of God's beauty by properly perceiving persons.

---

49. Augustine, *De trinitate*, 4.20.28, 5.5.6, 5.11.12.
50. Balthasar, *GL* I, 151; cf. *GL* I, 118.
51. Balthasar, *GL* VII, 115–61
52. Balthasar, *GL* I, 460.

The Subjectivity of God's Beauty

The intelligibility of God's beauty, as previously argued, rests not on our subjective experiences but on God's freedom to communicate himself to us, for God discloses his beauty at his appointed time, manner, and degree in accordance with his good pleasure (John 3:8). His eternal triune life "is intrinsically self-communicating" such that he "can be known to be true only because God has in fact extended the internal process of divine self-communication to include that which is not God."[53] Thus, God has created us in his image with various cognitive and affective abilities designed for communion and communication with him, others, and creation, what Anthony Hoekema refers to as humanity's "structural and functional" capacities.[54] Yet, is God's self-presentation of his beauty merely for our reflection and contemplation? Or, does God's beauty require a subjective response? If so, what are some of the subjective responses akin to God's beauty for properly perceiving subjects?

We learned from Peter's account of the transfiguration that Sublime Glory speaks; and in doing so, the Father expresses his delight in his Son with whom he is well-pleased (2 Pet 1:17; cf. Matt 17:5). Moreover, he commands those present to listen to his Son. In response to this direct encounter, Peter, James, and John fall prostrate to the ground in fear, overwhelmed and in awe of God's divine presence. No communication between God and humanity takes place as if God and humanity are equals. There is an asymmetrical relationship. Instead, humanity's encounters with God, as Balthasar maintains, "can occur only by virtue of a primary sense of being overawed by the undialogical presupposition of the dialogue that has started, namely, the divinity or glory of God."[55] Such actions require a response because God's beauty is not fit for disinterested contemplation. Rather, as Balthasar remarks, "the world can only respond, and hence 'understand,' through action on *its* part." Thus, when humanity is confronted with God's beauty, "there appears [God's] holiness and sinful man falls to the ground, only then does the contradiction between light and darkness, holiness and sin, come into full view, and the drama is begun which . . . is

---

53. MacFarland, *Divine Image*, 157.

54. Hoekema, *Created in God's Image*, 68–75. The structural aspect, according to Hoekema, includes the powers of the intellect and reason, humanity's moral sensitivity, aesthetic judgment, etc. while humanity's functional capacities include their ability "to worship God, to love the neighbor, to rule over creation, and so on" (69–70).

55. Balthasar, *GL*, VI, 11–12.

Panel Two: God's Beauty-in-Act

to lead to the reconciliation and redemption of the world."[56] God's beauty always demands a response such that the perceiving subject is confronted with the beauty of God's holiness and beckoned to perform his wisdom.

If Jesus Christ is incarnate Beauty, as we have argued, then we can reason theologically from this same biblical passage that one of the responses akin to God's beauty is delight, since the Father is pleased with his beloved Son. Notice, though, that the Father's delight is *not* in himself but in his Son such that when we properly perceive God's beauty our delight is oriented outward toward God and others and not bent inward upon ourselves. The Father's delight in the Son stems from the Son's loving obedience because the Son desires to do the will of the Father and not his own. In doing so, the Son experiences the fullness of the Father's overflowing joy, for this same joy is what the Son desires for us if we will only listen to him (John 15:11).[57] Hence, God's beauty evokes delight, not in ourselves, but in him such that our joy may be full.

Recall, from our previous discussions, what is beautiful about the cross—not the cruelties, suffering, pain, or agony of Christ's death, for such notions after Auschwitz are despicable and marginalize the millions who suffer today. No, what is beautiful about the cross is the *act* of self-giving love revealed through Christ's suffering, an act of supreme humility and compassion on our behalf. God's beauty *draws* (ἑλκύω) perceiving subjects out of themselves and into God's drama of redemption (John 12:20–33), not into some Romantic ideal that transports perceiving subjects out of themselves and into the realm of nostalgia, seeking hedonistic self-satisfaction or escape. God's beauty produces a sense of humility and

---

56. Balthasar, *TD* I, 15–16. Emphasis added. Balthasar also notes: "The glory of the God who disclosed himself always reveals his holiness as well . . . , and thus it discloses the full unholiness of the person beholding the glory: 'Woe is me! For I am lost; for I am a man of unclean lips' (Isa 6:5)" (*GL* VI, 13–14).

57. Begbie makes an important point, to which I substantially agree, demurring from the traditional notions of God's beauty merely in terms of proportion, perfection, integrity, and harmony that produce "closed harmonies." He contends that "if the 'measure' of beauty is outgoing love for the sake of the other, it will not be long before we are forced to come to terms with excess and uncontainability, the intratrinitarian life being one of ceaseless overflow of self-giving. There is still proportion and integrity, but it is the proportion and integrity of abundant love." Moreover, an overemphasis on closed harmonies "has the unfortunate effect of neglecting the Spirit's role as improviser, bringing about faithful novelty, fresh improvisations consistent with what has been achieved 'once and for all' in Christ. The other great danger of overharmonious models of beauty is that they will be singularly ill-equipped to take the evilness of evil seriously, evil's sheer irrationality" ("Created Beauty," 29–30).

self-denial such that we are attracted and drawn into the triune life of God, entering into the dramatic movements of the risen Christ in the Spirit.

Our previous investigations regarding God's μυστήριον also reveal an eschatological aspect such that God's beauty possesses a "hidden eschatological transfiguration" that points beyond itself through itself.[58] Creation and humanity are in bondage to the death and decay of sin (Gen 3) thereby deforming their existence with corruption and distortion (Rom 8:20–22). The resurrection of Christ and the sending of his Spirit as a Spirit of promise, though, indicate the inauguration of the *eschaton* whereby God's beauty unveiled in Christ through the Spirit is but a foretaste of what is to come when we will see God face-to-face. This eschatological tension in God's beauty produces an earnest *longing* for the beauty of the new heaven and the new earth, anticipating the *shalom* that is to be where there will be no more pain, no more suffering. Our present perceptions of reality should be oriented, then, towards the "future which makes whole, which is represented in an anticipatory way in the beautiful itself."[59]

The objective expressions of God's beauty evoke a variety of subjective responses dependent upon how God freely chooses to express (Word) and impress (Spirit) himself upon properly perceiving subjects. Such is the work and fruit of the Spirit to communicate God's beauty to the cosmos and the church, drawing perceiving subjects into communion with the Father through the Son. The continuity seen in all of these subjective encounters is, as David Bentley Hart suggests, "a desire for the other that delights in the distance of otherness," as seen in the perpetual self-giving love of God's triune life.[60] Throughout this discussion, though, we have presupposed *properly* perceiving subjects, insinuating that our faculties readily apprehend God's beauty. Is this the case? Let us look, now, at the proper subjective mode of perception that enables us to see God's beauty.

Perceiving God's Beauty Aright

Acknowledging God's beauty occurs when we are properly related to him. This does not mean that God's beauty is not present just because we do not perceive it. Rather, our perception of his beauty hinges on his self-expression and impression such that our perception is a receptive *response* to him. Balthasar states it this way: "The first desideratum for seeing

---

58. Balthasar, *GL* III, 341.
59. Jüngel, "'Even the Beautiful Must Die,'" 64–65.
60. Hart, *Beauty of the Infinite*, 20.

Panel Two: God's Beauty-in-Act

objectively is the 'letting be' of God's self-revelation . . . ; this first step is not to master the materials of perception by imposing our own categories on them but an attitude of service to the object"[61] The *proper* relationship stems from the position of our heart—one, though, that possesses proclivities for itself rather than the other—as well as an attentiveness to Christian virtues.

By all accounts, we are *unable* to perceive God's beauty on our own merits. Our natural human abilities of reason, imagination, perception, etc. are part of the created order that become *deformed* at the Fall, causing us to misperceive reality in illogical and fantastical ways. What is needed is *reform* by the One who *transforms* our minds so that we are able to perceive God's beauty. Our createdness affirms the reliability of human perception, although our finite, situated perspectives only see in part. Our fallenness guarantees distortion, deformation, and subversion, causing our human cognitive abilities to function improperly, necessitating redemption. Gregory of Nyssa similarly remarks that humanity possesses "dense minds, it seems . . . difficult . . . to distinguish logically and separate the matter from the beauty perceived in it, and to come to know the nature of beauty in itself" such that we misjudge what is beautiful and are unable by our own endeavors to discern God's beauty.[62] We are fallen creatures and our faculties of perception need proper orientation in order to see God's beauty aright, for the pure in heart will see God (Matt 5:8).

What we cannot see with our mind's eye we can only see with the *eyes of faith* in response to God's objective revelation. This should not lead us to conceive of faith, though, as static or fideistic but as movements of whole persons away from themselves toward God, "making *covenantal* contact,"[63] as we discussed in chapter two. We are in need of personal, more specifically, intellectual virtues such that knowledge of God "is less a matter of following correct procedures . . . than becoming the right sort of person," a person who follows after God's heart in the manner of Christ (Phil 2:1–18).[64] How, though, do we become this "beautiful person?"

Herein lies a crucial element in perceiving God's beauty, namely the *Gestaltungskraft* or shaping power of the Holy Spirit. Consistent with our previous remarks about the Holy Spirit not only as the communicator of God's beauty but also as the Beautifier of his church and cosmos, we see the

---

61. Balthasar, *My Work*, 81.
62. Gregory of Nyssa, *On Virginity*, 39.
63. Vanhoozer, *Drama of Doctrine*, 301.
64. Ibid., 301–5.

The Impossible Suffers as Incarnate Beauty

importance of the Spirit's work to *form* and *fashion* God's beauty into our lives, creating clean hearts and renewing a right spirit within us (Ps 51). This does not abdicate, though, our personal responsibility for imitating Christ by painting our lives with the vibrant colors of his supremely virtuous life (Eph 5:1; 1 Thess 1:6).[65] Yet, by acknowledging the Holy Spirit's work in our lives, we denounce our self-reliance, finding rest only in him (Heb 4). Dangers persist, though, which we must be aware.

Caution: The Golden Calf Speaks!

The people of Israel found themselves in a precarious situation waiting to hear from God's emissary, Moses, as he spoke with God on Mount Sinai (Exod 32). The people of God became restless and impatient, seeking to replace Yahweh's presence with the presence of a tangible idol—the golden calf (Exod 32:1–6). This fine craftsmanship of gold created by the hands of Aaron leads the people of God to worship the created rather than the Creator. In doing so, the beauty of the golden calf is a false beauty, denigrating and detracting from the worship and wisdom of Yahweh, thereby jeopardizing God's covenantal presence and marring the honor due to him. The Israelites, in short, act unfittingly in accordance with their obstinate hearts rather than with God's covenant ideal. Thus, the message of the golden calf warns us that our imaginations and human creative capacities, when oriented inward upon ourselves in accordance with our sinful proclivities rather than outward towards the other, produce fictitious realities that inhibit human flourishing and are unbecoming, lacking the very beauty God desires for us.

Our proclivities to possess, own, and seize what we desire should bring pause when it comes to perceiving God's beauty, ensuring that we delight in God rather than in ourselves.[66] Both, Gregory of Nyssa and Augustine, express this concern, suggesting that, because of our fallen, sinful condition, we become enamored with the pleasures of earthly beauty (and

---

65. Gregory of Nyssa says that the virtues of the Beatitudes (Matt 5:1–12) are like colorful paints that every person chooses to or not to paint on the canvas of their life. If we aspire to see God's beauty, then we must imitate Christ who became the image of the invisible God among us and fashioned a beauty consistent with the character of God (Gregory of Nyssa, *On Perfection*, 110).

66. A biblical example of the destructiveness of improperly ordered desires as they relate to the beautiful is King David and his lustful desires for Bathsheba that ended in the death of Uriah (2 Sam 11). Similarly, we see Amnon, David's son, desire to "possess" Tamor, forcing her to lie with him. In doing so, he despises her more than his previously expressed love (2 Sam 13:15).

Panel Two: God's Beauty-in-Act

define beauty by those pleasures) rather than *beholding* God's beauty to which the earthly points.[67] Karl Barth expresses his reservations this way: "Owing to its connexion with the ideas of pleasure, desire, and enjoyment . . . , the concept of the beautiful seems to be a particularly secular one, not at all adapted for introduction into the language of theology, and extremely dangerous," for "certainly we have every reason to be cautious here."[68]

These reservations are duly noted and must register not only in our theology of God's beauty, but also in all our theological discourse, for our tendency is to construct our own towers that attempt to reach God (Gen 11:1–9) and fashion idols in our own making (Exod 32:1–10). When we do, we succumb to Feuerbach's criticisms that all theology is really anthropology such that "we cannot conceive God otherwise than by attributing to him without limit all the real qualities which we find in ourselves."[69] Are we able, though, to eclipse Feuerbach's critique, or are we resigned to a beauty make over as we see fit?

One of the ways to ensure that God's beauty retains its proper place and avoids domestication is to *distinguish* beauty from her siblings such that beauty contributes to a thicker description of God's being-in-act, which is the nature of this proposal. Yet, this distinction should not dissolve into *separation* whereby God's truth and goodness are silenced. Rather, these transcendentals are an interconnected and interpenetrating triad that should not be compartmentalized. To separate beauty, truth, and goodness results in distortion not only of the triad but also of Christ himself. Thus, to see the act of Christ on the cross as merely beautiful is to turn towards sentimentality. To see the act of Christ on the cross as merely good is to understand Christ as a good moral example incapable of transforming humanity. To see the act of Christ on the cross as merely true is to reduce Christ to a brute unattractive historical fact that has no relevance for our lives. To keep beauty, truth, and goodness together, however, lifts up Christ's act of love on the cross, drawing humanity to himself so that we may participate fittingly in God's theo-drama.

The dramatic scene in Exodus 32 of Israel's apostasy, Moses's dialogue with Yahweh and intercession for the Israelites, and Yahweh's relenting from the calamity he threatened provide interludes of unfitting and fitting actions, all within the context of God's covenantal ideal that expresses the beauty of his wisdom and holiness. Israel's obstinate behavior

---

67. See my essay "Beauty and the Baptists," 104–24.
68. Barth, *CD* 2/1, 651.
69. Feuerbach, *Essence of Christianity*, 38.

demonstrates the unfittingness of their actions to Yahweh's wisdom expressed in the Decalogue. Moses's actions as an intercessor for God's people demonstrate his fitting participation within God's drama of redemption as he appeals to God's covenantal faithfulness and compassion to keep them from annihilation. Yahweh's fitting actions of relent manifest his character of longsuffering love and patient compassion amidst his holiness and justice, not unlike what we previously saw in the life of Jeremiah. Given our understanding of God's beauty in terms of fittingness and splendor, is there something peculiarly fitting about impassibility that radiates the splendor of God's triune love?

A Case Study: The Impossible Suffers as Incarnate Beauty

Relational theists contend, as we saw in the introduction, that the doctrine of divine impassibility is the linchpin that leads to the demise of the Trinity and the irrelevance of Christianity, which allows, as LaCugna asserts, "the attributes of God taken from [Greek] philosophy to remain intact, rather at odds with the living God of the Bible."[70] Moltmann concurs: "The adoption of the Greek philosophical concept of the 'God incapable of suffering' by the early church [has] led to difficulties in christology" whereby "as the perfect being, [God] is without emotion."[71] Relational theists maintain that the classical notion of God's impassibility is untenable. Yet, we noted that perfect being theology, both the static and dynamic sort, seems to have led some to misconstrue classical theism. Nevertheless, in light of other concerns, like God's love and the horrors of twentieth century suffering, is it even fitting to speak of God as impassible in light of Christ's redemptive-creative suffering on the cross?[72] Key to answering this question hinges on how we understand impassibility.

The complexity of the debate regarding God's impassibility is heightened by the disputed definition and varying usages of impassibility.[73]

70. LaCugna, *God for Us*, 300–301. Cf. Goetz, "Suffering God," 385–89.

71. Moltmann, *Crucified God*, 267–68. See also Castelo, "Moltmann's Dismissal of Divine Impassibility," 396–407, where he contends that Moltmann should have interpreted the Christ-event within the narrative logic of redemptive history rather than simply as a foundational starting point.

72. This case study is not intended to be exhaustive but rather suggestive of how God's beauty aids in articulating the contours of God's being.

73. The debate of God's suffering is not a new phenomenon as the annuls of church history attest. See Gavrilyuk, *Suffering of the Impassible God*, 64–171, Weinandy, *Does*

Panel Two: God's Beauty-in-Act

Moltmann, as we just mentioned, understands divine impassibility as God being incapable of suffering such that he is without emotions. Richard Creel, after offering eight possible definitions, delineates the core of divine impassibility as "the imperviousness to causal influence from external factors" such that God is immune to outside influences upon himself.[74] Marcel Sarot defines impassibility as "immutability with regard to one's feeling, or the quality of one's inner life."[75] Huw P. Owen's definition seems to encapsulate each of these by offering an external notion of impassibility such that God is incapable of being externally acted upon (i.e., immutable) and an internal notion in that God does not experience internal emotive states such as suffering, sorrow, or delight.[76] Yet, as we saw in our previous discussions regarding the Father's *delight* in the Son as well as God's *relenting* of the calamity that he threatened upon Israel in Exod 32, it appears that God is passible, that he experiences emotions and responds to external human circumstances.

There are, however, several latent assumptions in this conclusion presumed by relational theists, as well as some North American evangelicals, that lead to hasty generalizations and the dismissal of divine impassibility as fallacious.[77] For example, what exactly is an emotion and how do we identify what one is? How does the Christian tradition relate God's affections to his divine emotions? What role do God's covenantal expectations and ideals play in his disclosure of his pleasure or displeasure? How does the relationship between the immanent and economic Trinity affect our understanding of divine im/passibility? Addressing each of these

---

God Suffer?, 83–112, and the essays in Keating et al., *Divine Impassibility and the Mystery of Human Suffering*.

74. Creel, *Divine Impassibility*, 3–12. See also his essay "Immutability and Impassibility," 313–22.

75. Sarot, "Patripassianism, Theopaschitism and the Suffering of God," 368.

76. Owen, *Concepts of Deity*, 23. From this brief synopsis of defining impassibility, we can discern the intimate connection between immutability and impassibility. More importantly, immutability should not be mistaken as God being static or motionless because the living triune God of love is eternally and freely himself as the Father, Son, and Spirit, what Aquinas identifies as *actus purus* or what Barth entails by God's being-in-act.

77. Grudem asserts that "the idea that God has no passions or emotions *at all* clearly conflicts with much of the rest of Scripture, and for that reason I have not affirmed God's impassibility in this book" (*Systematic Theology*, 166). Grudem does give the proper theomorphic focus to human emotions by stating that they have their origin in God's emotions "who is the origin of our emotions and who created our emotions" (166). Yet, his lack of differentiation between emotion and affections leads him, in my estimation, to jettison divine impassibility unnecessarily.

questions deviates too far from our purpose; yet, they are the kinds of questions at the heart of the debate. We turn now to explicating Balthasar's position on divine impassibility to better frame our discussion of God's impassible being in light of his beauty.

The Name That Shall Not Be Named: Balthasar on Divine Impassibility

Balthasar is acutely aware of the contemporary situation in theology that attempts to locate the supposed abandonment of Christ on the cross, indicated by his "cry of dereliction," within the intratrinitarian life of God.[78] He seeks to negotiate a way between those who enmesh God with created processes and those who declare that God, in his transcendence, seems to be disinterested in the vicissitudes of human existence. Along these lines, Balthasar acknowledges the tension between those who "have no qualms about speaking of the pain of God" while noting that God's suffering appears to have some biblical warrant, particularly in light of various Old Testament passages, not to mention the christological debates of patristic fathers who formalized the notion that "'One of the Trinity has suffered' (and has died)."[79]

Balthasar asserts the following axioms regarding divine impassibility after a succinct review of the biblical and historical material: God can only experience *pathos* if his passivity is in accordance with some prior active, free decision to do so. The communicable divine attributes can be understood "on the analogy of human emotions, but this must not involve attributing 'mutability' to God."[80] Thus, Balthasar denies the univocal attributions of pain in God, for such notions are unacceptable because they compromise the Creator-creature distinction. He does affirm that God experiences emotion just not in the manner in which we experience them. Balthasar acknowledges that "the pain that comes to us in the world . . . has its origin, by analogy, in God as attested to in Scripture (*viscera misericordiae*)." Yet, we cannot "identify this essential attribute in God. We

---

78. See Yocum, "Cry of Dereliction?," 72–80.

79. Balthasar, *TD* V, 213–14.

80. Ibid., 222. Note that Balthasar also links God's impassibility with his immutability, which we noticed previously in other contemporary understandings. See O'Hanlon's seminal contribution, *Immutability of God in the Theology of Hans Urs von Balthasar* or his article "Does God Change?," 161–83, regarding this matter.

have no name for it."⁸¹ Following Jacques Maritain, Balthasar concludes that human sin does affect God and reaches into his divine being, "not by causing him to suffer something caused by the creature, but by causing the creature in its relationship with God to migrate to the side of that *unnamed* divine perfection, that eternal prototype in him, which in us is pain."⁸² Where, though, does Balthasar attempt to locate this "unnamed divine perfection" in God?

Balthasar turns to the relationship between the immanent and economic Trinity for his solution: "A way must be found to see the immanent Trinity as the ground of the world process (including the crucifixion) in such a way that it is neither a formal process of self-communication in God, as in Rahner, nor entangled in the world process, as in Moltmann."⁸³ The immanent Trinity, understood as "that eternal, absolute self-surrender whereby God is seen to be, in himself, absolute love," which explains why God does not need the world or its history to be who he is, and serves as the ontological basis for positing pain in God. That being the case, "the Father's self-utterance in the generation of the Son is an initial 'kenosis' within the Godhead that underpins all subsequent kenosis. For the Father strips himself without remainder, of his Godhead and hands it over to the Son."⁸⁴ This initial kenosis, according to Balthasar, is a divine act that posits an infinite distance between the persons of the Godhead, what I am calling a *divine eternal kenosis*. This "infinite 'distance' can contain and embrace all other distances that are possible within the world of finitude, including the distance of sin." It is here that "the *possibility* of such experience and suffering . . . is grounded in God."⁸⁵ Yet, is his position consistent with the biblical witness? Does his position allow him to retain the distinction between the immanent and economic Trinity, as he so desires? Finally, is he consistent with his own claims on divine simplicity?

Critiquing Balthasar's Divine Eternal Kenosis

The preceding account is a sketch of Balthasar's divine eternal kenosis that exposes the causal joints of his thought, particularly for his explanation of the pinnacle kenotic event of Christ's death on the cross and descent

81. Balthasar, *TD* V, 242. Emphasis added.
82. Ibid. Emphasis added.
83. Balthasar, *TD* IV, 322–23.
84. Ibid.
85. Ibid., 323–24. Emphasis added.

The Impossible Suffers as Incarnate Beauty

into hell. The primary basis for his divine kenotic ontology rests, not surprisingly, on his interpretation of Philippians 2 and commentary by early church fathers. Balthasar maintains that the first kenosis, where the preexistent Christ empties himself becoming incarnate, contains the second kenosis of the cross.[86] He extrapolates this kenotic moment deeper into the Godhead such that the Father and the Spirit have their own eternal kenotic moments.

Yet, his notion of divine eternal kenosis seems incompatible with the biblical witness. The apostle Paul in Philippians 2 associates the idea of kenosis *solely* with the Son, who takes on the form of a servant, and not with any other member of the Godhead. Balthasar, on the other hand, seems to transfer what is specifically identified with the Son to the Father such that the Father "strips himself without remainder, of his Godhead and hands it over to the Son," thereby going beyond what the text appears to be saying.[87] Such identification seems to equivocate on the meaning of kenosis, confusing the particularity of the Son with the Father. What, though, is the apostle Paul saying in and through the eternal Son's self-emptying about the Godhead? The incarnate Son's kenosis discloses the fact that the triune God is not selfish; and as such, we should emulate his humble attitude. Thus, "as love, he [God] is pure altruism, looking not on (or at) his own things, but at the things of others. From this point of view, the idea of *kenōsis* is revolutionary for our understanding of God."[88] With Balthasar, we can concur that God is self-giving love, but it seems best to demur from attributing eternal kenotic moments to all the trinitarian Persons to delineate such love.

If we grant Balthasar's reasoning thus far, his positing of an infinite distance within the eternal Godhead, which allows for "sin," "godlessness," and "nothingness," borders on the incomprehensible. The basis of Balthasar's divine eternal kenosis stems from the Father's absolute self-giving, *without remainder*, to the Son. Does this act include, though, the

---

86. See Balthasar's *Mysterium Paschale* where he gives a fuller account of his kenotic reasoning regarding Christ's death on the cross and its link with the Incarnation (11–48).

87. Balthasar, *TD* IV, 323.

88. Macleod, *Person of Christ*, 215 and his fuller discussion where he explicates the meaning of kenosis as self-emptying or making oneself nothing that entails Christ's preeminence, understands μορφή as that which presupposes and expresses the essence of Christ, and emphasizes the selflessness, actuality and assumption of humanity, and obedience of Christ. He continues suggesting that Christ's kenosis involved the obscuration of his divine glory, voluntary nature of his kenosis to the very end, and some notion of renunciation of his power without denouncing his deity (212–20).

Father's knowledge? In another passage, Balthasar remarks that "the Father shows the Son *less* his total knowledge than his total love, which conceals something whose concealment lets love radiate even more brightly."[89] How can this concealment though be consistent with his previous claims of total divesture? Balthasar endeavors to hold these opposites together analogously. Yet, as Matthew Levering aptly retorts, "once 'analogy' ultimately overturns the principle of contradiction, one wonders whether the limits of human language about God have been overstepped."[90] It seems difficult for Balthasar to maintain the distinction between the immanent and economic Trinity, as he so desires, leaving one to wonder whether he inadvertently entangles God's identity with world processes.

Finally, Balthasar draws upon the metaphor of drama to account for God's divine passion while attempting to avoid enmeshing God with world processes. The economic Trinity is the drama on the stage of "world theater" while the immanent Trinity is the underlying *Urdrama*, which "grounds and surpasses" the events of the cross.[91] The possibility of suffering, as we have seen, resides in Christ's self-emptying, not his temporal kenosis but eternal kenosis—an eternal divine distance within the immanent Trinity. This infinite difference entails, Balthasar contends, infinite mutual freedom so that the Father and the Son have the freedom to be who they are.[92] Yet, the Father's divesting himself of his "entire substance" to the Son seems to create, what John Milbank calls, a "suspended middle," whereby "the personal character of the divine essence as such ... is forgotten when von Balthasar so reduces the Trinitarian persons to free centers of being."[93] Thus, Balthasar struggles to articulate "what it means to think of one act of love throughout the dramatic processes he evokes," moving toward "something a bit like tritheism (the mutual worship of persons as Balthasar proposes)," thereby implicitly questioning God's divine simplicity.[94]

These inconsistencies with Balthasar's divine eternal kenosis emanate, perhaps, from Balthasar's perception of immutability and impassibility "as stumbling blocks that need to be overcome, as if, despite being immutable and impassible, God is nonetheless, in a dialectic fashion, still

---

89. Balthasar, *TD* V, 96. Emphasis added.
90. Levering, *Scripture and Metaphysics*, 132.
91. Balthasar, *TD* IV, 325.
92. Balthasar, *TD* II, 261.
93. Milbank, *Suspended Middle*, 74.
94. Williams, "Balthasar and the Trinity," 50.

loving and merciful," as Thomas Weinandy suggests.[95] Such seems to be the case when Balthasar declares that his position teeters on "a knife edge" because "it avoids all the fashionable talk of 'the pain of God' and yet is bound to say that something happens in God."[96] Moreover, Balthasar's presumption that Christ's cry of dereliction implies abandonment by the Father rather than lament seems to color his conclusions. What might we say, then, about divine impassibility in light of God's beauty?

The Beauty of the Triune God's Compassionate and Free Act

We can affirm up to this point that talk of God's suffering must not be due to some outside force. Otherwise, God becomes entangled with his creation, which dissolves the Creator-creature distinction, depicts God as capricious and whimsical, compromises his loving freedom, and domesticates God's glory. Something, though, does seem "to happen" within God, as Balthasar suggests. What, though, is that something that happens, why does it happen, and how does it happen? Contemporary theologians, like Paul Fiddes, surmise that the suffering of God "is both felt and received; it is both an emotion and an impression, a feeling-tone and a constraint." That "something" is a "feeling, an emotion, [or] an impulse" within God, produced by an external impression, that causes an "inner troubling or disturbance of equanimity," which "may be called 'pathos.'"[97] Fiddes's definition, despite its clear affinity with human emotions, reveals an important assumption regarding talk of God's emotive life, namely the association of emotions with pathos. Is this, though, the entirety of what the word emotion entails?

Contemporary understandings of "the category of emotions encompasses a vast variety of phenomena," that not only begs for distinction but also appears to be "exclusive to the modern era."[98] What clarifications might we make to help bring a measure of perspicuity to divine impassibility?[99] Augustine and other patristic fathers, like Tertullian (c.

95. Weinandy, *Does God Suffer?*, 163 n. 31.
96. Balthasar, *TD* IV, 324.
97. Fiddes, *The Creative Suffering of God*, 47.
98. Scrutton, "Emotion in Augustine of Hippo and Thomas Aquinas," 170. See also Dixon, *From Passion to Emotions*, where he discerns how linguistic conventions changed from talk of affections and passions to emotions.
99. See Spiegel, *Benefits of Divine Providence*, where he posits the notion "divine omnipathy" as a via media between impassibility and passibility. Vanhoozer also offers a unique proposal, appropriating Robert Roberts's notion of "concern-based

PANEL TWO: God's Beauty-in-Act

AD 160–240), offer an important distinction between *passiones* and *affectiones*. Throughout Augustine's writings, he tends "to use *passiones* (and related words such as *perturbationes*, *libido* and *morbos*) in a pejorative sense, and to contrast these with virtuous *affectus*, *motus*, and *affectiones*," although not exclusively.[100] Thus, "since these affections [*affectiones*], when they are exercised in a becoming way, follow the guidance of right reason," Augustine contends, "who will dare to say that they are diseases [*morbos*] or disordered passions [*passiones*]?"[101] Augustine associates *passiones* with the involuntary movements of the lower intellect that are not in accordance with right reason and *affectiones* with the voluntary movements that are in accordance with right reason.[102] How might this distinction inform our understanding of God's "emotive" life?

Lactantius (c. AD 240–320), another patristic father, provides us with an apt example as he endeavors to refute the Epicureans and Stoics who deny that God possesses anger. His opponents contend that God's benevolence precludes him from being angry because expressions of anger are morally reprehensible in that anger clouds judgment. Lactantius argues, to the contrary, that to prohibit God from being angry is to prohibit God's benevolence as well: "If God is not angry with the impious and the unrighteous, it is clear that he does not love the pious and the righteous."[103] God's affections toward the unrighteous do not change, for the unrepentant will still incur God's righteous justice. Yet, "because he is endued with the greatest excellence, He controls his anger, and is not ruled by it, but he regulates it according to his will."[104]

It seems that God does have feelings. He is not overcome or ruled by them as passions overcome and rule us. Rather, "God's feelings are *affections*—intentional affective attitudes that he eternally chooses to take

---

construals" with a covenantal and theodramatic twist—"covenantal concern-based theodramatic construals" (*Remythologizing Theology*, 408–12).

100. Scrutton, "Emotion in Augustine of Hippo and Thomas Aquinas," 170. See Tertullian's *Against Marcion*, II.16 where he distinguishes between God having *motus* and *passiones* such that God has *motus* like humanity yet unlike humanity he does not have *passiones*, which mar his character.

101. Augustine, *City of God*, XIV.9.

102. Scrutton makes an important point: "Despite being movements of the intellective soul, there is no lack of feeling in these affections. In contrast to modern views of emotion, Augustine does not contrast those emotions he knew as *affectus* and *affectiones* with reason. With respect to affections, there is no dichotomy between the heart and head" ("Emotion in Augustine of Hippo and Thomas Aquinas," 171).

103. Lactantius, *On the Anger of God*, §5.

104. Ibid., §21.

toward his creatures."[105] God's affections are active movements of his eternal being whereby "there is no lack of feeling in these affections."[106] If the triune God, whose being-is-in-act, possess affections rather than passions, what then of the incarnate Son's suffering on the cross?

The incarnate Son suffers on the cross, yet his suffering is not one in which he *involuntarily* endures, for Christ lays down his life on his *own initiative* (John 10:17). In doing so, the Father declares his love for the Son because of his obedience (John 10:18). The Son has freely become passive to the world in his mediation of the Father's will such that "the cross is the passion of the Son, but *as such* and in complete unity with it the omnipotent redemptive action of the Father." The cross of Christ "is not something suffered so much as something *achieved* through suffering."[107] What is the affective attitude operative in these moments of suffering?

In a word, *love* (John 3:16). Yet, we have seen that relational theists render this love in terms of mutuality or vulnerability such that, as Clark Pinnock claims, "God risked suffering when he decided to love and be loved by the creature."[108] This understanding of love mimics human experience and is not befitting of the triune God as a self-giving love that lies in obedience. Balthasar likens God's love to the "begetting" within God's triune life as the "absolute self-giving" such that "the 'love' of giving back in return can never be less than that of the begetting. From this we con-

---

105. Cooper, *Panentheism*, 332.

106. Scrutton, "Emotion in Augustine of Hippo and Thomas Aquinas," 171. Cole, in his article "Living God," 16–27, suggests that the distinction between anthropomorphism and anthropopathism is a distinction worth developing. Anthropomorphisms speak metaphorically (e.g., God's eyes are akin to his knowledge) while anthropopathisms speak literally (e.g., God grieves) about God. This distinction leads him to conclude that "when the Bible writers speak of God's grief it may not be so much a matter of God being anthropomorphic (human like) but of our being *theopathic* (God like) as bearers of the divine image" (24; Emphasis added). This seems to me the statement worth developing, and as such, is what appears to be the underlying basis for the patristic differentiation between passions and affections. Though Cole does not specifically make this connection, he all but alludes to it in his article when he refers to Tertullian's distinction "between God having emotion and feeling ('*motus*' and '*sensus*') as we do and God having passions ('*passiones*') which subvert His character as they do our own" (24n23).

107. Gunton, *Act and Being*, 126, 128. Barth puts it this way: "In it as a passion we have to do with action. That in it the subject of the Gospel story became an object does not alter this fact. For this took place in the freedom of this subject" (Barth, *CD* 4/1, 244).

108. Pinnock, "Systematic Theology," 119. Pinnock continues: "A lover's existence is inescapably affected by the other, especially when the loved one acts in ways that grieve and disappoint" (119).

Panel Two: God's Beauty-in-Act

clude that the interpenetration of love elicits that identity of love, equally powerfully in all three Persons," for "God is love and nothing else."[109] God's revelation of himself to Moses, then, in the burning bush as the identity of being finds its fullest expression in Jesus Christ who reveals God's triune life as love, which would otherwise not be known.

The persons of the Godhead, therefore, are "immutable and impassible in their love for one another, not because their love is static or inert, but because it is utterly dynamic and totally passionate in its self-giving."[110] God freely communicates this intratrinitarian love for the sake of the other. As Walter Kasper notes, "If God suffers, then he suffers in a divine manner, that is, his suffering is an expression of his freedom; suffering does not befall God, rather he freely allows it to touch him. He does not suffer, as creatures do, from a lack of being; he suffers out of love and by reason of his love, which is the overflow of his being."[111] God's love is active in that he freely communicates himself by giving himself through himself for the sake of the other.

To be sure, there are many aspects to this love of God where he expresses his love as patience, forgiveness, kindness, goodness, joy, compassion, mercy, sorrow, grief, justice, anger, reproof, etc. (1 Cor 13:4-7). God communicates these facets of his love supremely in his Son, Jesus Christ who is the New Covenant that must be understood in light of the Old while at the same time fulfilling and perfecting it. In other words, God's reconciling acts in Christ are not aimless or without intention, for "there was a driving purpose in the suffering and death of Christ stronger than just a show of solidarity with a suffering and dying world."[112] Christ's actions are not merely performed out of empathy or sympathy for that matter but because of the σπλάγχνα ἐλέους θεοῦ ἡμῶν (Luke 1:78)—a divine compassion that "arises . . . from a *covenantal identification* with God's suffering people, an identification that ultimately benefits the whole of creation (Rom 8:19–23)."[113] Divine compassion is the affective attitude that God eternally chooses to take toward his creatures, voluntarily taking on

---

109. Balthasar, *Epilogue*, 93.
110. Weinandy, *Does God Suffer?*, 161.
111. Kasper, *God of Jesus Christ*, 195.
112. DeYoung, "Divine Impassibility and the Passion of Christ, 47.
113. Vanhoozer, *Remythologizing Theology*, 444–48 Emphasis added. Empathy has the connotation of the attempt by one person to feel the same emotive states of another. Sympathy, on the other hand, connotes one's efforts to feel concern for someone rather than trying to place oneself into the same emotive state (See Eisenberg, "Empathy and Sympathy," 677–92).

The Impossible Suffers as Incarnate Beauty

the form of a Suffering Servant even to the point of death while not being overcome by his suffering like we are when we experience *passiones*. Through such suffering, God acting in Christ in the power of the Spirit accomplishes redemption, bringing comfort, peace, and hope to our suffering existence. Such is the beauty of God's compassion.[114]

What we see in the cross of Christ and his resurrection "is . . . the power and wisdom of God. It is the power of God in action because it is the means by which God meets evil on its own ground and defeats it without using its methods; it is divine wisdom in action because it is the only exercise of power that is proportionate to the need and condition of the sinner and successful in bringing about its end."[115] God's divine compassion is the consequence of his free, self-giving love exhibited in the act of Christ's death and resurrection that displays a fittingness between God's being and act that radiates the splendor of his triune love—*God's beauty-in-act*. In short, Christ, as incarnate Beauty, elucidates the contours of God's impossible suffering by demonstrating God's *compassion* in the face of suffering as he triumphs over death, all befitting actions of God who loves in freedom.

These conclusions regarding God's beauty as the attunement or fittingness of God's character and his actions that radiates the splendor of God's triune love provide a properly theological basis for articulating our participation in his beauty. In our final chapter, we will explore how God's beauty in the act of Christ's redemptive-creative suffering transforms our imaginations (2 Cor 3:18) and implores imaginative and fitting participation in God's drama of redemption set within the theater of his glory.

---

114. Davies's work, *Theology of Compassion*, surveys Western metaphysics, detailing how various periods have rendered compassion as unintelligible. He argues for a "metaphysics of compassion" or "kenotic ontology" such that the primary framework is a relational ontology oriented towards the other (xix). He bases this notion on the fact that "God is present where God speaks, and God's saving communication is the modality of God's being with God's people" (162). The question is whether Davies's understanding of divine compassion in terms of kenosis is commensurate with a God who not only "feels our pain" but also has the power to overcome it. Davies's kenotic compassion seems closer to the kind of compassion described by relational theists that ultimately is ineffective in addressing human suffering and accomplishing salvation.

115. Gunton, *Act and Being*, 126–27. See also Hart, *Beauty of the Infinite*, 167, 327–31.

5

Our Dramatic Participation in God's Awful Beauty

THE QUESTION, HOW CAN A LOVING GOD, IN LIGHT OF THE SUFFERING and turmoil of the twentieth century, not suffer *ad intra* with his creation thereby freely relinquishing his sovereignty to be immanently present, confounds relational theists, causing them to jettison any commitment to divine impassibility. Their conception of a truly loving God is a God who suffers and shares in our experiences such that "to love is to be in relationship where what the loved one does alters one's own experience," as Paul Fiddes remarks.[1] Yet, this notion of God's love entangles his being with his creation such that redemptive history *constitutes* who he is. God becomes a self-limiting God who restricts his power and knowledge in order to achieve the immanence required "to share in or suffer our experiences." Such notions actually render God's love as *ineffective* because he is mired and constrained by the very suffering that he acts to defeat.[2]

The biblical witness speaks of God as expressing anger, joy, mercy, compassion, love, etc., and relational theists are right to draw our attention to these passages, for contemporary conceptions of God that construe him as without emotions must account for this aspect of his self-revelation. We learned, though, from the patristic fathers to make an important distinction regarding God's emotions, namely *passiones* and *affectiones*. By construing God's feelings in terms of affections—intentional affective attitudes that he eternally chooses to take toward his creatures—God "feels

---

1. Fiddes, *Creative Suffering of God*, 50.
2. Balthasar remarks about God's effectual love that conquers death: "But God's proposal appears desperate only to the desperate will to live; in itself, it is pure love, which proves itself in death to be stronger than death, and thus to have conquered precisely that against which the world-will struggles in vain" (*Love Alone Is Credible*, 140).

our pain" in a divine manner, a *theomorphic* way that is in tune with who he is as the triune God who loves in freedom. *Such is God's beauty-in-act.*

The suffering cross does not overcome God, for out of his divine affective attitude of compassion he freely enters into it and triumphs over death such that Christ's obedience achieves that which God intended, namely the redemption of creature and cosmos. The attunement that radiates the splendor of God's self-giving, triune love, displayed in his impassible suffering, is the essence of his beauty. In light of these conclusions, though, are we glorifying suffering? Does the apostle Paul intimate as much when he declares that he rejoices (χαίρω) in his sufferings for the sake of the church (Col 1:24) or desires to share (κοινωνία) in Christ's suffering (Phil 3:10)?

Paul, in these contexts, is *not* glorifying suffering; he is rather taking every thought captive to Christ (2 Cor 10:5) such that he envisions his circumstances in light of the resurrection reality inaugurated by Christ and consummated by the Spirit. He endures suffering for the sake of the Gospel and the church so that he might know Christ and experience the power of the resurrection in a way he otherwise would not (Phil 3:10). Paul is able to rejoice in the midst of his sufferings because he lives in light of the hope of glory (Col 1:27) that he received by grace, changing his enmity towards God into peace. He can persevere through his sufferings, knowing that perseverance leads to character and character to hope. This hope will not disappoint, for God demonstrates his self-giving love in Christ crowning him with glory because of his loving obedience even to the very end (Rom 5:1–8).

In light of these conclusions, suffering is not to be sought, for it will find us (John 17:14; cf. 1 Pet 4:13–14). Rather, *when* suffering comes, we are able to persevere in joy (not enjoy) through the pain and suffering because we see our particular circumstances in light of the whole of God's drama of redemption, employing our Gospel-formed imagination. God, who is the God of all comfort, consoles us in the Spirit. Just as we share in his sufferings, we also share in his comfort, bringing peace and hope (2 Cor 1:1–5). Thus, this "joy and peace of Christ cannot be conjured up at will by an obsessive desire for happiness. They follow only from our deliverance out of a private abyss of illusion, and they are perfected by our groping attempt to be worthy of such a Lover: *Sic nos amantem quis non redamaret?*"[3]

---

3. Balthasar, *Heart of the World*, 9.

PANEL TWO: God's Beauty-in-Act

By rejoicing and persevering patiently in faith, we act fittingly in accordance with the One who suffered on our behalf thereby radiating his self-giving love. Christ poured this love into our hearts through the Spirit (Rom 5:5) in order to present us as holy and blameless before the Father (Col 1:22). Christ's glory in suffering fittingly brings many to glory (Heb 2:9–10) such that when we behold (κατοπτρίζω) Christ's beauty in faith we will be transformed (μεταμορφόω) by the shaping power of the Spirit into that same image (εἰκών) from glory to glory (2 Cor 3:18).[4] Does beholding Christ's beauty, though, merely imply introspection and reflection, or is more required?

Our forays into Balthasar's theological aesthetics in chapter two as well as our exposition of the biblical text in chapter three revealed that God's beauty is not merely for reflection. Rather, our encounters with God's beauty require a response—action! As such, the underlying notion of our beholding of Christ's beauty is the concept of participation, our fellowship with the risen Christ in the Spirit. This chapter seeks to explicate how we can participate in God's beauty through human imagining and the subsequent effects of our participation.[5] In renewing the imagination as a viable mode of human understanding necessary for fitting action, this chapter further suggests that the imagination is transformed by our participation in the beauty of God's life expressed in incarnate Beauty and impressed by the Beautifier (2 Cor 3:18). In doing so, properly perceiving subjects look outward away from themselves toward others in order to perform fittingly and flourish within the dramatic theater of God's glory.

---

4. I am grateful for a conversation with Keith E. Johnson regarding this passage of Scripture and its relationship to the imagination that helped to clarify my thoughts.

5. When discussing the imagination, I concur with Mary Warnock's assessment that "the heyday of faculty psychology is long behind us; we no longer believe in the functions of the mind compartmentalized, segregated, each with its own sphere. Nevertheless, as we approach the twenty-first century and should know better, it is still remarkably difficult to avoid dropping into the language of faculties, and talking about Reason, Emotion, Imagination each with its own part to play. Indeed, there seems no other language available to us. I firmly believe that it is impossible to make a precise conceptual distinction between reason and the emotions, and the imagination, often rightly taken to be the supreme property of the human animal, cannot be separated from either" ("Religious Imagination," 142). As such, our rhetoric will at times employ the language of "faculty" to make distinctions while at other times will speak of the imagination as a "disposition" or as "holistic" in order to capture its synthetic power.

Participating in the Beauty of God's Trinitarian Life

The apostle Paul appropriates this verse from Greek poetry, "in him we live and move and have our being" (Acts 17:28), for his apologetic sermon on Mars Hill, defending the one, true, living, and sovereign God of the universe. Similarly, Jesus says in John 17:21, "Father, just as you are in me and I am in you, may they also be in us." Do Paul and Jesus mean to imply that we are *ontologically* in God? John Webster shirks from the recent renaissance in the rhetoric of participation, for this very reason, and opts for the language of fellowship (κοινωνία). His concerns revolve around the dissolution of the Creator-creature distinction that leads to a symmetrical rather than an asymmetrical God-world relationship whereby the "*crassa mixtura*, the gross admixture of deity and humanity" ensues.[6] Should we follow Webster in jettisoning the participation metaphor? Or, can we use the metaphor in a way that captures the biblical idea of κοινωνία, Christ in you, and being in Christ while accounting for his concerns?

Ontological Participation: Perichoretic Dancing?

Relational theists, as we have seen, subscribe to a metaphysics of relationality, construing God's love for us in terms of mutuality, vulnerability, and interdependence—an ontological love between creature and Creator. The root metaphor for this metaphysics of relationality stems from the notion of *perichoresis*, which affirms the intimate union, communion, and mutual interpenetration between the divine persons of the Trinity.[7] The divine Persons share in the divine essence and act in unity without dissolving their distinctiveness. The Trinity is understood as "persons in communion" whereby "to-be is to be-in-relation."[8] These ideas become the bases for developing a social doctrine of the Trinity that attempts to eclipse the so-called substantialist metaphysics.[9] Consequently, a metaphysics of relationality, rooted in a social doctrine of the Trinity, "focuses on personhood, relationship, and communion as the modality of *all* existence," as LaCugna further contends.[10]

---

6. Webster, "Church and the Perfection of God," 91.

7. For the theological development of this concept, see Otto, "Use and Abuse of Perichoresis," 366–84.

8. LaCugna, *God for Us*, 248–50.

9. See Moltmann, *Trinity and the Kingdom*, 19.

10. LaCugna, *God for Us*, 250. Colin Gunton even goes so far as to identify perichoresis as a "transcendental" that is coextensive with all of being (*One, the Three, and the Many*, 152–53).

Panel Two: God's Beauty-in-Act

If a relational ontology is the modality of all existence, as LaCugna suggests, then the God-world relationship becomes one of mutual interdependence: "The economy of creation, salvation, and consummation is the place of encounter in which God and the creature exist together in one mystery of communion and interdependence."[11] The Trinity becomes, so says Moltmann, "open to men and women, and open to the world" such that the history of the world becomes constitutive of God's identity."[12] How does humanity participate, then, in the triune life of God? Paul Fiddes suggests that "no concept better expresses this [participation] than that of *perichoresis*" whereby "human persons are involved, that is, in the interweaving, mutual relations of the Trinity."[13]

Fiddes develops his notion of participation as perichoresis, drawing from the medieval notion of *circumincessio* whereby "the active participation . . . of the [trinitarian] persons in each other was occasionally described by the image of a divine dance."[14] The perichoresis of the Trinity is, according to Fiddes, a divine dance where "so intimate is the communion that they move in and through each other so that the pattern is all-inclusive. In fact, I suggest that the image of the dance makes the most sense when we understand the divine persons as movements of relationship, rather than as individual subjects who *have* relationships."[15] His emphasis on divine persons as movements suggests that the divine dance is more about *patterns* than persons. It is "the 'story' of the dancers ('the Father sends out the Son') [that] draws us in to participate in the movements of mission and worship with the dance." As such, the participation of humanity, and all creation for that matter, moves within these divine patterns such that "we find ourselves participating in a movement of mutual giving and receiving . . . [and] involved in the mission of God to the world."[16]

---

11. LaCugna, *God for Us*, 250.

12. Moltmann, *Trinity and Kingdom*, 19, 174.

13. Fiddes, "Participating in the Trinity," 379, 385; cf. Fiddes, *Participating in God*, 71–85.

14. Fiddes, "Participating in the Trinity," 385–86.

15. Ibid., 386.

16. Ibid., 386, 388. Fiddes continues arguing that humanity is not the only ones who participate in these movements: "In the vision of participation I have been commending everything created must be sharing all the time in the divine dance, not just human beings. This gives us a model for the creative activity of God in the world" (388).

Fiddes offers an intriguing proposal for participating in God that rightly emphasizes the movements or acts of God whereby we are caught up in God's mission to the world and worship of him. Yet, much hinges on Fiddes's definition of participation as perichoresis. Like other relational theists, Fiddes affirms that perichoresis means "the permeation of each person by the other, their coinherence without confusion" such that humanity participates in a "trinitarian" way, "that is, in the interweaving, mutual relations of the Trinity. It is as if God 'makes room' within God's own self for created beings to dwell."[17] Our mutual indwelling and movements within the divine patterns *affect* the identity of God, for "this is the humility of God: to allow the 'no' to be spoken within the life of the Trinity, and to suffer the pain that this causes."[18] Thus, "there appears to be no gap between the 'immanent' and the 'economic' Trinity . . . since there can be no other communion of persons than the one in which we are included; the dance returns to the Father carrying us with it."[19]

The kind of participation for which Fiddes contends is what concerns Webster—an ontological participation that collapses the immanent Trinity into the economic such that God's identity is yet to be complete. God's being is in his becoming. Fiddes seems to misstep by extrapolating the notion of perichoresis beyond the limits of the divine intratrinitarian relationships of the immanent Trinity, collapsing God's very being into the created order such that God has a real future, what Fiddes, as well as Moltmann, calls "the eschatological Trinity."[20] This collapse of divine proportion constrains God, as we saw in chapter four, questioning whether God is who he reveals himself to be through his speech and actions, calling into question the efficacy of those very actions. Yet, we can appropriate Fiddes's emphasis on participation in God's divine triune movements, in my estimation, so long as we understand that our participation is *not* constitutive

---

17. Ibid., 379.

18. Ibid., 389. Fiddes actually cites Balthasar throughout this paragraph referring to Balthasar's notion of divine eternal kenosis. Within Fiddes's framework, it seems that Balthasar would be a ready ally, given Balthasar's rhetoric of "godlessness" within the Godhead. Yet, an important element is missing in Fiddes's account that is essential for Balthasar—the notion of covenant. Covenant for Balthasar defines the parameters by which God and humanity interact, by which they enter into the drama. Covenant for Fiddes, it seems, has no functional value in articulating the God-world relationship.

19. Fiddes, *Participating in God*, 74–75.

20. Ibid., 260; cf. Moltmann, *Church in the Power of the Spirit*, 63. For further critiques of construing participation in terms of perichoresis, see Kilby, "Perichoresis and Projection," 432–45 and Cunningham, "Participation as a Trinitarian Virtue," 7–26.

PANEL TWO: God's Beauty-in-Act

of God's identity but rather *formative of ours* (Gal 2:20; 2 Cor 5:17).[21] What pattern or patterns might God's beauty beckon for us to participate?

The Call of God's Beauty

Recall, from our biblical exposition in chapter three, how Sublime Glory speaks; and in doing so, the Father expresses his delight in his Son with whom he is well pleased (2 Pet 1:17; cf. Matt 17:5). He commands those present to listen to his Son. In response to this direct encounter, Peter, James, and John fall prostrate to the ground in fear, overwhelmed and in awe of God's divine presence. Moreover, if Jesus Christ is incarnate Beauty, as we have argued, the beauty of the cross lies in the *act* of self-giving love revealed through Christ's suffering, an act of supreme humility and compassion on our behalf. God's beauty *draws* (ἑλκύω) perceiving subjects out of themselves and into God's drama of redemption (John 12:20–33), producing a sense of humility and self-denial such that we are attracted and drawn into the triune life of God, thereby entering into the dramatic movements of the risen Christ in the Spirit.

Such a call is not unlike Jeremiah's prophetic call where a dialogue between the prophet and God ensues in which Jeremiah bemoans his inadequacies and God reassures him of his presence and gives him a mission to call the people of Judah back to God by reminding them of their covenant privileges and responsibilities (Jer 1:5–10; cf. John 17). God's prophetic call to Jeremiah, though, has its roots in another, namely the call and response of Abraham (Gen 15:18, 17:2), whereby God in his freedom initiates his covenant and "*obligates himself* to Abraham and his descendents as Lord, Savior, and Protector in promising them a place (land, temple), people (Israel), and blessing (spiritual and material). Israel, [in turn], is called to covenant faithfulness (Gen 15:6), circumcision (ch. 17), and torah obedience (Ex 19–24; Deuteronomy)."[22] Thus, we are able to have

---

21. Here is an example of a suitable appropriation, so long as any connotation of human perichoretic participation within God's being, which Fiddes assumes, is removed: "The New Testament portrays prayer as being 'to' the Father, 'through' the Son and 'in' the Spirit. This means that when we pray to God as Father, we find our address fitting into the movement like that of speech between son and father, our response of 'yes' ('Amen') leaning upon a child-like 'yes' of humble obedience that is already there, glorifying the Father" (Fiddes, "Participating in the Trinity," 382). Bruce E. Benson alludes to something similar when he speaks of a "call-response" pattern in his essay "Call Forwarding," 70–83.

22. McKnight, "Covenant," 141–43.

"*covenantal contact*" with God in that "God contacts us, initiating a new kind of relationship," bringing promise and responsibility to his people.[23]

Balthasar sees the inherent connection between theological aesthetics and ethics within God's covenant because God's actions in and upon the world require a response and not simply disinterested contemplation because God's holiness intrudes in and upon the unholy. Humanity attains a performative understanding "through action on *its* part."[24] When we behold God's beauty in faith, "death turns into life, and this is something that also takes place in our hearts so that, drawn into the action, [we] can look toward the center in which all things are transformed" for "we have been appointed to play our part" in God's drama of redemption.[25]

God gives life within this dramatic moment, says Balthasar, by making space through a covenantal relationship, "an existence according to God's instructions . . . , a holiness within the space of God's own holiness."[26] This *covenant of love* gives life to those who live within it, to those who lovingly obey its stipulations, for "you shall be holy because I am holy" (Lev 20:26; 1 Pet 1:16). Therefore, God's covenant tethers together his beauty and requirement for action such that "all the creature's concepts are transformed thereby: a ray of God's glory touches them all, and this makes them more beautiful, but also heavier."[27]

---

23. Vanhoozer, *Drama of Doctrine*, 301.

24. Balthasar, *TD* I, 15. From this quotation, one might infer that we discern truth merely through performance. For Balthasar, this is simply not the case. Though there is a performative element to our understanding, we still must know something, although not absolutely, in order to act. Even in this quotation, our performance hinges on "God's revelation . . . his action in and on the world" (See especially Balthasar, *TL* II, 11–26). It is important to affirm, then, the interconnectedness of the true, the good, and the beautiful in Christ, who is after all "the way, the truth, and the life" (John 14:6) such that our knowledge of the true comes through his communicative actions, bringing a measure of understanding. Yet, a fuller understanding comes in our performance of what we know as we work out our salvation (Phil 2:12), demonstrating the wisdom of God.

25. Balthasar, *TD* I, 16.

26. Balthasar, *GL* VI, 13, 149. See Balthasar's extended discussion (*GL* VI, "God Allows His People Space," 149–77) on the nature of covenant whereby God's covenant creates space within the realm of God such that his people are "granted admittance to God's own royal realm" so long as they abide by his covenantal stipulations (149), for "in God's covenant, grace and demand are inseparably locked into one another" (177). Consequently, he contends that "the foundation of everything is the idea of 'covenant' between Yahweh and his people" (149).

27. Ibid., 177.

PANEL TWO: God's Beauty-in-Act

The call of God's beauty is to *life*—a covenantal life marked by the beauty of God's wisdom, for she calls us to "forsake our foolish ways and begin to live, walking in the way of understanding" (Prov 9:6; cf. Prov 8). This is the reason why the apostle Paul implores God's people to be filled with spiritual wisdom and understanding so that they may walk fittingly in a manner worthy of the Lord Jesus Christ. God's beauty beckons us to live a life of service, considering others more important than ourselves. Moreover, as God's beauty calls us to new life in Christ restoring the *imago Dei*, his beauty imparts a new reality, a new world from which we are to imagine how to live fittingly in an unjust world.

In doing so, God is pleased and delights in his people as we live in the power of the Spirit, bearing witness to the work of God in Christ and worshipping the triune God who qualifies us to share in his inheritance (Col 1:9–12). God's beauty always demands a covenantal response such that properly perceiving subjects are confronted with the beauty of God's holiness and beckoned to perform his wisdom, fulfilling our assigned part both fittingly and creatively within his drama of redemption. Such are the contours, patterns, and movements of the risen Christ in the Spirit. If ontological participation is to be avoided, how might we retrieve a notion of participation that retains the Creator-creature distinction while doing justice to the biblical language of κοινωνία, Christ in you, and being in Christ?

Missional Participation: Triplex Munus Christi

Balthasar, remarking about Paul's use of "in Christ," states that the phrase is "an all-encompassing and many-faceted formula, which is nevertheless held together by a single center," namely the life and work of Jesus Christ.[28] Fiddes is right to "shift our way of thinking away from the purely 'observational' which is characteristic of the split between the subject and object in our Western culture, and to introduce the aspect of 'participation' in what is real. This, we shall find, is linked with taking relationships seriously."[29] The root metaphor, though, for our participation in the real should be κοινωνία rather than perichoresis. Our fellowship with Christ in the Spirit hinges, as Fiddes so aptly pointed out, on being in *right relationship* with God. This relationship is not ontological, contra Fiddes, but covenantal, what John Calvin refers to as our "mystical union with Christ."[30]

28. Balthasar, *TD* III, 245–46.
29. Fiddes, *Participating in God*, 12.
30. Calvin, *Institutes*, 3.11.10. See also Horton, *Covenant and Salvation* where he

Our Dramatic Participation in God's Awful Beauty

Union with Christ is a multi-faceted covenantal communion predicated on the life and work of the risen Christ, communicated by the Spirit, received in faith, and consummated in the *eschaton*. Calvin further describes this union as a "fellowship of righteousness," as a "spiritual bond," whereby Christ "makes us sharers with him in the gifts with which he has been endowed."[31] There is a trinitarian structure to our union with Christ, as Calvin notes: "To share with us what he has received from the Father, he had to become ours and dwell within us." For "it is true that we obtain this by faith, yet since we see that not all indiscriminately embrace that communion with Christ which is offered through the gospel, . . . [it is] the energy of the Spirit by which we come to enjoy Christ and all his benefits."[32] We participate in these dramatic movements of God's trinitarian life by faith as covenantal partners, for we are a royal priesthood, a people belonging to God, such that we are to declare the excellencies of God who called us out of darkness and into his beautiful light (1 Pet 2:9-10).

A way in which we can participate in the mission of Christ in the Spirit is to participate in the beauty of the *Triplex Munus Christi*—the Threefold Office of Christ as Prophet, Priest, and King.[33] The apostle Paul seems to say and do as much in Col 1—2:5. Participating in Christ's prophetic office, Paul declares the incomparable riches of Christ in whom all wisdom and knowledge dwells (Col 2:2) such that he preaches God's μυστήριον among them so that they may know the glory of this mystery, which is Christ in you, the hope of glory (Col 1:25-27). Participating in Christ's priestly office, Paul suffers on behalf the church, fulfilling the sufferings of the body of Christ and giving thanks for the love of Christ among the people of the Lycus Valley such that he prays fervently for them to bear the spiritual fruit (Col 1:3-12, 24; 2:1-2). Participating in Christ's kingly office, he espouses the wisdom God, imploring them to be filled with all spiritual wisdom so that they might walk in a manner worthy

---

says that "Union with Christ and the covenant of grace are not simply related themes, but are different ways of talking about the one and the same reality" (181). Horton also offers an apt critique of ontological modes of participation in chapter eight (153-80) of his book and articulates well what I am arguing for in terms of covenantal participation in chapter nine of his book (181-215). Also, see Horton's essay "Participation and Covenant," 107-34.

31. Calvin, *Institutes*, 3.11.10.

32. Ibid., 3.1.1. See also Canlis, "Calvin, Osiander and Participation in God," 169-84 where she speaks to this very detail: "For Calvin, the mystical union is a masterpiece of the entire Trinity: our being brought by the Spirit into a form of the Son's relationship with the Father" (182 n. 48).

33. See Calvin, *Institutes*, 2.15.1-6 as well as Letham's *Work of Christ*.

Panel Two: God's Beauty-in-Act

of the Lord Jesus Christ. Therefore, let us be imitators of Paul, just as he imitates Christ (1 Cor 11:1).[34]

In chapter four, we saw Christ as Prophet akin to the prophets who went before him (e.g., Jeremiah) such that Luke identifies Christ as the Suffering Servant who takes away the sin of the world (Luke 13:31–35; Acts 8:32). Our participation in the beauty of the prophetic office of Christ compels us to *witness* to the resurrection reality of the risen Christ in the Spirit with joy, communicating the truth in love and attesting to the hope of the eucatastrophe of the Incarnation (Eph 3:15). Such joy in the Lord arises not from an egocentric desire to gain personal satisfaction, but by faith in Christ who redeems the totality of our beings, reorienting our affections toward God and giving us hope (Rom 5:1–5; Jas 1:2–6). This is the beauty of the Gospel, to which we witness, that quenches humanity's thirst for something greater than themselves. Without such beauty, as Barth maintains, we "will always have in a slight or dangerous degree something joyless, without sparkle or humour, not to say tedious and there finally neither persuasive nor convincing."[35]

Christ as Priest is our great High Priest after the order of Melchizedek (Gen 14:18–20; Ps 110:4; Heb 7) who intercedes on our behalf (Heb 7:25), who is the perfect atoning sacrifice (Heb 9:12), so that we may enter into God's presence. Our participation in the beauty of Christ's priestly work calls us to *worship* him as we enter into the holiness of his presence whereby we cry out, as with the apostle Peter, that Jesus is "the Christ, the Son of the living God" (Matt 16:15). In doing so, prayer becomes the means by which we are permitted to glimpse God's inner nature through an intimate dialogue where we listen to God's Word (Matt 17:5) and respond in love with the totality of our being (Matt 22:37–39). Moreover, we share in the sufferings of our great High Priest, for the sake of the other, and particularly his church, so that we might be presented before the Father as holy and blameless (Col 1:24). Therefore, our participation in the beauty of Christ's priestly office orders our affections as the *beauty of his holiness*

---

34. By arguing for participation in Christ's threefold office, I am not suggesting that this is the only way to participate in Christ's work. It seems to me a way in which to emphasize the multifarious ways in which we can participate in the mission of Christ in the Spirit as covenantal partners. A Gospel account of such participation is the story of Jesus' anointment at Bethany prior to his death. Jesus rebukes his disciples for chastising the woman who pours expensive oil on his head by saying that this woman "has done a beautiful thing to me" (Matt 26:10). Her act of self-giving, giving all that she had, participates in the mission of Christ in the Spirit such that her actions radiate the splendor Christ's self-giving love.

35. Barth, *CD* 2/1, 655.

shines into the darkness of our hearts, transforming us to love God and neighbor rather than merely ourselves (Matt 22:37–39) and drawing us in the Spirit out of realities of our own making and into something greater.

Christ as King acknowledges that the Father "has crowned him with glory and honor" putting all things under his rule (Heb 2:5–8), for he rules with all wisdom. Jesus is God's wisdom incarnate such that he is the agent of creation (Prov 8:27–31; Col 1:16), the mediator of reconciliation (Isa 33:6; Col 1:20), and the hope of consummation (Jer 32:39; Col 1:28). Our participation in the beauty of Christ's kingly status beckons us to embody the *wisdom* of God. Our fitting participation in God's drama of redemption bears the mark of creative fidelity to the true, the good, and the beautiful, for God created the world in and through Christ by the power of the Spirit. Moreover, our participation in Christ's reconciliation moves us to be peacemakers as we seek to act justly, love mercy, and walk humbly with God (Mic 6:8). Finally, such embodiment brings life as we obey Christ's commands and abide in his love (John 15), longing for the hope of his coming glory.

Yet, how are we to participate in the mission of the Spirit? Recall from chapter four the Spirit's mission to glorify Christ by producing fruit in the world. As we participate in the mission of Christ, we are simultaneously participating in the mission of the Spirit, for the Spirit, as the Beautifier, glorifies Christ by producing fruit in the life of the church. As we participate fittingly in Christ's threefold office, *in the Spirit*, we glorify Christ thereby beautifying the church and society not only becoming beautiful ourselves, but also portraying the wisdom of God that brings color, vibrancy, and light, namely *beauty* to the world.[36]

Our participation in the beauty of the *Triplex Munus Christi* provides us, then, with a way to articulate our covenantal participation in Christ by the Spirit. Through this kind of participation, we enjoy the benefits of the covenant and discover our true identity in Christ while incurring great responsibility.[37] The church's mission to the world is part of Christ's mis-

---

36. Note too, Balthasar's similar identification: "'Sanctification for mission' is sought explicitly by Christ for his disciples, and after Easter he himself bestows it sovereignly. Mission as the conferral of full authority corresponds again to the handing over of the Holy Spirit (Jn 20: 21–22). The Spirit that has been bestowed on the Church is the Spirit both of sanctification and mission. Everyone who counts himself a member of the Church of Christ must in his particular way be both saint and witness" ("Theology and Holiness," 344–45).

37. Balthasar also speaks to discovering our true identity in Christ when we are obedient to God's calling such that we become who we were created to be when we participate fittingly within God's drama of redemption. See Balthasar, *TD* II, 302–11

sion to reconcile all things to himself whereby the Spirit equips the church to fulfill her task (1 Cor 12). Hence, when the church acts in accordance with Christ's mission in the power of the Spirit, she participates creatively and fittingly in God's drama of redemption. *How beautiful are the feet that bring good news* (Rom 10:15; Isa 52:7). Such actions, therefore, are not ontological whereby God is formed by our actions; rather, they are *missional*, forming us into the image of God's Son through the shaping power of the Holy Spirit.

Now that we have delineated the extent to which we can participate in God's beauty, let us examine the human disposition that enables our fitting participation, namely human imagining. In other words, how we might be able to behold (κατοπτρίζω) the beauty of Christ in faith whereby we are transformed (μεταμορφόω) by the shaping power of the Spirit into that same image (εἰκών) from glory to glory (2 Cor 3:18).

Renewing the Imagination

We observed, in chapter one, that beauty may be awakening from her slumber although the vast majority of Protestant theology still has little regard for beauty as an aspect of God's divine identity. We also discussed the deleterious effects of beauty's beleaguered status for theological discourse, citing the lack of reflection upon God's beauty as that which hinders our worship, witness, and wisdom. Consequently, such disdain for beauty diminishes the synthetic power of human imagining that "grasps the goal of the venture of faith as a whole, integrating all those elements that relate specifically to the thinking or feeling or willing faculties."[38] Let us reiterate with further detail, how some trends in contemporary Protestant theology either leash or release the imagination, given certain presumptions about reality, the human person, and theological method. In doing so, we are able to suggest that God's beauty renews the human imagination as a viable way of knowing reality that is necessary for envisioning how to participate fittingly in God's drama of redemption.

---

and *Word Made Flesh*, 11–148. Such obedience is predicated on the prior obedience of Christ and is the essence of Balthasar's Christology.

38. Avis, *God and the Creative Imagination*, 79. See also Gouwens's article "Kierkegaard on the Ethical Imagination," 204–20 where he argues for "Kierkegaard's wider attempt to redeem the aesthetic in the ethical such that the imagination, as a legitimate cognitive faculty, is in harmony with the other elements of human thinking like reason, volition, and feeling" (205).

Leashing or Releasing the Imagination?

Contemporary renderings of perfect being theology understand God by maximizing, negating, or reasoning from human traits rather than beginning with God's self-revelation. Such an approach is indebted, in part, to Enlightenment rationalism and empiricism where human reason becomes the supreme human cognitive faculty for knowing reality. Neither approach "could adequately account for the faculty of imagination or for aesthetics as a realm of activity. For rationalism, the imagination did not possess the clarity of rational ideas; for empiricism, the imagination seemed to lack the concreteness and vividness of sense-impression."[39] Consequently, the imagination concerns itself with felicity and feelings, with fascination and emotion, rather than the exactitude of human reason, thereby *leashing* the imagination's cognitive operations to the non-real where beauty ultimately resides. Such characteristics are indicative of amorphous theology.

Aesthetic theology, on the other hand, conceptualizes God by playing freely with culturally instantiated theological signs *ad infinitum* that have no apparent connection to reality, much less God's self-revelation. Aesthetic theology values the formalism found in literary criticism as well as the linguistic-logical impulse of analytic philosophy, all the while lacking commitment to some form of objective reality. The imagination, in turn, becomes a part of "the New Age of openness to the non-rational" as Paul Avis notes: "Along with this goes a new receptivity to images, symbols, and myths. Combined with consumer-led capitalism, this generates a market-place of images where metaphors, symbols, and myths are freely and arbitrarily created, traded, and syncretised and dissolved—especially in the mass media, advertising, and information technology."[40]

Richard Kearney recognizes the irony of the situation: "One of the greatest paradoxes of contemporary culture is that at a time when the image reigns supreme the very notion of a creative human imagination seems under mounting threat." There is no reality, only vain imaginings, for "we are at an impasse where the very rapport between imagination and reality seems not only inverted but subverted altogether."[41] The *releasing*

---

39. Gouwens, *Kierkegaard's Dialectic of the Imagination*, 17. Avis also makes the point: "The modernity that stems from the Enlightenment . . . privileges *logos* over against *eidos*. The former is hailed as the vehicle of knowledge, mastery, and progress; the latter dismissed as the source of ignorance, superstition, and illusion. The first path to truth; the second to falsity (Avis, *God and the Creative Imagination*, 22).

40. Avis, *God and the Creative Imagination*, 23.

41. Kearney, *Wake of the Imagination*, 3. Kearney's work is an historical account

of the imagination *ad infinitum* that allows one to construct one's own reality in search of meaning is ironically a net loss since there is nothing real in the first place.

North American Evangelical theology, as suggested in chapter one, seems to be some permutation of amorphous theology with proclivities for certain aspects of perfect being theology, particularly in light of its theological method, the absence of theological discourse on beauty, and its tacit ascription of supremacy to human reason and logic. This is most evident in how some evangelical theologians construe the Bible as Scripture, often approaching the text in search of the facts, not unlike Mr. Thomas Gradgrind in Charles Dickens's novel *Hard Times*.[42] Such an approach *overlooks form for content* by placing value primarily on propositions as the "clearer" portions of Scripture to the neglect of other genres. As Trevor Hart notes, "what is of permanent value for faith must be reducible in the final analysis either to fact (history) or to eternal truths that can be shown to be rationally and morally satisfying."[43] John Stackhouse makes a similar observation of the problem: "Evangelicals already prize truth and goodness. Our tradition emphasizes honesty and charity. We practice doctrinal fidelity, straightforward evangelism, and plainspoken preaching. . . . But why? . . . Many of us lack even an adequate vocabulary by which to make beauty part of our shared life."[44] Consequently, evangelicals, in many quarters, are exceedingly suspicious of the imagination, fearing it to be an idol-producing factory prone to manufacturing golden calves and making God in our own image.

Charles Hodge's section entitled, "The Scriptures contain all the Facts of Theology," is indicative of this kind of amorphous theology.[45] Even the renowned theologian Carl F. H. Henry, who courageously championed the inerrancy of Scripture during his day, follows the way of modernity by advocating a propositional theology because the "Scriptures contain a body of divinely given information actually expressed or capable of being

---

of various views of the imagination that ultimately leads to a somber account of the imagination in contemporary postmodern culture. Based on his historical study, he distinguishes three different paradigms: "the *mimetic* paradigm of the premodern (i.e., biblical, classical, medieval) imagination; the *productive* paradigm of the modern imagination; and the *parodic* paradigm of the postmodern imagination" (17).

42. Dickens, *Hard Times*.
43. Hart, "Imagining Evangelical Theology," 193.
44. Stackhouse, "True, the Good, and the Beautiful Christian," 60–61.
45. Hodge, *Systematic Theology*, I.15.

expressed in propositions."[46] A more contemporary example is Wayne Grudem's approach where systematic theology has "its focus ... on the collection and then the summary of the teaching of all the biblical passages on a particular subject" whereby we use our reason "*to draw deductions from any passage of Scripture so long as these deductions do not contradict the clear teaching of some other passage of Scripture.*"[47]

The clear implication in each of these approaches to theology is that propositional statements in Scripture are the *clearest and most informative* parts of Scripture from which we reason and thus systematically arrange our thoughts on any one particular subject matter. But is this the only genre in Scripture? To be sure, *there is propositional content in Scripture*, for it too possesses a unique form and communicates God's voice in a particular manner. There is more in Scripture, though, than simply propositions. And it is this *more* that theology needs to attend to without *reducing* it to propositions, for God communicates himself to us in a variety of ways through a variety of genres. To strip his communicative acts in Holy Scripture of these various forms is to muddle the content, distort the meaning of the text, and exalt one form over another in the name of clarity. Such emphases actually diminish and deteriorate the authority of Scripture no matter how vigorously or vociferously one makes that claim. Rather, we need to understand how each of these genres communicates God's truth, goodness, and beauty such that our theology reflects these nuances. Doing so requires a robust imagination, "our natural mode of reasoning [that] is not from propositions to propositions, but from things to things, from concrete to concrete, from wholes to wholes."[48]

These overarching trends in contemporary theology, along with its various emendations and combinations, subscribe to a fundamental axiom stemming from the Enlightenment, namely the dichotomy between "rational discourse, on the one hand, and imagistic thinking on the other."[49] Perfect being theology and amorphous theology champion word

---

46. Henry, *God, Revelation, and Authority*, 3:457.

47. Grudem, *Systematic Theology*, 23, 34.

48. Newman, *Grammar of Assent*, 323. Newman understands the imagination to be part of rational thinking such that both reason and the imagination are but "two modes of assent" (93). Newman does not subscribe, though, to the false dichotomy of modernity that assigns reason to the real and the imagination to the non-real. Rather, since we think as whole persons, the entire mind is needed to know reality. This phenomenon, Newman postulates, is called the *illative sense* as we will see shortly.

49. Avis, *God and the Creative Imagination*, 22. For further support of this particular narrative regarding the denigration of the imagination and its association with the imaginary, see Green, *Imagining God*, 1–40.

over image, reason over the imagination, while aesthetic theology values image over discourse, the imagination over reason. Must we acquiesce, though, to this dichotomy? Is this the war within, between reason and the imagination, to which Paul alludes (Rom 7:23); or, are reason and imagination innate, human modes of thought that entail one another, which ultimately concern our humanity?

We warned, in chapter four, of our sinful proclivities to possess that which we desire, fashioning golden calves after our own conceptualities. These dangers, though, are no more damning for beauty and the imagination than logical fallacies are for our capacity to reason. By being aware of the limitations of the imagination, the inherent dangers of earthly beauty, and our sinful condition, we can elude these hazardous trappings. To *circumvent* them, though, we must *take captive every thought to Christ* (2 Cor 10:5) such that our imaginations are captivated by God's theo-drama and not extra-biblical frameworks, marketing schemes, or secular worldviews.

The Gospel is our control story that frames our thinking about God, the world, and ourselves. Our theological discourse should trend toward *perfect-fit theology* rather than perfect being theology as we seek to attune our theological discourse with God's divine triune discourse attested to in Holy Scripture. Such endeavors require a Gospel *form*-ed imagination whereby God's beauty, through the shaping power of the Holy Spirit, draws us out of our misconceptions of reality and into the movements and patterns of his dramatic triune life. Let us briefly examine, then, what constitutes the human cognitive mode of thought known as the imagination.

Human Perception and the Theological Imagination

William Alston in his work, *Perceiving God*, offers us guidance for understanding our faculties of perception as they relate to knowing God. He argues that we possess a faculty of perception akin to our sense perceptions called Christian mystical perception where "the fact of *presentation* and *givenness*, the fact that something is presented to consciousness, is something of which I am *directly* aware" such that these perceptions are of God.[50] He argues, as an extension of reformed epistemology's properly basic beliefs and realism, that the formulation and epistemic justification of beliefs based on Christian mystical perception are justified and reliable through doxastic practices. These practices are non-voluntary systems of

---

50. Alston, *Perceiving God*, 27.

belief formation related to a particular input that does not determine truth or reality but serves as a source of criteria for justification and rationality.[51]

His model is limited, though, because these doxastic practices are *only* socially established and unrelated to a transcultural *norming norm* such that what one perceives of God in one community is just as justifiable as what another perceives in another community, even if they are diametrically opposed. Yet, if we consider how God presents himself and what he says about himself in Scripture as the *norming norm*, Alston provides us with a robust argument for the viability of truthful perceptions of God. How might our imaginations relate to our perceptions of God?

Recall, from chapter two, how Balthasar brings together two important acts of theological perception, namely seeing and hearing. Seeing often implies a grasping, taking possession, or control while hearing has the least control of the sense perceptions, having to submit to the self-communication of the other. Yet, Balthasar contends that, in one instance, seeing loses its power to seize the other when perceiving beauty. In doing so, he brings together seeing and hearing under the notion of perception (*Wahrnehmung*) such that "sight is not in as much control as it might first seem. Beauty by its very nature always elicits a response: one simply cannot experience a form or phenomenon as beautiful without responding, without *assenting*." Through Balthasar's analysis, "we see how sight and hearing can be fused into one total of assent to God's gift of creation and revelation."[52]

This passive reception of God's beauty by our sense perceptions of hearing and seeing is, for Balthasar, the movement that gives primacy to the objectivity of God's self-revelation. At this point, Balthasar invokes the imagination where he seemingly inverts the Romantic emphasis on the purely creative imagination: "This is why the *Einbildungskraft* ("imagination") which primarily projects from within toward the exterior, ought rather to be called *Ausbildungskraft* ("power-to-externalize-images"), whereas the process of *Ausbildung* ("education," "formation," "development,"), in which the objective content of images is assimilated from the outside to the interior, ought rather to be called *Einbildung* ("imaging," or "imag-ining," that is, interiorizing external images)."[53] The theologi-

---

51. Ibid., 153.

52. Oakes, *Pattern of Redemption*, 142. See also Balthasar, *Spouse of the Word*, 473–90 and *GL* I, 119–21.

53. Balthasar, *GL* I, 178–79. For an introductory survey of the imagination see Hart's entry in "Imagination," 321–23. For a historical survey, see Kearney, *Wake of the Imagination* or Mackey, *Religious Imagination*, 29–124.

cal imagination assimilates God's self-revelation such that "the maturing person gradually learns to acquire the art of discrimination, that is, the art of perceiving what is beautiful in itself."[54] The act of contemplation, according to Balthasar, becomes ever more important as believers enter into (i.e., indwell) the triune life of God such that "the theological imagination (*Einbildungskraft* = 'power to shape an image') lies with Christ, who is at once the image (*Bild*) and the power (*Kraft*) of God."[55]

With E. L. Mascall, it must be said that this respective/passive aspect of the mind is not merely concerned about comprehending the spiritual but also "is concerned equally with the perception of the everyday world of material things."[56] Contemplation is not merely introspection or disinterested reflection such is the way of aestheticism. Rather, as Balthasar rightly notes, contemplation "is a stimulus to something further" and "is always measured by whether it bears fruit in an existence that is an appropriately active response to that revelation." Therefore, "contemplation flows into action."[57] How, though, does the imagination facilitate such action?

John Henry Cardinal Newman, although he struggles to articulate what he means by imagination, asserts that it, as "an intellectual act, . . . has the means, which pure intellect has not, of stimulating those powers of the mind from which action proceeds."[58] Those powers of the mind from which action proceeds are the motive powers shaped by the affective aspects of our being "by providing a supply of objects strong enough to stimulate them." In this sense, "the imagination may be said . . . to be of a practical nature, inasmuch as it leads to practice indirectly by the action of its object upon the affections."[59] *The active power of the imagination stirs*

---

54. Balthasar, *GL* I, 178.

55. Ibid., 490. Balthasar, with his redefinition of *Einbildungskraft*, seems to counter the Kantian notion of *Einbildungskraft* that emphasizes the subjective human power of making images, yet not entirely. He does think that Kant's description of the creative power of the imagination is appropriate so long as it is prepared by the Spirit in its obedient orientation to Christ (*GL* I, 177). Thus, Balthasar does not negate the power of imagination but argues for its fulfillment in Christ (*GL* I, 179).

56. Mascall, *Words and Images*, 64. Here, Mascall is drawing upon the medieval distinction of *ratio* and *intellectus* that sees both as two aspects of the mind necessary for human knowing.

57. Quash, "Theo-drama," 143–44.

58. Newman, *Grammar of Assent*, 86. Bronowski, in his book *Origins of Knowledge and Imagination*, 109–12, speaks of a similar notion when describing the imagination as that innate ability to detect the hidden likeness in things that connects various parts together and produces a new likeness.

59. Newman, *Grammar of Assent*, 82. Given what Newman says about our

the affections toward action, providing us with an important element for connecting aesthetics and ethics. What else might be said about how the imagination stirs us toward action?

Much more can be said, and has been said about the imagination, particularly regarding the creative or active nature of our imaginations. As alluded to previously, the Romantic period (e.g., Coleridge, Wordsworth, etc.) describes the creative imagination as active in perceiving the whole in light of the parts and parts in light of the whole by enabling us to envision "an image, as symbolic, as meaning something beyond itself." It also has the power that *"brings* ideas together, and which is at work to create the forms of things which seem to speak to us of the universal, and which at the same time necessarily cause in us feelings of love and awe."[60] Mary Warnock, renders an apt account of the active and creative imagination:

> There is a power in the human mind which is at work in our everyday perception of the world, and is also at work in our thoughts about what is absent; which enables us to see the world, whether present or absent as significant, and also to present this vision to others, for them to share or reject. And this power, though it gives us "thought-imbued" perception (it "keeps the thought alive in the perception"), is not only intellectual. Its impetus comes from the emotions as much as from the reason, from the heart as much as from the head.[61]

What seems to emerge is the idea that the imagination is a "holistic faculty . . . that relates specifically to the thinking or feeling or willing faculties." It seems to possess a "heuristic power [that] enables imagination to see the end from the beginning and to anticipate what it will be like to arrive at our destination."[62] Such notions are similar to what Newman calls the

---

imaginative power to stir our affections, is it possible that such is a theomorphic phenomenon? In other words, does God have an imagination? If so, how might his imagination function in stirring his actions? How, for example, might his imagination enlighten our understanding of the Gospel, "for God so loved (his intentional affection) that he gave (consequent action) his only Son . . . ?" Further research is necessary to explore these questions and would take us beyond the scope of this project; yet, these are the kinds of questions that may prove worthy in our efforts to renew the imagination. See George MacDonald's little known essay, "The Imagination," in his *Dish of Orts*, 11–43 as well as McIntyre, *Faith, Theology and Imagination*, 41–64.

60. Warnock, *Imagination*, 83–84. Cf. Scruton, *Art and Imagination*.

61. Ibid., 196.

62. Avis, *God and the Creative Imagination*, 79. The imagination and faith do overlap, for faith, like the imagination, relates to the thinking, feeling, and willing faculties. We see these relationships in the writer of the Hebrews definition of faith (Heb 11:1–3).

Panel Two: God's Beauty-in-Act

illative sense.[63] By contending for a the viability of the imagination to know the real, such efforts rehumanize humanity as human persons connect the past with the present in light of the future. In doing so, "the imagination emerges as a *disposition*" such that "one who with originality and vision adheres to the picture of the ideal self and allows it to inform his entire life."[64]

The human imagination is clearly instrumental to human identity, for it is "at the core of what it means to be human."[65] Diminished views of the imagination only denigrate the human self, dehumanizing humanity with a mechanistic and legalistic worldview that leads to an emaciated existence and inhibiting human flourishing. On the other hand, an uninhibited imagination leads to a pompous and solipsistic understanding of the human self as one proceeds to play with various images *ad infinitum*, constructing fantastical worlds disconnected from the true, the good, and the beautiful. Balthasar endeavors to walk between this polarity, recognizing both the passive and active nature of the imagination without overestimating "the active-constructive synthetic power ... to the detriment of God's own power, which expresses and imposes itself in its historical witness."[66] How might God work his shaping power into the lives of believers?

As we mentioned previously, Balthasar defines the theological imagination (*Einbildungskraft*) christologically whereby Christ "is at once the image (*Bild*) and the power (*Kraft*) of God."[67] He redefines *Einbildungskraft* in terms of *Ausbildungskraft* thereby privileging objective reality as that which educates, forms, shapes, or develops our imaginations. In my estimation, it seems apropos to combine these notions such that God's self-presentation of his beauty in Christ possesses the *Ausbildungskraft* to transform our *Einbildungskraft* through the *Gestaltungskraft* of the Holy Spirit. For those who are in Christ, he, as the Lord of Glory, has taken away the veil that shrouds our imaginations such that when we behold

---

63. Newman, *Grammar of Assent*, 270–99. Cf. Kevin Vanhoozer's discussion of the imagination in his *Drama of Doctrine*, 278–85, 337, 377–78, 416 where he gives a theo-dramatic rendering.

64. Gouwens, "Kierkegaard on the Ethical Imagination," 216. Emphasis added. Gouwens is summarizing Kierkegaard's understanding of the ethical person who pursues the "ideal self" where "Christ presents himself to the ethical imagination not as a glorious internally-generated ideal, but as the suffering God-man who atones for sin—an offense to the self-reliance of the imagination as well as the reason. The imagination cannot, any more than the reason, grasp the divine" (217).

65. Hart, "Imagining Evangelical Theology," 198–99.

66. Balthasar, *GL* I, 176–77.

67. Balthasar, *GL* I, 490.

(κατοπτρίζω) his beauty we are transformed (μεταμορφόω) by the Holy Spirit into Christ's likeness with an ever-increasing beauty (2 Cor 3:18). Let us endeavor to explore this notion further.

Incarnate Beauty and the Transformation of the Imagination

George MacDonald, in his essay "The Imagination: Its Function and Its Culture," begins by offering a definition of the imagination as "that faculty which gives form to thought—not necessarily uttered form, but form capable of being uttered form, but form capable of being uttered in shape or in sound, or in any mode upon which the senses can lay hold."[68] Like Balthasar, he characterizes the imagination as both active and passive, while privileging the passive: "The forms which man uses in creative imagination are not themselves created by him; they are already prepared for him." Yet, humanity's creative imagination is analogous to God's creativity such that "the imagination of man is made in the image of the imagination of God."[69] He predicates his assertions theologically in the *imago Dei*, contending that the imagination is its primary locus that links to God's creative activity.

MacDonald subsequently connects the imagination with the life of faith: "a wise imagination, which is the presence of the Spirit of God, is the best guide that man or woman can have, for it is not the things we see the most clearly that influence us the most powerfully." After all, we "walk by faith and not by sight" (2 Cor 5:7). The integration of the imagination into the life of faith, for MacDonald, is the "ordering of our life toward the harmony with its ideal in the mind of God" such that as believers face uncertainty in life they learn to "imagine greatly," following and worshipping God.[70] "The end of the imagination," says MacDonald, "is *harmony*. A right imagination, being the reflex of the creation, will fall in with the divine order of things as the highest form of its own operation."[71] The imagination, according to MacDonald, is shaped by the divine order of creation, is the locus for the *imago Dei*, is a conduit for the Spirit of God, and is essential to living a life a faith.

John McIntyre uses MacDonald's essay as a blueprint to further the discussion "that will prove remarkably pertinent to our purpose in

---

68. MacDonald, *Dish of Orts*, 12.
69. Ibid.
70. Ibid., 32–33, 38.
71. Ibid., 38.

PANEL TWO: God's Beauty-in-Act

touching upon some of the philosophical themes that will concern us, and also taking the investigation of the nature of imagination into the centre of theology itself."[72] He develops the notion of a "parabolic imagination" by examining the parables of Jesus in the New Testament, claiming that Jesus' use of parables provides a strong basis for developing "the subject of the imagination as a biblical category" in order to attain "fresh insights into familiar topics" of theology "without producing any distortion or falsification of doctrine."[73] He briefly explores the imagination's relationship to the attributes of God, Creation, the Incarnation, Atonement, and the Holy Spirit. Pertinent for our discussions, though, are his comments regarding the relationship of the imagination to God's attributes.[74]

McIntyre begins his discussion by summarizing Karl Barth's understanding of the divine attributes as "perfections" in order to "draw attention to those parts in Barth's exposition where, to my mind, the notion of the imagination could be introduced, or where alternatively it is implied."[75] In doing so, he gives a theological account of the imagination as "an attribute of God" that "is a direct derivative of the love of God, which therefore acts as a control upon all that we say concerning [the] imagination. Equally, it gives [the] imagination access to the whole range of the actions of the God who is loving." It is through God's "imaginative penetration" that demonstrates how God's love, freedom, mercy, and patience enter "into the plight and condition of the loved one, worthless as he is." McIntyre concludes saying that "there is a sense in which it is [God's] imagination which initiates several other activities and sustains them, through the point where the relief of the distress is complete."[76]

MacDonald and McIntyre offer us fruitful lines of thought for fresh insights into the relationship of the imagination to faith and theology that deserve further exploration. What is peculiarly absent from both of their accounts, though, yet wholly conceivable, is *the relationship between God's beauty and the imagination*, both God's and humanity's. To be sure, either could have made the argument that it is God's imaginative penetration of his beauty where "the Holy Spirit is God's imagination let loose and working with all the freedom of God in the world, and in the lives, the words

72. McIntyre, *Faith, Theology, and the Imagination*, 13.

73. Ibid., 19, 41.

74. Ibid., 41–64. McIntyre continues to flesh out his understanding of the imagination by exploring the ethical and philosophical dimensions of the imagination in chapters four and five, respectively.

75. Ibid., 44. Cf. Barth, *CD* 2/1, 322–677.

76. McIntyre, *Faith, Theology, and Imagination*, 45–48.

and actions, of the men and women of our time."[77] In fact, "that imaginative creativity which God showed in forming the beauty of the world about us, he demonstrated once again in novel style of his intervention in human history in the form of the Word made flesh, an event so unexpected, so unpredictable," as McIntyre claims.[78] Not surprisingly, McIntyre connects the Holy Spirit with the beauty of creation.

McIntyre also makes no mention of the relationship between God's beauty and human imagining in his chapter entitled "The Ethical Dimension," although he speaks to the significance of "the role which imagination has to play in the understanding of how the Christian life is to be lived."[79] MacDonald also does not make the connection, though he makes an interesting observation, drawing from Goethe, about how to develop the human aesthetic faculty. MacDonald remarks: "Goethe has told us that the way to develop the aesthetic faculty is to have constantly before our eyes, that is, in the room we most frequent, some work of the best attainable art. This will teach us to refuse evil and choose the good."[80] MacDonald, at times, seems to link the "wise imagination" with "the spirit of God," insinuating that human creations may contain more meaning than an author intended at the time of its creation.[81] Such may be true given the Holy Spirit's mission to communicate God's beauty to the world. Yet, how are we to distinguish the human spirit from the Holy Spirit, in light our proclivities for vain imaginings? It seems more appropriate for incarnate Beauty to be the object communicated to our imaginations by the Spirit as our pedagogue for refusing evil and doing the good. How might God's beauty, then, transform our imaginations?

Karl Barth and Emil Brunner in the early twentieth century ardently contested the relationship between nature and grace, arguing over the epistemological and methodological implications of the so-called *Anknüpfungspunkt*—the human point of contact for God's self-revelation. Garrett Green attempts to resolve this dispute "by identifying the point of divine-human contact as imagination" whereby "the challenge is rather to find a way of describing the *Anknüpfungspunkt* that not only does justice

77. Ibid., 64.

78. Ibid., 55. Note McIntyre's emphasis is not on beauty but the demonstration of God's imaginative actions, intervening in the most unimaginable of ways as the God-man.

79. Ibid., 65.

80. MacDonald, *Dish of Orts*, 39.

81. Ibid., 32, 263. MacDonald further suggests that the best way to develop the imagination is through the reading of books.

Panel Two: God's Beauty-in-Act

to the character of revelation as grace but also makes clear in purely 'formal' or theologically neutral terms what it means to say that human beings receive that revelation."[82] Green reconfigures Barth's redefinition of *Anknüpfungspunkt* as *Gottförmigkeit* in terms of the imagination since Barth's "language shifts from static and local metaphors to dynamic images of shaping and forming." In doing so, "Barth's account of how revelation is received can be redescribed as a conversion of the imagination."[83] Perhaps, then, this is the passive moment, which we spoke of earlier whereby God freely discloses his beauty such that, as Newman suggests, "the heart is reached, not through reason, but through the imagination" without any bifurcation between reason and the imagination.[84] Could this be what the holy fool, Prince Myshkin, had in mind when he said, "Beauty will save the world?"[85]

As we have seen, God's beauty, understood through the actions of his Son in the Spirit attested to in Scripture, displays a fittingness that radiates the splendor of God's triune self-giving love that not only demands a response but also convinces, persuades, and attracts, drawing us out of our illusory realities and into God's dramatic triune life. God's beauty in the *Gestalt Christi* possesses the *Ausbildungskraft* to shape our *Einbildungskraft* through the *Gestaltungskraft* of the Holy Spirit. These fitting movements of the risen Christ in the Spirit serve as the patterns that educate and form the imaginations of properly perceiving subjects such that "the subjective elements of perception . . . more and more pass into the service" of incarnate Beauty.[86]

This transformation that comes by the expression of incarnate Beauty through the impression of the Beautifier occurs in such a way that, as Jonathan Edwards remarks, "it is as if a new world opens to its view"

---

82. Green, *Imagining God*, 34–35.

83. Ibid., 37-38. Barth redefines *Anknüpfungspunkt* as *Gottförmigkeit*: "The image of God in man . . . that forms the actual point of contact of the Word of God is the newly created *rectitudo*, awakened by Christ from actual death to life and thus 'restored,' now actually as the possibility of man for the Word of God" (Barth, CD 1/1, 238–39).

84. Newman, *Grammar of Assent*, 89. This is not to suggest that reason remains unconverted or that the imagination is the necessary entry point because God's shaping power transforms the heart—the very seat of our emotional (Col 4:8), intellectual (Matt 12:34), and spiritual life (Matt 13:15). See Mascall, *Words and Images*, where he argues that the medieval distinction of *ratio* and *intellectus* are two aspects of our understanding.

85. Dostoyevsky, *Idiot*, 382.

86. Balthasar, GL I, 178.

such that "when a person has this sense knowledge given him, he will view nothing as he did before."[87] Christ, as the Lord of Glory, has taken away the veil that shrouds our imaginations, for he is "the ideal, the 'Pattern,' [that] quickens the imagination and directs the will to imitation and obedience in renewed ethical passion."[88] Such an encounter with God's beauty captivates our imaginations with the authentic life of faith in Christ lived in the Spirit. Thus, as we behold God's beauty, we are transformed by the Holy Spirit into Christ's likeness with an ever-increasing beauty (2 Cor 3:18). How might these redemptive-creative actions affect our performances within God's drama of redemption?

Becoming Beautiful: Imaginative Performances within the Theater of God's Glory

We have suggested that our redemptive-creative remaking reaches into our hearts—the very seat of our emotional (Col 4:8), intellectual (Matt 12:34), and spiritual life (Matt 13:15)—not simply via reason but also our imagination. God's beauty, as "the intruding lordliness of him who comes to confront the world, both judging it and gracing it,"[89] beckons us to participate in the dramatic movements of his triune life. When we behold God's beauty in faith, "death turns into life, and this is something that also takes place in our hearts so that, drawn into the action, [we] can look toward the center in which all things are transformed" for "we have been appointed to play our part" in God's drama of redemption.[90] Our participation in God's beauty is covenantal such that "all the creature's concepts are transformed thereby: a ray of God's glory touches them all, and this makes them more beautiful, but also heavier."[91] As God's beauty beckons and we behold it in faith, how does his beauty shape our imaginations? How do our imaginations enable fitting participation in the movements of God's triune life, and what might that look like?

---

87. Edwards, *Treatise Concerning Religious Affections*, 275.
88. Gouwens, "Kierkegaard on the Ethical Imagination," 217.
89. Balthasar, *GL* VI, 14.
90. Balthasar, *TD* I, 16.
91. Balthasar, *GL* VI, 177.

PANEL TWO: God's Beauty-in-Act

Fitting Participation in the Life of Incarnate Beauty

Participating in God's beauty follows the call-response pattern not only what we saw in the call-response pattern of Jeremiah elucidated in chapter three but also the call-response found in the establishment of the Abrahamic covenant. Part of that pattern is God sending his servants to accomplish an appointed task, according to his good pleasure. Jesus, in his high priestly prayer, says as much when he asks the Father to sanctify God's people by setting them apart, by making them holy through the truth, for his word (λόγος) is truth (John 17:17). Christ sends his followers into the world, just as the Father sent him (John 17:18). As servants respond and perform their appointed parts, they become who God intended them to be. Yet, how can we discern God's call and ascertain what a fitting response might be?

The spiritual disciplines (e.g., prayer, fasting, communion, *lectio divina*, etc.), which have long been part of the church's practices, play an important part in becoming beautiful after the likeness of Christ. "Prayer," as Balthasar notes, "is a conversation in which God's word has the initiative and we, for the moment, can be nothing more than listeners. The essential thing is for us to hear God's word and discover from it how to respond to him." In doing so, "we have been permitted to glimpse his inner nature, to enter into it, into the core of eternal truth; bathed in this light which radiates upon us from God, we ourselves become light and transparent before him."[92] The ancient monastic discipline of *lectio divina* where one reads the Scriptures in small portions slowly and thoroughly can also aid in the process of becoming beautiful.[93] Through such practices, God shapes and forms our imaginations so that we become attuned to his movements and patterns of thinking, saying, and doing.

Crucial to the process of forming our imaginations is Holy Scripture, for the Scriptures are the "spectacles" through which we view God, the world, and ourselves, thereby bringing into focus the truth, goodness, and

---

92. Balthasar, *Prayer*, 15. Oliver Davies in his book, *Living Beauty*, offers a way of integrating God's beauty into our lives through various forms of prayer: silence, freedom, powerlessness, poverty, love, delight, and transfiguration. Moreover, this process of becoming beautiful after the likeness of Christ is akin to what typically is known as sanctification.

93. *Lectio divina* is a dynamic way of reading Scripture that begins with *lectio* (reading for *prima facie* understanding), proceeds to *meditatio* (reflection on a passage such that one internalizes the text's meaning), and concludes with *contemplatio* (moments of spiritual communion with God).

Our Dramatic Participation in God's Awful Beauty

beauty of God.[94] The Bible is filled with a variety of forms (e.g., narrative, poetry, didactic, parabolic, apocalyptic, etc.) through which God communicates his triune life to us. These various forms train our imaginations to perceive what God is saying and doing in Christ by the Spirit so that we may join him as covenantal partners in his mission to the world. That being the case, "Scripture . . . is the vehicle that impresses the Christ-form in the hearts of men," stretching our imaginations to understand the parts of Scripture in light of the whole such that we think with and along the text, seeking to ascertain God's wisdom.[95] Through this process, the Spirit enlightens the eyes of our hearts so that we will know the hope to which God has called us (Eph 1:18). Kevin Vanhoozer aptly makes the point: "The various books of the Bible train the reader in certain 'habits' of seeing, feeling, and most important judging, . . . [enabling us to] discern the ultimate meaning of things . . . by seeing them in relation to God and the kingdom of God—by placing them in theo-dramtic context."[96] By training our imaginations in this manner, "we will learn to see, feel, think about, and act in the world in ways similar to those of the biblical authors, the commissioned witnesses to the event of Jesus Christ."[97]

Disciplining our imaginations leads us into strict training (1 Cor 9:24–27) as we seek to break old habits and ways of thinking that inhibit flourishing akin to the days when we were alienated from God and hostile in mind towards him (Col 1:21), for "we humans are addicts, and our deepest addiction is to a mistaken identity, to a false self."[98] By disentangling our identity from illusory notions "through God's beauty we are unselfed, thus formed . . . [by] the cross, . . . a beauty that we cannot possess but only suffer. By suffering such a beauty, a beauty that hides not its suffering, we

---

94. Calvin, *Institutes*, 1.6.1. Calvin remarks: "Just as old or bleary-eyed men and those with weak vision, if you thrust before them the most beautiful volume, even if they recognize it to be some sort of writing, yet can scarcely construe two words, but with the aid of spectacles will begin to read distinctly; so Scripture, gathering up the otherwise confused knowledge of God in our minds, having dispersed our dullness, clearly shows us the true God" (1.6.1).

95. Balthasar, *GL* I, 530.

96. Vanhoozer, *Drama of Doctrine*, 377.

97. Ibid. Although there are numerous inappropriate examples, the faithful saints found in the annals of church history serve as illustrative examples of other embodied and imaginative instantiations of God's wisdom, "the great cloud of witnesses" (Heb 11) who performed their parts in God's drama of redemption. We turn to them to glean wisdom from their fitting or unfit performances in order to eclipse our biases and better understand our location in God's theo-drama.

98. Mitchell, *Liturgy and the Social Sciences*, 76.

Panel Two: God's Beauty-in-Act

are possessed and thus saved from the ugliness of our sin. In short, we are made holy."[99] When we give ourselves "wholeheartedly" to participating imaginatively in the movements of the risen Christ in the Spirit, performing our assigned parts, discipleship becomes real, manifesting authentic expressions of the living Christ in the Spirit through worship, witness and wisdom.[100] How do our imaginations enable such fitting participation?

Do This in Remembrance of Me: Remembering the Past, Envisaging the Future, and Living in the Present

The imagination, as we have discussed, has the ability to envision various parts in light of the whole, often making that which is absent present to the mind. The imagination is also a disposition and is instrumental to human identity. David Gouwens remarks, "The imagination gives continuity to a person's life and links one day to another by grasping the dimensions of the past and the future." This continuity "requires the imagination to bring the past before one in memory; it requires the imagination to be related to the future. And yet both must be done in a way which avoids negating the present and dissolving oneself in the medium of imagination."[101] If our imaginations are transformed by God's beauty as we have argued, then how does the renewed imagination shape our identity in Christ for understanding how to act fittingly in God's drama of redemption?

The apostle Paul often draws the attention of his readers to the life that they once lived, calling them to *remember* the time when they were separated from Christ, excluded from the Kingdom of God, foreigners to

---

99. Hauerwas, *Performing the Faith*, 163–64.

100. Graham, "Liturgy as Drama," 79. Authentic expressions of Christ have nothing to do with the popular notion of being "authentic to oneself," for such expressions are unfitting. Rather, our performances are beautiful when our lives are attuned to the life of Christ in the Spirit. It is possible to "fit" into another storyline, but such fittingness does not radiate the self-giving love exhibited by the triune life of God. See also Vanhoozer's discussion of "The Disciple's Vocation: Being Real," in *Drama of Doctrine*, 394–97.

101. Gouwens, "Kierkegaard on the Ethical Imagination," 215–16. Paul Ricoeur's protracted argument in *Memory, History, and Forgetting* also suggests memory to be constitutive of our identity and thus formative of our interpersonal and social actions (see especially chapter three, "Personal Memory, Collective Memory"). These notions build upon his previous work, *Oneself as Another*, where he argues for the validity of narrative identity over personal identity (see his fifth study, "Personal Identity and Narrative Identity") such that narrative identity is "no longer considered from the perspective of its relation to the constitution of human time, . . . but from that of its contribution to the constitution of the self" (114).

Our Dramatic Participation in God's Awful Beauty

the covenant of promise, and without hope (Eph 2:12). Such recollections not only involve memory but also invoke the imagination as we recall our former existence apart from Christ. Yet, such evocations are in *contrast* to another memory that Paul evokes, namely the finished work of Christ on the cross where Christ's completed work brought peace and justice, breaking down walls of division, enmity, and strife (Eph 2:14).

Paul appeals to redemptive history in such a way that the Gentiles, to whom he was addressing in his letter to the Ephesians, share in the same history of the apostles and the prophets (Eph 2:20). Such appeals invoke the symbolic, poetic, metaphoric images, and narrative accounts of that history, all of which the Spirit uses to fashion a *sacred memory* (i.e., *sacra memoria*) that serves to remind God's people of his communicative actions on their behalf (John 14:26), spurring them on to further action.[102] These images are not to remain within our collective memory as a reminder of some sentimental past. Rather, our imaginations must bring this sacred memory into the present in order to form and fashion our identities in Christ, directing our actions in the present for fitting participation in God's drama of redemption.

Bringing redemptive history into the present, though, is not sufficient for becoming beautiful or for fitting participation in God's drama of redemption. Visions of the coming kingdom of God are also necessary. Paul expresses this eschatological component as the hope of glory, when Christ by the power of the Spirit will make all things anew. The risen Christ is the first fruits of this new creation (Col 1:18) while the Spirit is the seal of promise who is the guarantee of our future inheritance (Eph 1:13–14). This future inheritance is the hope of glory when there will be no more suffering, no more pain. It is a time when we live in the fullness of God's beauty, worshipping the triune God singing, "Holy, Holy, Holy, is the Lord God the Almighty, who was and who is and who is to come" (Rev 4:8). As our imaginations look forward, with confident expectations of the Second Advent, these images of our future glory engender hope as we groan along with creation in the midst of our present sufferings for a future glory, hoping for what we do not see and persevering until we do (Rom 8:18–25). Such is the nature of our eschatological imagination that

---

102. *Memoria* is more than simple recall of past events but involves "the essential roles of emotion, imagination, and cogitation within the activity of recollection" (Carruthers, *Craft of Thought*, 2). See also Carruthers's book, *Book of Memory* for further detail about the medieval concept of *memoria*.

makes the future present, orienting our actions toward that ever-greater glory when we see God face-to-face.[103]

On the night before Jesus' died on the cross, he sat around a table, sharing the Passover meal with his disciples. At some point during the evening, he took a piece of bread and a cup of wine, instituting what the church now calls the Eucharist. Jesus' instructions to "do this in remembrance of me" (Luke 22:19) are formative and essential to living fittingly in the present. Jesus' command is, first, to *do* something. It is a call to action, a call to perform the drama of redemption in the here and now. Yet, his command is protological as we remember what he has done for us, giving shape to what we are to do now. His command is also eschatological in that he will not drink of the cup again until we are with him in glory, orienting our present actions toward the future kingdom of God. Thus, *our performance of the Eucharist serves to triangulate our actions in the present as we live in the presence of the risen Christ in the Spirit with reference to redemptive history yet in light of his eschatological glory.*[104] A robust imagination is necessary to integrate our remembering and envisaging—what *was* with what *is* and *is to come*, bringing a sense of meaning and understanding to the present so we can participate fittingly and creatively in the dramatic movements of God's triune life.[105]

A Call for Reconciliation and Creativity

Our investigations to this point have highlighted several dramatic movements within the triune life of God—the call of God's beauty and our response, Christ's humble descent culminating in the laying down of his life and taking it up again in his triumphant ascent, and the Spirit's mission of being sent to glorify the Son through the church. Another movement involving both the Son and the Spirit is the broader redemptive-creative

---

103. See Vanhoozer, "Praising God in Song," 119 where he speaks about living as "being-towards-resurrection" and our lives as "living hymns," all oriented toward "living beautifully."

104. Although I have worked out these ideas differently, see Smith, *Radical Orthodoxy and the Reformed Tradition*, 205–76 that flesh out the implications of this assertion.

105. Gregor, "Thinking Through Kierkegaard's Anti-Climacus," 448–65 where he details three important roles the imagination plays in Christian living: 1. The awareness of a range of possibilities, 2. the envisioning of perfection, and 3. the subjective appropriation of the image of Christ.

motif we outlined in chapter four.[106] Christ's redemptive work in the Spirit that creates anew calls for properly perceiving subjects, not to mimic his actions in identical form, but to improvise faithfully from these actions to promote and instigate human flourishing in new contexts and situations.

Bruce Ellis Benson, in his essay "Call Forwarding: Improvising the Response to the Call of Beauty," suggests that improvisation is an apt way of conceiving how to respond to God's beauty. He draws upon black spirituals and jazz music to make his point: "To improvise in jazz . . . is to respond to a call, to join in something that is always already in progress" whereby we "cultivate a habitus, a way of being that is both nurtured by and results in what [Pierre] Bourdieu terms 'regulated improvisation.'" For us "to be able to improvise means one is steeped in the tradition and knows how to respond to the call of other improvisers."[107] Such notions are in contrast to modern and romantic ideals that suggest improvisers are to be "original" where one "is to carve out a place for oneself by overcoming the influence of previous artists."[108] Improvisation is not a performance *ex nihilo* but "requires both training (formation) and discernment (imagination)."[109]

Our responses to God's beauty necessitate that we learn from God by listening, first, to his Son (Matt 17:5), discerning the dramatic movements of his life in the Spirit as attested to in Scripture. We receive training from past and present improvisers of the church as we note their fidelity or infidelity to Christ's sayings and doings. Therefore, as we respond in new contexts and situations to God's call/leading, we seek beautiful improvisations on the Word in the Spirit that are faithful to the dramatic movements of God's triune life attested to in Holy Scripture and guided by previous improvisers of that great cloud of witnesses (Heb 11). That being the case,

---

106. Adrienne Chaplin echoes similar sentiments in her essay, "The Invisible and the Sublime," in *Radical Orthodoxy and the Reformed Tradition*, 89–106.

107. Benson, "Call Forwarding," 74–76. Benson draws upon his work as a musician to illustrate further what he means by improvisation: "Composers 'improvise' on the conventions of their music genre (not to mention the work of previous composers); performers improvise certain elements of their performances (more or less, depending on prevailing conventions); and listeners are part of the improvisatory practice by how they listen." He then draws upon the specific genres of black spirituals and jazz "to illumine what takes place in the call and the response" (75).

108. Ibid., 78.

109. Vanhoozer, *Drama of Doctrine*, 337. Cf. Vanhoozer, "What Has Vienna to Do with Jerusalem?," 123–50, where he contends that our creative artifacts should be authentic expressions of the Gospel such that "art and music [should] aid the eucatastrophic imagination when they take sin and suffering seriously, but not so seriously as to lose sight of the joy of the gospel, which stands like bookends on either side of the human story. The church needs the tonic, the discipline, of suffering tonality" (149).

Panel Two: God's Beauty-in-Act

how might we imaginatively improvise on Christ's redemptive-creative actions in the Spirit?

The apostle Paul, in his letter to the Ephesians, refers to the actions of Christ on the cross as the defining moment that removed the dividing wall between Jews and Gentiles, bringing peace and unity by crucifying their hostility (Eph 2:14–18). Christ accomplishes this peace with the poverty of spirit necessary to bring about reconciliation and to impart his riches out of his poverty (2 Cor 8:9).[110] When God's beauty draws us out of ourselves, our focus turns toward the other whereby we are able to enter the situation of the other through the imagination, enabling us to seek understanding first before being understood. Such poverty of spirit, such humility is essential for tearing down walls that divide families, marriages, ethnicities, and socio-economic groups. In doing so, the act of forgiveness becomes the key response to incarnate Beauty's call to deny oneself, take up your cross and follow me (Luke 9:23). Such is the beauty of forgiveness and the ministry of reconciliation (2 Cor 5:18).[111]

Christ's redemptive acts on the cross not only bring peace to his creatures, but also redeem his creation, for he is the mediator, sustainer, and goal of all creation (John 1:3; Eph 1:3–14; Col 1:15–20). Such actions demonstrate God's commitment to his "good" creation (Gen 1–2) as Creator. Yet, the created order is in bondage to death and decay, which is why creation groans for its transfiguration (Rom 8:20–22). The dramatic movements of Christ's creative and re-creative actions call us to a renewed sense of human creativity in order to "voice creation's praise" (Ps 19:1).[112] Our human creativity, though, must also account for the death and decay present in the world to avoid creating a false reality of sentimentality and nostalgia. Such practices, which take seriously Christ's redemptive-creative work, will seek to portray "beauty in the transformation of the disfigured," what some are now calling "A Broken Beauty"[113] that "strives to show the mystery and mess of a *story* that is far from over—one that is ever more complex and problematic, yet moving toward a sense of

---

110. Balthasar, "Die Armut Christi," 385–87. Cf. Wells, *Improvisation*.

111. David Kelsey in his book *Imagining Redemption* offers a compelling account of how our imaginations participate in Christ's redemptive acts that sees Christ's work as a whole and envisions "what we can do for another and about another's life" (105). To imagine redemption is to see how Jesus' ministry, death, and resurrection can rebuild, renew, and restore.

112. Begbie, *Voicing Creation's Praise*, 179.

113. Walford, "Case for a Broken Beauty," 103.

resolution."[114] This is the beauty of the "old, old story of Jesus Christ and his love"—a story of three trees that reveal (Gen 3), redeem (Gal 3), and renew (Rev 22), beckoning us to participate imaginatively and fittingly in the dramatic movements of God's triune life.[115]

---

114. Herman, "Foreword," *Broken Beauty*, x.
115. Hankey, *Old, Old Story*.

Conclusion

THIS PROJECT IS DESIGNED TO ADDRESS, IN PART, THE DELETERIOUS effects of contemporary emanations of perfect being theology that anesthetize God's beauty, stifle human imagining, and inhibit human flourishing. These effects perpetuate a gap in our understanding of God, dehumanize humanity, and hinder Christian worship, witness, and wisdom. To rectify these matters, in part, I offered a trinitarian account of God's beauty noting particularly how it artfully renews human imagining, which is essential not only for human being but also for creative expression and ethical action. The key idea, God's beauty-in-act, was understood through the risen Christ's actions in the Spirit by following a biblical trajectory found in the pattern of the Suffering Servant motif in the Old Testament and Christ's death and resurrection in the New. Hence, we saw how God's beauty-in-act radiates the splendor of his multifaceted, self-giving, dynamic love that draws perceivers into these divine patterns of living and being. These fitting movements of the risen Christ in the Spirit serve as the patterns that educate and form the imaginations of properly perceiving subjects, enabling them to envision how to perform their parts creatively and fittingly in God's drama of redemption. In doing so, human beings flourish as they jettison false identities and realities of their own making that are incommensurate with God's purpose found in Christ by the Spirit.

A Synopsis of the Argument

The first panel of the diptych structure of our argument examined whether the cross of Christ is a dilemma for classical theism. Relational theists, like Jürgen Moltmann, Wolfhart Pannenberg, Catherine Mowry LaCugna, argue that the cross is a dilemma that creates a metaphysical gap between who God is *ad extra* in Christ and who he is *in se*. They indict classical theism for smuggling in Greek philosophy—chiefly the doctrine of impassibility—through Augustine, Anselm, and Aquinas that construes God as unaffected and unconcerned about his creation. In doing so, the Gospel is rendered impotent as Christianity faces a dual crisis of identity and relevance in the modern world, unable to address the suffering of the twentieth century and the widening gulf between theology and life.

Relational theism's depictions of classical theism as well as their solution to the supposed dilemma revealed that perfect being theology appears to be the culprit rather than traditional classical theism per se, as we saw in the introduction. Regarding their depiction of classical theism, it seemed that relational theists have read the Christian tradition through the lenses of a Cartesian variety of perfect being theology. Yet, their critiques of *contemporary* renderings of classical theism may not be too far afield, since these renderings appear to have imbibed aspects of perfect being theology. Regarding their solution to the supposed dilemma, relational theists appeared to have exchanged an Enlightenment variety of perfect being theology for another, namely a panentheistic or process model. God is still a maximally perfect being, just a maximally and perfectly related one. Consequently, Feuerbach's critique, where all theology is anthropology, seemed fitting. Contemporary conceptions of perfect being theology also tended to mimic the precision of modern science and analytic philosophy, both of which inherently *restrict* reality to the true and/or the good while ignoring other aspects that may address, in part, some of the concerns of relational theism—namely God's beauty.

Retrieving an understanding of God's beauty for theological discourse, though, is a difficult endeavor. As we saw in chapter one, contemporary theology perceives beauty as having a checkered past unable to articulate the metaphysical realities of this world, much less God's divine being. Such omissions diminish our prayers and love of God and neighbor, thwart our *fruitio Dei* in serving others, and impede our fitting participation in God's drama of redemption. Although there are dangers and pitfalls to avoid, can we afford not to speak of God's beauty? Indeed we cannot. To do otherwise, Karl Barth maintains, is to perpetuate "a gap in our knowledge" of God.[1] Thus, any incorporation of beauty into theological discourse must avoid sentimental, nostalgic, and hedonistic motifs. Such rhetoric presumes a subjectivist ideal where beauty loses its ability to convey meaning beyond the realm of personal taste, relegating beauty to the ornamental and innocuous pleasant. Rather, any notion of God's beauty apt for theological discourse must privilege God's self-revelation attested to in Holy Scripture.

We turned in chapter two to converse with Hans Urs von Balthasar's theological aesthetics that seeks to counteract the effects of the

---

1. Barth, *CD* 2/1, 651–52.

God's Beauty-in-Act

cosmological and anthropological reductions that ensued from the *esse univocum* of Duns Scotus (Being as a Concept) and Meister Eckhart (Being as God). Balthasar addresses these issues by advocating a theological understanding of beauty that draws perceivers out of themselves and into a direct encounter with God's beauty. Such action elicits a response and demonstrates the interconnectedness between aesthetics and ethics—*the theological aesthetics of Christian living*.

We critically engaged the heart of Balthasar's theological aesthetics where he identifies Jesus Christ as *Herrlichkeit* and *Übergestalt*, christocentric terms that allude to Christ's singularity, God's divine freedom and trinitarian nature, and the inherent connections between creation and redemption. Yet, Balthasar blunts the force of these christological terms and their intended outcomes as he blurs the lines between justification and sanctification by predicating human ontology on God's act of creation rather than God's electing purpose to reconcile the world in and through Christ. Consequently, humanity maintains its relationship to God on the basis of the created order, even if it is a negative relationship. Such notions tend to minimize the destructive effects of sin on humanity and the created order, leaving open the possibility for human self-justification. Hence, Balthasar's desire to retain the viability of the created order, provisional as it may be, distinct from God's electing purpose and reconciling act in Christ seems to undermine the efficacy of God's glory because Christ as the Lord of Glory only *fulfills* or *perfects* the created order rather than *trans*forming or *re*forming it from the destruction of sin.

If we maintain, though, a redemptive-creative emphasis that privileges God's electing purpose and reconciling act in Christ (not only of human persons but also for the whole of creation), life is understood as a gift and human persons find their identity, hopeless as it may be, in the One who is life and gives his life on our behalf. Christ is our justification and not we ourselves. Moreover, human actions are not mere epiphenomena, for not only do we live and move and have our being in Christ but all things hold together in him (Acts 17:8; Col 1:17). Hence, Jesus Christ is Lord of covenant and creation, preserving the efficacy of God's glory and allowing us to employ *Herrlichkeit* and *Übergestalt* constructively as the theological loci of a trinitarian understanding of God's beauty.

In chapter three, the hinge that connects parts one and two, we developed a relevant biblical motif through the thematic patterning of the Suffering Servant in Jeremiah. Jeremiah's lamentations led to discerning Christ's "cry of dereliction" on the cross as a movement *toward* God rather

Conclusion

than a separation from him. We observed Jeremiah's obedience to deliver Yahweh's message to the people of Judah while enduring senseless suffering. Such obedience in the face of adversity demonstrated a deep wisdom, a counterintuitive wisdom, embodied in Jeremiah's laments as he cried out to Yahweh in agony while continuing to fulfill his calling faithfully. Although Yahweh did not always answer his prayers as expected, Jeremiah had *the privilege of presence* that allowed him to call upon Yahweh and sustained him in the midst of his suffering.

Having traced this thematic patterning in Jeremiah, we fleshed out this pattern by explicating the Christ-form in the New Testament, noting the prophetic mission, priestly dimension, and kingly status of Christ's unexpected fulfillment of what Israel could not as the Servant of Yahweh. We concluded our biblical trajectory with a focused theological exposition of Col 1—2:5 as we tried to understand why it was fitting for God to glorify his Son through his death and resurrection *without* glorifying suffering. We looked specifically at a cluster of themes—μυστήριον, δόξα, σοφία, and πάθημα—that Paul utilizes for articulating the performance knowledge necessary for living lives fitting of Jesus Christ. Lines connecting Christ's glory, wisdom, and redemptive-creative suffering begin to emerge, elucidating the contours of God's beauty. We were able, then, to suggest how to understand the relationship between God's glory and his beauty, noting that Sublime Glory speaks (2 Pet 1:16–21), instructing us to listen to his Son, Jesus Christ, who is incarnate Beauty in whom he delights. Consequently, we advocated a communicative God-world relationship whereby God's beauty is the form of his sublime glory that attracts, persuades, convinces, and draws us unto himself, imploring a response.

The second panel of the diptych structure of our argument, beginning with chapter four, conceptually expanded upon God's beauty-in-act through the notion of incarnate Beauty, which allowed us to explicate its objective, subjective, and relational components. We concluded that *God's beauty is the attunement or fittingness of the incarnate Son's actions in the Spirit to the Father's will that radiates the splendor of God's triune love.* As such, the incarnate Son, as the *expression* of God's beauty, makes God's beauty perceptible, for he is the *form* or image of the invisible God; and, the Holy Spirit, as the *impression* of God's beauty, communicates and affects the *splendor* of God's beauty in the cosmos and the church through his *Gestaltungskraft*. We also learned that our encounters with God's graciously and freely bestowed beauty evokes a variety of subjective responses, summarized in David Bentley Hart's suggestion, as "a desire for

God's Beauty-in-Act

the other that delights in the distance of otherness," which is seen in the perpetual self-giving love of God's triune life.[2] Yet, our proper acknowledgment God's beauty stems from the position of our heart—one, though, that possesses proclivities for itself rather than the other. What we need are *eyes of faith* that respond to God's objective revelation as movements of whole persons away from themselves toward God, "making *covenantal* contact" with him.[3] In doing so, we become beautiful as God's Spirit forms and fashions us into the image of his Son.

We ended chapter four with a brief case study of Balthasar's position on divine impassibility, critiquing his notion of divine eternal kenosis while intimating what we can learn of God's impassibility in light of his beauty. Balthasar's position seemed to equivocate on the meaning of kenosis as he moved beyond the biblical witness, ascribing the particular kenosis of the Son to all three Persons of the Trinity. As a result, he blurs the distinction between the immanent and the economic Trinity, that he so desires to maintain, seemingly rupturing the analogical relationship. Moreover, his positing of an infinite distance between each Person of the Trinity seems incomprehensible as he struggles to maintain the Godhead's unity of action. In an effort to bring a measure of perspicuity to the debate on divine impassibility, we appropriated the patristic distinction between *passiones* and *affectiones* to clarify God's emotive life. In doing so, divine compassion is the affective attitude that God eternally chooses to take toward his creatures such that he voluntarily takes on the form of a Suffering Servant even to the point of death while not being overcome by his suffering like we are when we experience *passiones*. Through such suffering, God acting in Christ in the power of the Spirit accomplishes redemption, bringing comfort, peace, and hope to our suffering existence. Such is God's beauty-in-act and the beauty of his compassion.

The final chapter explored how God's beauty in the act of Christ's redemptive-creative suffering transforms our imaginations (2 Cor 3:18) and implores imaginative and fitting participation in God's drama of redemption. Our participation in God's beauty, as we learned, is not ontological whereby our actions shape God in such a way that he has a future. Rather, his actions shape us as we participate fittingly in the dramatic patterns and movements of his triune life. One way in which we can participate in the mission of Christ in the Spirit is to participate in the beauty of the *Triplex Munus Christi*—the threefold office of Christ as Prophet, Priest, and King.

2. Hart, *Beauty of the Infinite*, 20.
3. Vanhoozer, *Drama of Doctrine*, 301.

Conclusion

These participatory actions transfigure our imaginations whereby God's self-presentation of his beauty in the *Gestalt Christi* possesses the *Ausbildungskraft* to transform our *Einbildungskraft* through the *Gestaltungskraft* of the Spirit.

Christ, as *Herrlichkeit*, has taken away the veil that shrouds our imaginations such that as we behold (κατοπτρίζω) his beauty we are transformed (μεταμορφόω) by the Spirit into Christ's likeness with an ever-increasing beauty (2 Cor 3:18). The performance of the Eucharist becomes essential as it serves to triangulate our actions in the present as we live in the presence of the risen Christ in the Spirit with reference to redemptive history yet in light of his eschatological glory. A robust imagination is necessary to integrate our remembering and envisioning—what *was* with what *is* and *is to come*, bringing a sense of meaning and understanding to the present so that we might fittingly and creatively participate in the dramatic movements of God's triune life.

As we live in the present, our ever-changing and demanding world requires the use of our Gospel-formed imaginations to flourish in an unjust world, necessitating that we improvise from the dramatic patterns and movements of the triune God attested to in Holy Scripture. When God's beauty draws us out of ourselves, our focus turns toward the other, enabling us to enter the situation of the other through the imagination as we seek to understand before being understood. Such poverty of spirit, such humility, is essential for tearing down walls that divide families, marriages, ethnicities, and socio-economic groups. These dramatic movements of Christ's creative and re-creative actions call us to a renewed sense of human creativity that voices creation's praise while attending to the brokenness of the world until Christ comes again to make all things new.

We have concluded a long journey through treacherous paths as we have attempted to avoid turning God's beauty into graven images of golden calves, on the one hand, and glorifying suffering on the other. We have endeavored to contribute to the ongoing discussion regarding the necessity of restoring beauty to her place within theological discourse to relieve theology from its unfortunate caricature as being formalistic, dull, lifeless, and boring. We have sought to dissolve the unfortunate and supposed divide between theology and the Christian life as we saw how God's beauty transforms our worship, witness, and wisdom. We have also contributed to the renewal of the imagination for living creative and fitting lives in accordance with the dramatic movements of God's triune life by linking the redemption of the imagination to God's beauty. Thus, as God's people perform their parts, they flourish and become who God designed them to be, thereby becoming a beautiful community and a community of the beautiful.

Tracing Further Lines of Inquiry

In all, we have sought to make good on the claim that God's beauty is the attunement or fittingness of the incarnate Son's actions in the Spirit to the Father's will that radiates God's glory and enraptures properly perceiving subjects, transforming the imagination through the shaping power of the Spirit and drawing them to participate in God's drama of redemption. We have come to this conclusion by grace—by way of the old rugged cross—although stained with divine blood, is beauty for all to see. Such is the deep and *counterintuitive* wisdom of incarnate Beauty, of the living and resurrected Christ. What might be some of the implications of such a claim for the interpretation of Scripture, other Christian doctrines, and the formation of the church?

The Implications of Form (and Content) for the Interpretation of Scripture

Richard Harries, in his work *Art and the Beauty of God*, aptly stresses the importance of form: "It is the form which distinguishes a painting from a splurge of paint, music from a cacophony of sound, a novel or play from a rambling anecdote. In them all, the details relate to one another and the whole in a way which achieves a satisfying unity."[4] Moreover, Barth provides us with a properly theological explanation for the importance of form and content: God "is the perfect content of the divine being, which also makes His form perfect" because "the form is necessary to the content, because it belongs to it. And in this form the perfect content, God Himself, shines out."[5] In short, Harries and Barth argue that *what* (content) is known about God cannot be dismembered from *how* (form) God reveals himself such that our understanding depends upon the unity of the various parts to the whole. As we begin to consider how God's beauty impacts biblical interpretative practices, these theological suppositions presume a theological ontology of Scripture that sees the Bible as part of God's triune

---

4. Harries, *Art and the Beauty of God*, 22.
5. Barth, *CD* 2/1, 659.

communicative economy, as part of his divine triune discourse, to communicate himself through himself to the world.

One implication of keeping God's beauty in mind when interpreting Scripture entails that genre plays a seminal part in communicating the meaning of a text rather than merely reducing a particular genre, say narrative, to a set of propositions in order to distill its meaning. There is more in Scripture than simply propositions. And it is this *more* that theology needs to account for without *reducing* it to propositions, for God reveals himself not as a proposition nor as a virtue but as a Person who calls us to follow him. To strip his communicative acts in Holy Scripture of these various forms is to muddle the content, distort the meaning of the text, and exalt one form over another. Additionally, the interpreter who considers God's beauty seeks to understand the various parts of Scripture in light of the whole. Such an approach understands a particular passage of Scripture within its immediate context as well as in it canonical context. More work needs to be done, though, on how each of these genres communicates God's truth, goodness, and beauty such that our theology reflects the nuances of these parts in light of the whole. In doing so, theology is less about organizing an airtight system of propositions and more about demonstrating the interconnectedness of doctrine that reveals the wisdom or performance knowledge necessary to live fittingly in the theater of God's glory, "for the church lives by the biblical narrative" and her "imagination catches fire in encountering that narrative rather than displacing it."[6]

The Implication of God's Beauty for Other Christian Doctrines

In chapter one, we discussed two contemporary trends in theology that fail to consider the objective reality of God's beauty for their discourse, namely aesthetic and amorphous theology. Aesthetic theology implicitly embraces a Romantic understanding of beauty by exploring the fruitfulness of categories like narrative, metaphor, poetry, the imagination, and other aesthetic concepts for theological discourse, all the while lacking commitment to some form of objective reality. In doing so, aesthetic theology produces a plurality, *ad infinitum*, of theological discourses deficient in expressing the harmony of God's self-revelation attested to in Holy Scripture. Amorphous theology, to the extent that it subscribes to the

---

6. Stafford, "Imagination and Scripture: Seeing the Unseen," 165. Though the quotation uses the phrase "biblical narrative," the entire compendium of biblical genres is necessary not only for the life of the church but to map reality in such a way that we see from a variety of vistas.

methodology or ethos of modern science and analytic philosophy, seeks to articulate a titanium proof system that results in the atomization of the knowledge of God. Such theologies ensue from commitments to articulating the true and/or the good without considering their other sibling, namely beauty.

That being the case, one implication of God's beauty for Christian doctrine leads to its integrative unity or its simple-complex reality such that what we say about one area of theology has repercussions for other areas. No doctrine is an island. What we say about God affects what we say about Scripture; what we say about eschatology affects how we understand creation; what we say about creation affects our understanding of redemption; and, so on. Moreover, there is a familial resemblance between a plurality of theologies such that each voice harmoniously resounds God's self-revelation attested to in Holy Scripture. In other words, each theology committed to explicating the subject of theology, namely the being and acts of the triune God, plays its part in the grand symphony that produces a rich harmony between a plurality of voices akin to the four canonical Gospels of the New Testament that witness to the life of Christ. The Gospel is our control story that frames our thinking about God, the world, and ourselves. Thus, our theological discourse should trend toward *perfect-fit theology* rather than perfect being theology as we seek to attune our theological discourse with God's divine triune discourse attested to in Holy Scripture.

The Implications of Sacred Memory and the Imagination for the Bildung *of the Church*

C. S. Lewis once remarked, "Reason is the natural order of truth; but imagination is the organ of meaning."[7] How we make sense of the world depends on many factors, but one in particular is our self-understanding. The Protestant Church, though, is often confused about her identity, denigrating the imagination and mixing it with secular ideologies as we discussed in chapter one. Paul Ricoeur, in his *Memory, History, and Forgetting*, suggests memory to be constitutive of our identity and thus formative of our interpersonal and social actions.[8] Yet, connecting who we are (identity) with what we do (actions) depends upon our ability to synthesize various parts into a collective whole. This ability is the active component

---

7. Lewis, "Bluspels and Flalansferes," 265.
8. Ricoeur, *Memory, History, and Forgetting*.

of the imagination as we learned in chapter five. Memory and the imagination function with significant overlap. Memory, in part, recalls what *was* while the imagination envisions what *is* and *can be*, bringing a sense of meaning and understanding to the present. Both, therefore, are essential to the formation of the human beings.

One implication of God's beauty for the formation of the church stems from the *Gestaltungskraft* of the Holy Spirit to form and fashion God's beauty into the life of the church such that she becomes the beautiful bride God intends for her to be. Part of this formative process involves the symbolic, poetic, and metaphoric images and narrative accounts that require the imagination to understand the reality communicated through these forms. These images serve to fashion a *sacred memory* (i.e., *sacra memoria*), reminding us of God's communicative actions on our behalf (e.g., God's redemption of Israel from Egypt, Christ's ordination of the sacraments, etc.). As we learned in chapter five, our performance of the Eucharist—to do this in remembrance of Christ—serves to triangulate our actions in the present as we live in the presence of the risen Christ in the Spirit with reference to redemptive history yet in light of his eschatological glory. These images, though, are not to remain within our collective memory as a reminder of some sentimental past; rather, they should evoke fitting and creative action within God's drama of redemption. Thus, to see how sacred memory leads to fitting action, a Gospel-formed *imagination* is necessary to integrate what *was* with what *is* and *is to come*.

These closing remarks regarding the implications of God's beauty for theology and life are woefully underdeveloped and are merely suggestive of the possibilities and significance for doing so. Moreover, I was unfortunately only able to intimate in passing throughout the book the implications of God's beauty for human flourishing. My scant remarks are not indicative of the importance God's beauty has for re-humanizing humanity as the imagination becomes integral to creative expression and ethical action in an unjust world. Hence, when human beings jettison false identities and fictitious realities of their own making and fittingly and creatively participate in the movements of God's dramatic triune life, humanity flourishes in ways commensurate with Christ's actions in the Spirit. Through these sketches, though, I have tried to capture the imagination, intimating at the fittingness of God's beauty-in-act as it radiates its splendor into every corner of our existence.

Bibliography

Aalen, Sverre. "Glory." In *The New International Dictionary of New Testament Theology*, 4 vols., edited by Collin Brown, 2:44–48. Grand Rapids: Zondervan, 1986.
Addison, Joseph. "Pleasures of the Imagination." In *The Spectator*, 3 vols., edited by Henry Morley, 2:411–16, 3:417–21. London: Routledge, 1891.
Aertsen, Jan. "Beauty in the Middle Ages: A Forgotten Transcendental?" *Medieval Philosophy and Theology* 1 (1991) 68–97.
Alston, William. *Perceiving God: The Epistemology of Religious Experience*. Ithaca, NY: Cornell University Press, 1991.
Anderson, William. *Cecil Collins: The Quest for the Great Happiness*. London: Barrie & Jenkins, 1990.
Anselm. *Cur Deus homo*. Translated by Janet Fairweather. In *Anselm of Canterbury: The Major Works*, edited by Brian Davies and G. R. Evans. Oxford: Oxford University Press, 1998.
———. *A New Interpretive Translation of St. Anselm's Monologion and Proslogion*. Translated by Jasper Hopkins. Minneapolis: A. J. Banning, 1987.
Aquinas, Thomas. *De ente et essentia*. Translated by Joseph Bobik. South Bend, IN: Notre Dame University Press, 1965.
———. *Quaestiones disputatae de veritate*. 3 vols. Translated by R. W. Mulligan et al. Chicago: H. Regnery Co., 1952–1954.
———. *Summa theologica*. 5 vols. Translated by the Fathers of the English Dominican Province. Westminster, MD: Christian Classics, 1981.
———. *Thomas Aquinas's Earliest Treatment of the Divine Essence: Scriptum super libros Sententiarum Book I, Distinction* 8. Translated by E. M. Macierowski. Binghamton, NY: Binghamton University, 1998.
Aristotle. *Metaphysics*. Translated by W. D. Ross. In *Wadsworth Philosophy Source* 3.0, CD-ROM, edited by Daniel Kolak. New York: Wadsworth.
———. *Poetics*. Translated by S. H. Butcher. In *Wadsworth Philosophy Source* 3.0, CD-ROM, edited by Daniel Kolak. New York: Wadsworth.
Augustine. *City of God*. Translated by Marcus Dods et al. In *Wadsworth Philosophy Source* 3.0, CD-ROM, edited by Daniel Kolak. New York: Wadsworth.
———. *The Confessions*. Translated by Maria Boulding. The Works of Saint Augustine: A Translation for the 21st Century I/1. Hyde Park, NY: New City Press, 1997.
———. *Expositions on the Book of Psalms by Augustine, Bishop of Hippo*. Translated by members of the English Church. A Library of the Holy Catholic Church 2. Oxford, 1848.
———. *On the Trinity*. Translated by Arthur W. Haddan. Nicene and Post-Nicene Fathers 3. MA: Hendrickson, 1999.
Austin, John L. "A Plea for Excuses." In *Philosophical Papers*, 3rd ed., edited by J. O. Urmson and G. J. Warnock, 175–204. Oxford: Oxford University Press, 1979.

Bibliography

Avis, Paul. *God and the Creative Imagination: Metaphor, Symbol and Myth in Religion and Theology*. London: Routledge, 1999.

Ayres, Lewis. "Augustine, Christology, and God as Love: An Introduction to the Homilies on 1 John." In *Nothing Greater, Nothing Better: Theological Essays on the Love of God*, edited by Kevin J. Vanhoozer, 67–93. Grand Rapids: Eerdmans, 2001.

———. *Nicaea and Its Legacy: An Approach to Fourth-century Trinitarian Theology*. Oxford: Oxford University Press, 2004.

Bacon, Francis. *The Advancement of Learning*. London: Lowe & Brydone, 1915.

———. *The New Organon and Related Writings*. New York: Bobbs-Merrill, 1960.

———. *Selected Writings*. New York: Random House, 1955.

Balentine, Samuel E. "Jeremiah, Prophet of Prayer." *Review and Expositor* 78 (Summer 1981) 331–44.

Balthasar, Hans Urs von. "Christian Prayer." *Communio* 5 (Spring 1978) 15–22.

———. *Creator Spirit*. Translated by Brian McNeil. Vol. 3 of *Explorations in Theology*. San Francisco: Ignatius, 1993.

———. "Current Trends in Catholic Theology." *Communio* 5 (1978) 77–85.

———. "Death Is Swallowed Up by Life." *Communio* 14 (Spring 1987) 49–54.

———. "Die Armut Christi." *Internationale katholische Zeitschrift* 15 (1986) 385–87.

———. *Epilogue*. Translated by Edward T. Oakes. San Francisco: Ignatius, 2004.

———. "Eternal Life and the Human Condition." *Communio* 18 (Spring 1991) 4–23.

———. *The Glory of the Lord: A Theological Aesthetics*. 7 vols. Edited by Joseph Fessio, and John Riches. Translated by Erasmo Leiva-Merikakis et al. San Francisco: Ignatius, 1982–1991.

———. "God Is His Own Exegete." *Communio* 4 (Winter 1986) 280–87.

———. *The God Question and Modern Man*. Translated by Hilda Graef. New York: Seabury Press, 1967.

———. *Heart of the World*. Translated by Erasmo S. Leiva. San Francisco: Ignatius, 1979.

———. *Love Alone Is Credible*. Translated by D. C. Schindler. San Francisco: Ignatius, 2004.

———. *My Work: In Retrospect*. No Translator. San Francisco: Ignatius, 1993.

———. *Mysterium Paschale: The Mystery of Easter*. Translated by Aidan Nichols. San Francisco: Ignatius, 1990.

———. *Prayer*. Translated by Graham Harrison. San Francisco: Ignatius, 1986.

———. *Spouse of the Word*. No Translator. Vol. 2 of *Explorations in Theology*. San Francisco: Ignatius, 1993.

———. *Theo-Drama: Theological Dramatic Theory*. 5 vols. Translated by Graham Harrison. San Francisco: Ignatius, 1989–1998.

———. *Theo-Logic*. 3 vols. Translated by Adrian J. Walker. San Francisco, Ignatius, 2000–2005.

———. "Theology and Aesthetic." *Communio* 8 (Spring 1981) 62–71.

———. "Theology and Holiness." *Communio* 14 (1987) 341–50.

———. *A Theology of History*. No Translator. New York: Sheed & Ward, 1963.

———. *The Theology of Karl Barth: Exposition and Interpretation*. Translated by Edward T. Oakes. San Francisco: Ignatius, 1992.

———. "Toward a Theology of Christian Prayer." *Communio* 12 (1985) 245–57.

———. "Weltliche Schönheit und göttliche Herrlichkeit." *Internationale katholische Zeitschrift* 11 (1982) 513–17.

———. *The Word Made Flesh*. Translated by A. V. Littledale and Alexander Dru. Vol. 1 of *Explorations in Theology*. San Francisco: Ignatius, 1989.

Baltzer, Klaus. *Deutro-Isaiah: A Commentary on Isaiah 40-55*. Hermeneia. Translated by Margaret Kohl. Minneapolis: Fortress, 2001.

Barnes, Michel. "Augustine in Contemporary Trinitarian Theology." *Theological Studies* 56 (1995) 237–50.

Barth, Karl. *The Doctrine of Creation*. Translated by J. W. Edwards et al. Vol. 3/1 of *Church Dogmatics*. Edited by Geoffrey W. Bromiley and Thomas F. Torrance. New York: T. & T. Clark, 1958; New York: T. & T. Clark, 2004.

———. *The Doctrine of Creation*. Translated by J. W. Edwards et al. Vol. 3/2 of *Church Dogmatics*. Edited by Geoffrey W. Bromiley and Thomas F. Torrance. New York: T. & T. Clark, 1958; New York: T. & T. Clark, 2004.

———. *The Doctrine of God*. Translated by T. H. L Parker et al. Vol. 2/1 of *Church Dogmatics*. Edited by Geoffrey W. Bromiley and Thomas F. Torrance. New York: T. & T. Clark, 1956; New York: T. & T. Clark, 2004.

———. *The Doctrine of Reconciliation*. Translated by Geoffrey W. Bromiley. Vol. 4/1 of *Church Dogmatics*. Edited by Geoffrey W. Bromiley and Thomas F. Torrance. New York: T. & T. Clark, 1956; New York: T. & T. Clark, 2004.

———. *The Doctrine of the Word of God*. Translated by Geoffrey W. Bromiley. Vol. 1/1 of *Church Dogmatics*. Edited by Geoffrey W. Bromiley and Thomas F. Torrance. New York: T. & T. Clark, 1956; New York: T. & T. Clark, 2004.

———. *The Holy Spirit and the Christian Life*. Translated by R. Birch Hoyle. London: Frederick Muller, 1938.

Bartholomew, Craig G., and Michael W. Goheen. *The Drama of Scripture: Finding our Place in the Biblical Story*. Grand Rapids: Baker Academic, 2004.

Basil. *Letters and Selected Works*. Translated by Bloomfield Jackson. Nicene and Post-Nicene Fathers 9. Peabody, MA: Hendrickson, 1994.

Bauerschmidt, Frederick. "Aesthetics: The Theological Sublime." In *Radical Orthodoxy: A New Theology*, edited by J. K. A. Smith, 201–19. London: Routledge, 1999.

Baumgardner, Walter. *Die Klagedichte des Jeremia*. Giessen: Topelmann, 1917.

Baumgarten, Alexander. *Aesthetica*. Hildesheim, NY: G. Olms, 1970.

———. *Reflection on Poetry*. Translated by Karl Aschenbrenner and William B. Holther. Los Angeles: University of California Press, 1954.

Beardsley, Monroe C. *Aesthetics: From Classical Greece to the Present*. Tuscaloosa: Alabama University Press, 1966.

———. "Beauty Since the Nineteenth Century." In *Dictionary of the History of Ideas*, edited by Philip Wiener, 1:207–14. New York: Scribner, 1974.

Begbie, Jeremy. "Beauty, Sentimentality, and the Arts." In *The Beauty of God: Theology and the Arts*, edited by Daniel J. Treier et al., 19–44. Downers Grove, IL: IVP Academic, 2007.

———. "Created Beauty." In *The Beauty of God: Theology and the Arts*, edited by Daniel J. Treier, et al., 25–31. Downers Grove, IL: IVP Academic, 2007.

———. *Voicing Creation's Praise: Towards a Theology of the Arts*. Edinburgh: T. & T. Clark, 1991.

Bellinger, Jr., William H., and William R. Farmer, editors. *Jesus and the Suffering Servant: Isaiah 53 and Christian Origins*. Eugene, OR: Wipf & Stock, 1998.

Bibliography

Benner, Drayton C. "Augustine and Karl Rahner on the Relationship between the Immanent Trinity and the Economic Trinity." *International Journal of Systematic Theology* 9 (2007) 24–38.

Benson, Bruce E. "Call Forwarding: Improvising the Response to the Call of Beauty." In *The Beauty of God: Theology and the Arts*, edited by Daniel J. Treier, et al., 70–83. Downers Grove, IL: InterVarsity, 2007.

Bernstein, J. M. *Fate of Art: Aesthetic Alienation from Kant to Derrida and Adorno*. University Park, PA: Pennsylvania State University Press, 1992.

Betz, John. "Beyond the Sublime: The Aesthetics of the Analogy of Being (Part Two)." *Modern Theology* 22 (January 2006) 12–20.

Blenkinsopp, Joseph. *Isaiah 40-55: A New Translation with Introduction and Commentary*. Anchor Bible Commentary 19. New York: Doubleday, 2000.

Bockmuehl, Markus N. A. *Revelation and Mystery in Ancient Judaism and Pauline Christianity*. Tübingen: Mohr Siebeck, 1990.

Bonaventure. *The Soul's Journey into God*. Translated by Ewert Cousins. New York: Paulist, 1978.

———. *The Tree of Life*. Translated by Ewert Cousins. New York: Paulist, 1978.

Bora, C. M. *The Romantic Imagination*. New York: Galaxy, 1961.

Bornkamm, Günter. "μυστήριον." In *Theological Dictionary of the New Testament*, 10 vols., edited by Gerhard Kittel and Gerhard Friedrich, 4:820. Grand Rapids: Eerdmans, 1964–1976.

Bray, Gerald. "Has the Christian Doctrine of God Been Corrupted by Greek Philosophy?" In *God Under Fire: Modern Scholarship Reinvents God*, edited by Douglas S. Huffman and Eric L. Johnson, 105–18. Grand Rapids: Zondervan, 2002.

Bredin, Hugh, and Liberato Santoro-Brienza. *Philosophies of Art and Beauty: Introducing Aesthetics*. Edinburgh: Edinburgh University Press, 2000.

Brierley, Michael. "Naming a Quiet Revolution: The Panentheistic Turn in Modern Theology." In *In Whom We Live and Move and Have Our Being: Panentheistic Reflections on God's Presence in a Scientific World*, edited by Philip Clayton and Arthur Peacocke, 1–18. Grand Rapids: Eerdmans, 2004.

Bright, John. "A Prophet's Lament and Its Answer: Jeremiah 15:10–21." *Interpretation* 28 (January 1974) 59–74.

Bronowski, Jacob. *The Origins of Knowledge and Imagination*. New Haven, CT: Yale University Press, 1978.

Brotton, Jerry. *The Renaissance: A Very Short Introduction*. Oxford: Oxford University Press, 2006.

Brown, Colin, editor. *The New International Dictionary of New Testament Theology*. 4 vols. Grand Rapids: Zondervan, 1986.

Brown, Frank B. "The Beauty of Hell: Anselm on God's Eternal Design." *The Journal of Religion* 73 (1993) 329–56.

———. *Religious Aesthetics: A Theological Study of Making and Meaning*. Princeton: Princeton University Press, 1989.

Brown, Montague. *Restoration of Reason: The Eclipse and Recovery of Truth, Goodness, and Beauty*. Grand Rapids: Baker Academic, 2006.

Brubaker, Leslie, and John Haldon. *Byzantium in the Iconoclast Era: An Annotated Survey*. Aldershot, England: Ashgate, 2001.

Bruce, F. F. *Ephesians and Colossians*. The New International Commentary on the New Testament, edited by Ned Stonehouse. Grand Rapids: Eerdmans, 1957.
Brueggemann, Walter. "The Book of Jeremiah: Portrait of a Prophet." *Interpretation* 37 (1983) 130–45.
———. "From Hurt to Joy, From Death to Life." *Interpretation* 28 (January 1974) 3–19.
Bychkov, Oleg V., and James Fodor, editors. *Theological Aesthetics After von Balthasar*. Aldershot, England: Ashgate, 2008.
Calvin, John. *Commentary on the Book of the Prophet Isaiah*. Translated by William Pringle. Edinburgh: Calvin Translation Society, 1853.
———. *The Institutes of the Christian Religion*. 2 vols. Translated by Ford Lewis Battles. Philadelphia: Westminster, 1960.
Canlis, Julie. "Calvin, Osiander and Participation in God." *International Journal of Systematic Theology* 6 (2004) 169–84.
Caputo, John, editor. *Deconstruction in a Nutshell: A Conversation with Jacques Derrida*. New York: Fordham University Press, 1997.
Carpenter, Eugene. "עבד." In *New International Dictionary of Old Testament Theology and Exegesis*, 5 vols., edited by Willem VanGemeren, 3:304–9. Grand Rapids: Zondervan, 1997.
Carrol, Robert P. *From Chaos to Covenant, Prophecy in the Book of Jeremiah*. New York: Crossroad, 1981.
Carruthers, Mary. *Book of Memory: A Study of Memory in Medieval Culture*. Cambridge: Cambridge University Press, 1990.
———. *Craft of Thought: Meditation, Rhetoric, and the Making of Images, 400–1200*. Cambridge: Cambridge University Press, 1998.
Carson, Donald A. "Mystery and Fulfillment: Toward a More Comprehensive Paradigm of Paul's Understanding of the Old and the New." In *The Paradoxes of Paul*, vol. 2 of *Justification and Variegated Nomism*, edited by Donald A. Carson et al., 393–436. Tübingen: Mohr Siebeck, 2004.
Castelo, Daniel. "Moltmann's Dismissal of Divine Impassibility: Warranted?" *Scottish Journal of Theology* 61 (2008) 396–407.
Chaplin, Adrienne Dengerink. "The Invisible and the Sublime: From Participation to Reconciliation." In *Radical Orthodoxy and the Reformed Tradition: Creation, Covenant, and Participation*, edited by James K. A. Smith and James H. Olthuis, 89–106. Grand Rapids: Baker Academic, 2005.
Charry, Ellen. "The Soteriological Importance of the Divine Perfections." In *God the Holy Trinity: Reflections on Christian Faith and Practice*, edited by Timothy George, 129–48. Grand Rapids: Baker Academic, 2006.
Chia, Roland. "Theological Aesthetics or Aesthetic Theology? Some Reflections on the Theology of Hans Urs von Balthasar." *Scottish Journal of Theology* 49 (1996) 75–95.
Chrysostom, Saint John. *On the Incomprehensible Nature of God*. Translated by Paul W. Harkins. The Fathers of the Church 72. Washington, DC: Catholic University of America Press, 1984.
Clark, David. *To Know and Love God*. Wheaton, IL: Crossway, 2003.
Clarke, W. Norris. *The One and the Many: A Contemporary Thomistic Metaphysics*. South Bend, IN: Notre Dame University Press, 2006.
Clayton, Philip D. *The Problem of God in Modern Thought*. Grand Rapids: Eerdmans, 2000.

Bibliography

Clowney, Edmund. "Living Art: Christian Experience and the Arts." In *God and Culture: Essays in Honor of Carl F. H. Henry*, edited by Donald A. Carson and John D. Woodbridge, 235–53. Grand Rapids: Eerdmans, 1993.

Coffey, David M. "A Proper Mission of the Holy Spirit." *Theological Studies* 47 (1986) 227–50.

Cole, Graham A. *He Who Gives Life: The Doctrine of the Holy Spirit*. Wheaton, IL: Crossway, 2007.

———. "The Living God: Anthropomorphic or Anthropopathic?" *The Reformed Theological Journal* 59 (April 2000) 16–27.

———. "Towards a New Metaphysic of the Exodus." *The Reformed Theological Review* 42 (1983) 75–84.

Cooper, John. *Panentheism: The Other God of the Philosophers*. Grand Rapids: Baker Academic, 2006.

Coulton, G. *Art and the Reformation*. Cambridge: Cambridge University Press, 1953.

Crain, Chris T. "Turning the Beast into a Beauty: Towards an Evangelical Theological Aesthetics." *Presbyterian* 29 (Spring 2003) 27–41.

Creel, Richard. *Divine Impassibility*. Cambridge: Cambridge University Press, 1986.

———. "Immutability and Impassibility." In *A Companion to Philosophy of Religion*, edited by Philip Quinn, 313–22. Oxford: Blackwell, 1997.

Crisp, Oliver. "On the Fittingness of the Virgin Birth." *Heythrop Journal* 49 (2008) 197–221.

Cullmann, Oscar. *The Christology of the New Testament*. Translated by Shirley C. Guthrie and Charles A. M. Hall. London: SCM, 1963.

Cunningham, David. "Participation as a Trinitarian Virtue: Challenging the Current 'Relational' Consensus." *Toronto Journal of Theology* 14 (1998) 7–26.

Davidson, Jo Ann. "Toward a Theology of Beauty: A Biblical Aesthetic." PhD diss., Trinity Evangelical Divinity School, 2000.

Davies, Oliver. *Living Beauty: Ways of Mystical Prayer*. London: Darton Longman & Todd, 1990.

———. *A Theology of Compassion: Metaphysics of Difference and the Renewal of Tradition*. Grand Rapids: Eerdmans, 2003.

Delattre, Roland A. *Beauty and Sensibility in the Thought of Jonathan Edwards: An Essay in Aesthetics and Theological Ethics*. 1968. Reprint, Eugene, OR: Wipf & Stock, 2006.

Dennis, John. *The Grounds of Criticism in Poetry*. In *The Critical Works of John Dennis*, edited by E. N. Hooker. Baltimore: Johns Hopkins Press, 1937.

———. *A Large Account of the Taste in Poetry and the Degeneration of It*. In *The Critical Works of John Dennis*, edited by E. N. Hooker. Baltimore: Johns Hopkins Press, 1937.

Derrida, Jacques. "Structure, Sign, and Play in the Discourse of the Human Sciences." In *The Structuralist Controversy: The Languages of Criticism and the Sciences of Man*, edited by Richard Macksey and Eugenio Donato, 247–64. Baltimore: Johns Hopkins University Press, 1972.

———. *Writing and Difference*. Translated by Alan Bass. Chicago: University of Chicago Press, 1978.

Descartes, René. *Discourse on the Method for Rightly for Rightly Conducting the Reason and Seeking the Truth in the Sciences*. Translated by Elizabeth Haldane. In *Wadsworth Philosophy Source* 3.0, CD-ROM, edited by Daniel Kolak. New York: Wadsworth.

———. *Meditations on First Philosophy: In which the Existence of God and the Distinction of the Soul from the Body are Demonstrated*. Translated by Elizabeth Haldane. In *Wadsworth Philosophy Source* 3.0, CD-ROM, edited by Daniel Kolak. New York: Wadsworth.

Deterding, Paul E. *Colossians: A Theological Exposition of Sacred Scripture*. Saint Louis: Concordia, 2003.

DeYoung, Kevin. "Divine Impassibility and the Passion of Christ in the Book of Hebrews." *Westminster Theological Journal* 68 (2006) 41–50.

Dickens, Charles. *Hard Times*. Oxford: Oxford University Press, 2008.

Dickens, W. T. *Hans Urs von Balthasar's Theological Aesthetics: A Model for Post-Critical Biblical Interpretation*. South Bend, IN: University of Notre Dame Press, 2003.

Dillenberger, John. *A Theology of Artistic Sensibilities: The Visual Arts and the Church*. New York: Crossroads, 1986.

Dixon, Thomas. *From Passion to Emotions: The Creation of a Secular Psychological Category*. Cambridge: Cambridge University Press, 2003.

Dodaro, Robert, and George Lawless, editors. *Augustine and His Critics*. New York: Routledge, 2000.

Donnelly, Veronica. *Saving Beauty: Form as the Key to Balthasar's Christology*. Oxford: Peter Lang, 2007.

Dostoyevsky, Fyodor. *The Idiot*. Translated by Richard Pevear and Larissa Volokhonsky. New York: Everyman's Library, 2001.

Dreyfus, Hubert L., and Mark A. Wrathall, editors. *A Companion to Heidegger*. Oxford: Blackwell, 2005.

Dunn, James D. G. *The Epistles to the Colossians and to Philemon: A Commentary on the Greek Text*. Grand Rapids: Eerdmans, 1996.

Dupré, Louis. "The Glory of the Lord: Hans Urs von Balthasar's Theological Aesthetic." *Communio* 16 (Fall 1989) 384–412.

Dyrness, William. "Aesthetics in the Old Testament: Beauty in Context." *Journal of the Evangelical Theological Society* 28 (December 1985) 421–32.

———. *Visual Faith: Art, Theology, and Worship in Dialogue*. Grand Rapids: Baker Academic, 2001.

Eco, Umberto. *The Aesthetics of Thomas Aquinas*. Translated by Hugh Bredin. Cambridge: Harvard University Press, 1988.

Edwards, Jonathan. *Discourse on the Trinity*. Vol. 21 of *The Works of Jonathan Edwards*, edited by Sang H. Lee. New Haven: Yale University Press, 2003.

———. *The Nature of True Virtue*. Ann Arbor: University of Michigan Press, 1960.

———. *A Treatise Concerning Religious Affections*. Vol. 2 of *The Works of Jonathan Edwards*, edited by John E. Smith. New Haven, CT: Yale University Press, 1959.

Eisenberg, Nancy. "Empathy and Sympathy." In *Handbook of Emotions*, edited by Michael Lewis and Jeannette Haviland-Jones, 677–92. New York: Guilford, 2000.

Elliot, Mark, editor. *Isaiah 40–66*. Vol. 11 of *Ancient Christian Commentary on Scripture*. Downer's Grove, IL: InterVarsity, 2007.

Evdokimov, Paul. *The Art of the Icon: A Theology of Beauty*. Redondo Beach, CA: Oakwood, 1990.

Farley, Edward. *Deep Symbols: Their Postmodern Effacement and Reclamation*. Valley Forge, PA: Trinity, 1996.

———. *Faith and Beauty: A Theological Aesthetic*. Aldershot, England: Ashgate, 2001.

Ferguson, Sinclair. *The Holy Spirit*. Downers Grove, IL: InterVarsity, 1996.

Bibliography

Feuerbach, Ludwig. *The Essence of Christianity*. Translated by George Eliot. New York: Harper & Row, 1957.

Fiddes, Paul. *The Creative Suffering of God*. Oxford: Oxford University Press, 1992.

———. *Participating in God: A Pastoral Doctrine of the Trinity*. Louisville: Westminster John Knox, 2000.

———. "Participating in the Trinity." *Perspectives in Religions Studies* 33 (Fall 2006) 375–91.

Finan, Barbara A. "Review Symposium: God for Us." *Horizons* 20 (1993) 134–35.

Franks, Christopher. "The Simplicity of the Living God: Aquinas, Barth, and Some Philosophers." *Modern Theology* 21 (April 2005) 275–300.

Fretheim, Terence E. *The Suffering God: An Old Testament Perspective*. Philadelphia: Fortress, 1984.

Gallagher, Daniel. "The Analogy of Beauty and the Limits of Theological Aesthetics." *Theandros: An Online Journal of Orthodox Christian Theology and Philosophy* 3 (Spring/Summer, 2006). No pages. Online: http://www.theandros.com/beauty.html.

García-Rivera, Alejandro. *The Community of the Beautiful: A Theological Aesthetics*. Collegville, MN: Liturgical, 1999.

Garrett, Stephen M. "Beauty." In *Encyclopedia of Christian Civilization*, edited by George T. Kurian, 1:218–20. Oxford: Blackwell, 2011.

———. "Beauty and the Baptists: The Significance for Recovering a Theology of Beauty." In *Tradition and the Baptist Academy*, edited by Roger Ward, 104–24. Bletchley, England: Paternoster, 2011.

———. "God's Beauty-in-Act: An Artful Renewal of the Imagination." *International Journal of Systematic Theology*. Online: http://onlinelibrary.wiley.com/doi/10.1111/j.1468-2400.2012.00650.x/full.

———. "Theological Aesthetics." In *Encyclopedia of Christian Civilization*, edited by George T. Kurian, 4:2344–46. Oxford: Blackwell, 2011.

Gavrilyuk, Paul. *The Suffering of the Impassible God: The Dialectics of Patristic Thought*. Oxford: Oxford University Press, 2004.

Gerth, Hans, and C. Wright Mills, editors. *From Max Weber: Essays in Sociology*. Oxford: Oxford University Press, 1946.

Gilson, Étienne. *Being and Some Philosophers*. Toronto: Pontifical Institute of Medieval Studies, 1952.

———. "The Forgotten Transcendental: *Pulchrum*." In *Elements of Christian Philosophy*, 159–63. New York: Doubleday, 1960.

Goetz, Ronald. "The Suffering God: The Rise of the New Orthodoxy." *Christian Century* 103 (April 1986) 385–89.

Goldingay, John. *God's Prophet, God's Servant: A Study in Jeremiah and Isaiah 40–55*. Carlisle, England: Paternoster, 1994.

Goodall, Lawrence. "Hans Urs von Balthasar: A Respectful Critique." *Pro Ecclesia* 8 (Fall 1999) 423–36.

Goppelt, Leonhard. *TYPOS: The Typological Interpretation of the Old Testament in the New*. Translated by Donald H. Madvig. Grand Rapids: Eerdmans, 1982.

Gordley, Matthew E. *The Colossian Hymn in Context: An Exegesis in Light of Jewish and Greco-Roman Hymnic and Epistolary Conventions*. Tübingen: Mohr Siebeck, 2007.

Gouwens, David J. *Kierkegaard's Dialectic of the Imagination*. New York: Peter Lang, 1989.

———. "Kierkegaard on the Ethical Imagination." *The Journal of Religious Ethics* 10 (1982) 204–20.
Graham, Gordon. "Liturgy as Drama." *Theology Today* 64 (2007) 71–79.
———. *Philosophy of the Arts: An Introduction to Aesthetics*. London: Routledge, 1997.
Green, Garrett. *Imagining God: Theology and the Religious Imagination*. Grand Rapids: Eerdmans, 1989.
Gregor, Brian. "Thinking Through Kierkegaard's Anti-Climacus: Art, Imagination, and Imitation." *Heythrop Journal* 50 (May 2009) 448–65.
Gregory of Nyssa. *Ascetical Works: On Perfection*. Translated by Virginia W. Callahan. In *The Fathers of the Church*, edited by Ludwig Schopp. Washington, DC: Catholic University of America Press, 1967.
———. *Ascetical Works: On Virginity*. Translated by Virginia W. Callahan. In *The Fathers of the Church*, edited by Ludwig Schopp. Washington, DC: Catholic University of America Press, 1967.
———. *Life of Moses*. Translated by Abraham J. Malherebe and Everett Ferguson. New York: Paulist, 1978.
Grenz, Stanley. *Rediscovering the Triune God: The Trinity in Contemporary Theology*. Minneapolis: Fortress, 2004.
Grogan, Geoffrey. "A Biblical Theology of the Love of God." In *Nothing Greater, Nothing Better: Theological Essays on the Love of God*, edited by Kevin J. Vanhoozer, 47–66. Grand Rapids: Eerdmans, 2001.
Grudem, Wayne. *Systematic Theology: An Introduction to Biblical Doctrine*. Grand Rapids: Zondervan, 1994.
Gunton, Colin. *Act and Being: Towards a Theology of Divine Attributes*. Grand Rapids: Eerdmans, 2002.
———. "Augustine, The Trinity, and the Theological Crisis of the West." *Scottish Theological Journal* 43 (1990) 33–58.
———. *The One, The Three, and the Many*. Cambridge: Cambridge University Press, 1993.
———. *The Promise of Trinitarian Theology*. 2nd ed. London: T. & T. Clark, 2003.
———. "Review of *God for Us*." *Scottish Journal of Theology* 47 (1994) 136–37.
Guthrie, Donald. *New Testament Theology*. Downers Grove, IL: InterVarsity, 1981.
Halík, Tomáš. *Patience with God: The Story of Zacchaeus Continuing in Us*. New York: Doubleday, 2009.
Hankey, Arabella. *The Old, Old Story: In Two Parts*. London: William MacIntosh, 1875.
Harries, Richard. *Art and the Beauty of God: A Christian Understanding*. London: Continuum, 2005.
Harris, Murray. *Colossians and Philemon*. Grand Rapids: Eerdmans, 1991.
Harrison, Carol. *Beauty and Revelation in the Thought of St. Augustine*. Oxford: Clarendon, 1992.
Hart, David Bentley. *The Beauty of the Infinite: The Aesthetics of Christian Truth*. Grand Rapids: Eerdmans, 2003.
Hart, Kevin. "Without Derrida." *The European Legacy* 12 (2007) 419–29.
Hart, Trevor. "How Do We Define the Nature of God's Love?" In *Nothing Greater, Nothing Better: Theological Essays on the Love of God*, edited by Kevin J. Vanhoozer, 94–113. Grand Rapids: Eerdmans, 2001.
———. "Imagination." In *Dictionary for the Theological Interpretation of the Bible*, edited by Kevin J. Vanhoozer et al., 321–23. Grand Rapids: Baker, 2005.

Bibliography

———. "Imagining Evangelical Theology." In *Evangelical Futures: A Conversation on Theological Method*, edited by John Stackhouse, 191–200. Grand Rapids: Baker, 2000.

Hauerwas, Stanley. *Performing the Faith: Bonhoeffer and the Practice of Nonviolence*. Grand Rapids: Brazos, 2004.

Hegel, George. *Aesthetics: Lectures in Fine Art*. Translated by T. M. Knox. Oxford: Clarendon Press, 1975.

Heidegger, Martin. *Being and Time*. Translated by Joan Stambaugh. In *Basic Writings*, edited by David F. Krell. New York: Harper & Row, 1977.

———. *The Origin of the Work of Art*. Translated by Albert Hofstadter. In *Basic Writings*, edited by David F. Krell. New York: Harper & Row, 1977.

———. *The Will to Power as Art*. Translated by David F. Krell. Vol. 1 of *Nietzsche*. San Francisco: Harper & Row, 1979.

Henry, Carl F. H. *God, Revelation, and Authority*. 6 vols. Waco, TX: Word, 1976-1983.

Herman, Bruce. Foreward to *Broken Beauty*. Edited by Theodore L. Prescott, viii–x. Grand Rapids: Eerdmans, 2005.

Heschel, Abraham. *The Prophets*. New York: Harper & Row, 2007.

Hodge, Charles. *Systematic Theology*. 3 vols. Grand Rapids: Eerdmans, 1979.

Hodges, John Mason. "Aesthetics and the Place of Beauty in Worship." *Reformation and Revival* 9 (Summer 2000) 59–74.

Hoekema, Anthony A. *Created in God's Image*. Grand Rapids: Eerdmans, 1986.

Hogg, David S. *Anselm of Canterbury: The Beauty of Theology*. Aldershot, England: Ashgate, 2004.

Holmes, Stephen R. "'Something Much Too Plain to Say:' Towards a Defence of the Doctrine of Divine Simplicity." *Neue Zeitschrift für Systematische Theologie* 43 (2001) 137–54.

Holladay, William L. "Background of Jeremiah's Self-Understanding: Moses, Samuel, and Psalm 22." *Journal of Biblical Literature* 83 (1964) 153–64.

Hooker, Morna D. *Jesus and the Servant*. London: SPCK, 1959.

Horton, Michael. *Covenant and Salvation*. Louisville: Westminster John Knox, 2007.

———. "Participation and Covenant." In *Radical Orthodoxy and the Reformed Tradition: Creation, Covenant, and Participation*, edited by James K. A. Smith and James H. Olthuis, 107–34. Grand Rapids: Baker Academic, 2005.

Huffmon, Herbert B. "The Covenant Lawsuit in the Prophets." *Journal of Biblical Literature* 78 (1959) 285–95.

Hume, David. *A Standard of Taste and Other Essays*. Edited by John E. Lentz. Indianapolis: Bobbs-Merill, 1965.

———. *Enquiry Concerning Human Understanding*. Edited by Eric Steinberg. Indianapolis: Hackett, 1977.

Hutcheson, Francis. *An Inquiry into the Original of Our Ideas of Beauty and Virtue*. Edited by Wolfgang Leidhold. Indianapolis: Liberty Fund, 2004.

Ingraffia, Brian. "Deconstructing the Tower of Babel: Ontotheology and the Postmodern Bible." In *Renewing Biblical Interpretation*, edited by Craig Bartholomew et al., 284–306. Grand Rapids: Zondervan, 2000.

Irenaeus. *Adversus haereses*. Translated by Dominic J. Unger and John J. Dillon. Ancient Christian Writers 55. New York: Paulist, 1992.

Jameson, Frederic. *The Postmodern Turn: Essays in Postmodern Theory and Culture*. Durham: Duke University Press, 1991.

Janowski, Bernd. "He Bore Our Sins: Isaiah 53 and the Drama of Taking Another's Place." In *The Suffering Servant: Isaiah 53 in Jewish and Christian Sources*, edited by Bernd Janowski and Peter Stuhlmacher, translated by Daniel P. Bailey, 48–74. Grand Rapids: Eerdmans, 2004.

Janowski, Bernd and Peter Stuhlmacher, editors. *The Suffering Servant: Isaiah 53 in Jewish and Christian Sources*. Translated by Daniel P. Bailey. Grand Rapids: Eerdmans, 2004.

Jenks, Charles. *What Is Postmodernism?* New York: St. Martin's, 1987.

Jenson, Robert W. *The Triune God*. Vol. 1 of *Systematic Theology*. Oxford: Oxford University Press, 1997.

Johnson, Keith L. *Karl Barth and the Analogia Entis*. Edinburgh: T. & T. Clark, 2010.

Justin Martyr. *The First Apology, The Second Apology, Dialogue with Trypho, Exhortation to the Greeks, Dialogue to the Greeks, The Monarchy, The Rule of God*. Translated by Thomas B. Falls. Vol. 6 of *The Fathers of the Church*. Washington, DC: Catholic University of America Press, 1965.

Jüngel, Eberhard. "Even the Beautiful Must Die." Translated by Arnold Neufeldt-Fast and John Webster. In *Theological Essays II*, edited by John Webster, 59–82. Edinburgh: T. & T. Clark, 1995.

———. *Justification: The Heart of the Christian Faith*. Translated by Jeffery F. Cayzer. London: T. & T. Clark, 2001.

Kant, Immanuel. *Critique of Judgment*. Translated by James C. Meredith. In *Wadsworth Philosophy Source* 3.0, CD-ROM, edited by Daniel Kolak. New York: Wadsworth.

———. *Critique of Pure Reason*. Translated by J. M. D. Meiklejohn. In *Wadsworth Philosophy Source* 3.0, CD-ROM, edited by Daniel Kolak. New York: Wadsworth.

———. *Prolegomena to Any Future Metaphysics*. Translated by Paul Carus. In *Wadsworth Philosophy Source* 3.0, CD-ROM, edited by Daniel Kolak. New York: Wadsworth.

———. *Religion within the Boundaries of Mere Reason: And Other Writings*. Translated by Alan Wood and George di Giovanni. Cambridge: Cambridge University Press, 2004.

Kasper, Walter. *The God of Jesus Christ*. London: SCM, 1984.

Kaufman, Gordon D. *The Theological Imagination: Constructing the Concept of God*. Philadelphia: Westminster, 1981.

Kearney, Richard. *The Wake of the Imagination: Toward a Postmodern Culture*. Minneapolis: University of Minnesota Press, 1988.

Kearsley, Roy. "The Impact of Greek Concepts of God on the Christology of Cyril of Alexandria." *Tyndale Bulletin* 43 (1992) 307–29.

Keating, James F., and Thomas Joseph White, editors. *Divine Impassibility and the Mystery of Human Suffering*. Grand Rapids: Eerdmans, 2009.

Kelsey, David. *Imagining Redemption*. Louisville: Westminster John Knox, 2005.

Kerr, Fergus. *After Aquinas: Versions of Thomism*. Oxford: Blackwell, 2002.

———. "Foreward: Assessing This 'Giddy Synthesis.'" In *Balthasar at the End of Modernity*, edited by Lucy Gardner et al., 1–14. London: T. & T. Clark, 2001.

Kettler. Christian D. "The Vicarious Beauty of Christ: The Aesthetics of the Atonement." *Theology Today* 64 (2007) 14–24.

Kilby, Karen. "Perichoresis and Projection: Problems with Social Doctrines of the Trinity." *New Blackfriars* 81 (October 2000) 432–45.

Bibliography

Kittel, Gerhard, and Geoffrey W. Bromiley, editors. *Theological Dictionary of the New Testament*. 10 vols. Translated by Geoffrey W. Bromiley. Grand Rapids: Eerdmans, 1964–1976.

Kristeller, Paul O. *Renaissance Thought and Its Sources*. New York: Columbia University Press, 1979.

Lactantius. *On the Anger of God*. Translated by Alexander Roberts and James Donaldson. Vol. 7 of *Ante-Nicene Fathers*. Peabody, MA: Hendrickson, 1994.

LaCugna, Cathrine M. *God for Us: The Trinity and Christian Life*. San Francisco: HarperCollins, 1991.

———. "Philosophers and Theologians on the Trinity." *Modern Theology* 2 (1986) 169–81.

———. "Re-Conceiving the Trinity as the Mystery of Salvation." *Scottish Theological Journal* 38 (1985) 1–23.

———. "The Relational God: Aquinas and Beyond." *Theological Studies* 46 (1985) 647–63.

———. "Returning from 'The Far Country': Theses for a Contemporary Trinitarian Theology." *Scottish Journal of Theology* 41 (1988) 191–215.

Leith, John. *Creeds of the Churches: A Reader in Christian Doctrine, from the Bible to the Present*. Louisville: Westminster John Knox, 1983.

Leiva, Erasmos. Translator's note to *Heart of the World*, by Hans Urs von Balthasar. San Francisco: Ignatius, 1979.

Letham, Robert. *The Work of Christ*. Downers Grove, IL: InterVarsity, 1993.

Levering, Matthew. *Scripture and Metaphysics: Aquinas and the Renewal of Trinitarian Theology*. Oxford: Blackwell, 2004.

Lewis, C. S. *Surprised By Joy: The Shape of My Early Life*. New York: Bruce Harcourt, 1956.

———. "Bluspels and Flalansferes: A Semantic Nightmare." In *Selected Literary Essays*, edited by Walter Hooper, 251–65. Cambridge: Cambridge University Press, 1979.

———. "The Weight of Glory." In *The Weight of Glory and Other Addresses*, 25–46. San Francisco: HarperCollins, 2001.

Locke, John. *An Essay Concerning Human Understanding*. In *Wadsworth Philosophy Source* 3.0, CD-ROM, edited by Daniel Kolak. New York: Wadsworth.

Lohse, Eduard. *Colossians and Philemon: A Commentary on the Epistles to the Colossians and to Philemon*. Translated by William R. Poehlmann and Robert J. Karris. Hermeneia. Philadelphia: Fortress, 1971.

Lundbom, Jack R. *Jeremiah: A New Translation with Introduction and Commentary*. Vol. 21 of Anchor Bible Commentary. New York: Doubleday, 1999.

Luther, Martin. *Liturgy and Hymns*. Translated by Paul Z. Strodach. Vol. 53 of *Luther's Works*, edited by Helmut T. Lehmann. Philadelphia: Fortress, 1958.

Lyotard, Jean-François. *The Postmodern Condition: A Report on Knowledge*. Manchester: Manchester University Press, 1984.

MacDonald, George. *A Dish of Orts*. London: Edwin Dalton, 1908. Reprint, BiblioBazaar Reproductions, 2007.

MacFarland, Ian M. *The Divine Image: Envisioning the Invisible God*. Philadelphia: Fortress, 2005.

Mackey, James P., editor. *Religious Imagination*. Edinburgh: Edinburgh University Press, 1986.

Macleod, Donald. *The Person of Christ*. Downers Grove, IL: InterVarsity, 1998.

Bibliography

Macquarrie, John. "Heidegger's Earlier and Later Work Compared." *Anglican Theological Review* 49 (1967) 3–16.

Malamat, Abraham. "The Last Kings of Judah and the Fall of Jerusalem: An Historical-Chronological Study." *Israel Exploration Journal* 18 (1968) 137–56.

———. "The Twilight of Judah: In the Egyptian-Babylonian Maelstrom." *Supplements to Vetus Testamentum* 28 (1975) 123–45.

Marion, Jean-Luc. *God Without Being*. Translated by Thomas A. Carlson. Chicago: University of Chicago Press, 1991.

Martin, Alfred J. "The Significance of Aesthetics for Theology as Imaginative Construction." *Journal of the American Academy of Religion* 50 (1982) 81–85.

Martin, Jr., James A. *Beauty and Holiness: The Dialogue between Aesthetics and Religion*. Princeton: Princeton University Press, 1990.

Mascall, E. L. *Words and Images: A Study in Theological Discourse*. London: Longman, Greens, 1957.

McCall, Thomas H. *Whose Trinity? Which Monotheism? Philosophical and Systematic Theologians on the Metaphysics of the Trinitarian Theology*. Grand Rapids: Eerdmans, 2010.

McCormack, Bruce. *Karl Barth's Critically Realistic Dialectical Theology: Its Genesis and Development 1909-1936*. Oxford: Oxford University Press, 1995.

McConville, J. Gordon. "Theology of Jeremiah." In *New International Dictionary of Old Testament Theology and Exegesis*. 5 vols. Edited by Willem VanGemeren, 4:755–67. Grand Rapids: Zondervan, 1997.

McFague, Sallie. *Metaphorical Theology: Models of God in Religious Language*. Philadelphia: Fortress, 1982.

———. *Models of God: Theology for an Ecological, Nuclear Age*. Philadelphia: Fortress, 1987.

———. *Speaking in Parables: A Study in Metaphor and Theology*. Philadelphia: Fortress, 1975.

McGrath, Alister. *Iustitia Dei: A History of the Christian Doctrine of Justification*. 3rd ed. Cambridge: Cambridge University Press, 2005.

McIntyre, John. *Faith, Theology and Imagination*. Edinburgh: Handsel Press, 1987.

McKane, William A. *A Critical and Exegetical Commentary on Jeremiah*. 2 vols. International Critical Commentary. Edited by J. A. Emerton, et al. Edinburgh: T. & T. Clark, 1986.

McKnight, Scot. "Covenant." In *Dictionary for the Theological Interpretation of the Bible*, edited by Kevin J. Vanhoozer, et al., 141–43. Grand Rapids: Baker, 2005.

Milbank, John. "Beauty and Soul." In *Theological Perspectives on Beauty*, 1–34. Harrisburg, PA: Trinity Press International, 2003.

———. *The Suspended Middle: Henri de Lubac and the Debate Concerning the Supernatural*. Grand Rapids: Eerdmans, 2005.

Milbank, John, et al., eds., *Radical Orthodoxy: A New Theology*. London: Routledge, 1999.

Milbank, John, et al. *Theological Perspectives on God and Beauty*. Harrisburg, PA: Trinity Press International, 2003.

Miller, Patrick D. "Trouble and Woe: Interpreting the Biblical Laments." *Interpretation* 37 (January 1983) 32–45.

Mitchell, Nathan. *Liturgy and the Social Sciences*. Collegeville, MN: Liturgical, 1999.

Bibliography

Molnar, Paul. *Divine Freedom and the Doctrine of the Immanent Trinity: In Dialogue with Karl Barth and Contemporary Theology.* London: T. & T. Clark, 2002.

Moltmann, Jürgen. *The Church in the Power of the Spirit.* Translated by M. Kohl. London: SCM, 1977.

———. *The Crucified God: The Cross of Christ as the Foundation and Criticism of Christian Theology.* Minneapolis: Fortress, 1974.

———. "The Passion of Christ and the Suffering of God." *Asbury Theological Journal* 48 (1993) 19–28.

———. *Theology and Joy.* Translated by Reinhard Ulrich. London: SCM, 1973.

———. *The Trinity and the Kingdom: The Doctrine of God.* Minneapolis: Fortress, 1981.

Mongrain, Kevin. "Von Balthasar's Way from Doxology to Theology." *Theology Today* 64 (2007) 58–70.

Moo, Douglas. *The Epistle to the Romans.* New International Commentary on the New Testament. Grand Rapids: Eerdmans, 1996.

Moule, C. F. D. *The Epistles of Paul the Apostle to the Colossians and to Philemon.* London: Cambridge University Press, 1957.

Muller, Earl. "The Science of Theology: A Review of Catherine LaCugna's God For Us." *Gregorianum* 75 (1994) 311–41.

Muller, Richard. "Incarnation, Immutability, and the Case for Classical Theism." *Westminster Theological Journal* 45 (1983) 22–40.

Murphy, Francesca. *Christ the Form of Beauty: A Study in Theology and Literature.* Edinburgh: T. & T. Clark, 1995.

Navone, John. *Toward a Theology of Beauty.* Collegeville, MN: Liturgical, 1996.

Newman, John Henry Cardinal. *An Essay in Aid of a Grammar of Assent.* South Bend, IN: Notre Dame University Press, 2006.

Nicholas of Cusa. *On Learned Ignorance.* Translated by Jasper Hopkins. Minneapolis: A. J. Benning Press, 1981.

———. *On the Vision of God.* Translated by John P. H. Clark. In *An Introduction to the Medieval Mystics of Europe: Fourteen Original Essays*, edited by Paul E. Szarmach. Albany, NY: State University of New York Press, 1984.

Nichols, Aidan. *The Word Has Been Abroad: A Guide Through Balthasar's Aesthetics.* Washington, DC: Catholic University Press of America, 1998.

Nickelsburg, George. "Reading the Hebrew Scriptures in the First Century: Christian Interpretations in Their Jewish Context." *Word and World* 3 (1983) 238–50.

Niehaus, Jeffery. "Theology of Theophany." In *New International Dictionary of Old Testament Theology and Exegesis*, 5 vols., edited by Willem VanGemeren, 4:1247–49. Grand Rapids: Zondervan, 1997.

Nietzsche, Friedrich. *The Birth of Tragedy.* Translated by Walter Kaufmann. New York: Vintage, 1967.

———. *The Gay Science: With a Prelude in Rhymes and an Appendix of Songs.* Translated by Walter Kaufmann. New York: Vintage, 1974.

———. *Thus Spake Zarathustra.* Translated by Thomas Common. In *Wadsworth Philosophy Source* 3.0, CD-ROM, edited by Daniel Kolak. New York: Wadsworth.

———. *Will to Power.* Translated by Walter Kaufmann and R. J. Hollingdale. New York: Vintage, 1968.

North, Christopher R. *The Suffering Servant in Deutero-Isaiah: An Historical and Critical Study.* 2nd ed. Eugene, OR: Wipf & Stock, 1956.

Nygren, Anders. *Agape and Eros.* London: SPCK, 1953.

Oakes, Edward T. *Pattern of Redemption: The Theology of Hans Urs von Balthasar*. New York: Continuum, 2005.

O'Brien, Peter T. *Colossians, Philemon*. Word Biblical Commentary 44. Waco, TX: Word, 1982.

O'Conner, John D. "Theological Aesthetics and Revelatory Tension." *New Blackfriars* 29 (July 2008) 399–417.

O'Connor, Kathleen. "Lamenting Back to Life." *Interpretation* 62 (January 2008) 34–47.

O'Donnell, John. "Hans Urs von Balthasar: The Form of His Theology." *Communio* 16 (Fall 1989) 458–74.

O'Hanlon, Gerard F. "Does God Change?—H. U. von Balthasar on the Immutability of God." *Irish Theological Quarterly* 53 (1987) 161–83.

———. *The Immutability of God in the Theology of Hans Urs von Balthasar*. 1990. Reprint, Cambridge: Cambridge University Press, 2007.

Olsen, Glenn W. "Hans Urs von Balthasar and the Rehabilitation of St. Anselm's Doctrine of the Atonement." *Scottish Journal of Theology* 34 (1981) 49–61.

Origen. *De Principiis*. Translated by G. W. Butterworth. Gloucester, MA: Peter Smith, 1973.

Otto, Randell E. "The Use and the Abuse of Perichoresis in Recent Theology." *Scottish Journal of Theology* 54 (2001) 366–84.

Ouellet, Marc. "The Message of Balthasar's Theology to Modern Theology." *Communio* 23 (Summer 1996) 270–99.

Owen, Huw P. *Concepts of Deity*. New York: Herder & Herder, 1971.

Owen, Owen T. "Does God Suffer?" *Church Quarterly Review* 158 (1957) 176–84.

Pannenberg, Wolfhart. "Father, Son, and Spirit: Problems of a Trinitarian Doctrine of God." *Dialog* 26 (Fall 1987) 250–57.

———. *Metaphysics and the Idea of God*. Translated by Philip Clayton. Grand Rapids: Eerdmans, 1988.

———. *Systematic Theology*. 3 vols. Grand Rapids: Eerdmans, 1991–1998.

Parsons, Mikeal C. "Isaiah 53 in Acts 8: A Reply to Professor Morna Hooker." In *Jesus and the Suffering Servant: Isaiah 53 and Christian Origins*, edited by William H. Bellinger Jr. and William R. Farmer, 104–19. Eugene, OR: Wipf & Stock, 1998.

Pecknold, Chad C. "How Augustine Used the Trinity: Functionalism and Development of Doctrine." *Anglican Theological Review* 85 (2003) 127–41.

Pelikan, Jaroslav. *Fools for Christ: Essays on the True, the Good, and the Beautiful*. Eugene, OR: Wipf & Stock, 2001.

Peters, Ted. *God as Trinity: Relationality and Temporality in Divine Life*. Louisville: Westminster John Knox, 1993.

Pinnock, Clark. "Systematic Theology." In *The Openness of God: A Biblical Challenge to the Traditional Understanding of God*, edited by Clark Pinnock, 101–25. Downers Grove, IL: InterVarsity, 1995.

Placher, William. *The Domestication of Transcendence: How Modern Thinking About God Went Wrong*. Louisville: Westminster John Knox, 1996.

Plantinga, C. "Deep Wisdom." In *God the Holy Trinity: Reflections on Christian Faith and Practice*, edited by Timothy George, 149–58. Grand Rapids: Baker Academic, 2006.

Plato. *The Republic*. Translated by Benjamin Jowett. In *Wadsworth Philosophy Source 3.0*, CD-ROM, edited by Daniel Kolak. New York: Wadsworth.

Bibliography

———. *Symposium*. Translated by Benjamin Jowett. In *Wadsworth Philosophy Source 3.0*, CD-ROM, edited by Daniel Kolak. New York: Wadsworth.

Powell, Samuel. *The Trinity in German Thought*. Cambridge: Cambridge University Press, 2001.

Quash, Ben. "The Theo-drama." In *The Cambridge Companion to Hans Urs von Balthasar*, edited by David Moss and Edward T. Oakes, 143–57. Cambridge: Cambridge University Press, 2004.

Rad, Gerhard von. *Old Testament Theology*. New York: Harper, 1962.

Rahner, Karl. *The Trinity*. Translated by J. Donceel. New York: Herder & Herder, 2005.

Raschke, Carl. *The Next Reformation: Why Evangelicals Must Embrace Postmodernity*. Grand Rapids: Baker, 2004.

Reumann, John H. "Psalm 22 at the Cross." *Interpretation* 28 (January 1974) 39–58.

Ricoeur, Paul. *Memory, History, and Forgetting*. Translated by Kathleen Blamey. Chicago: University of Chicago Press, 2004.

———. *Oneself as Another*. Translated by Kathleen Blamey. Chicago: University of Chicago Press, 1992.

Rogers, Katherine. *Perfect Being Theology*. Edinburgh: Edinburgh University Press, 2000.

Rossi, Philip. "The Metaphysics of the Sublime: Old Wine, New Wineskin?" *Philosophy and Theology* 16 (2004) 101–11.

Rowe, W. V. "Adolf von Harnack and the Concept of Hellenization." In *Hellenization Revisited: Shaping a Christian Response with the Greco-Roman World*, 69–98. Lanham, MD: University Press of America, 1994.

Sanders, Fred. *The Image of the Immanent Trinity: Rahner's Rule and the Theological Interpretation of Scripture*. New York: Peter Lang, 2005.

———. "The State of the Doctrine of the Trinity in Evangelical Theology." *Southwestern Journal of Theology* 47 (2005) 153–75.

Sarot, Marcel. "Patripassianism, Theopaschitism and the Suffering of God: Some Historical and Systematic Considerations." *Religious Studies* 26 (1990) 363–75.

Scalise, Pamela J. "The Logic of Covenant and the Logic of Lament in the Book of Jeremiah." *Perspectives in Religious Studies* 28 (Winter 2001) 395–401.

Scary, Elaine. *On Beauty and Being Just*. Princeton: Princeton University Press, 1999.

Schelling, Friedrich. *Philosophy of Art*. Translated by D. W. Stott. Minneapolis: University of Minnesota Press, 1989.

Schiller, Friedrich. "Letters on the Aesthetic Education of Man." Translated by Elizabeth Wilkinson and L. A. Willoughby. In *Essays*, edited by Walter Hinderer and Daniel O. Dahlstrom, 86–178. New York: Continuum, 2005.

Schlegel, Friedrich. "The Limits of the Beautiful." In *The Aesthetic and Miscellaneous Works of Friedrich Schlegel*, translated by E. J. Millington, 413–24. London: H. G. Bohn, 1849.

Schwöbel, Christop. "A Theological Ontology of Communicative Relations." In *Theology and Conversation: Towards a Relational Theology*, edited by J. Haers and P. De Mey, 43–67. Leuven: Leuven University Press, 2003.

Schopenhauer, Arthur. *Welt als Wille und Vorstellung*. New York: Dover Publications, 1966.

Schultz, Richard. "Servant, Slave." In *New International Dictionary of Old Testament Theology and Exegesis*. 5 vols. Edited by Willem VanGemeren, 4:1183–97. Grand Rapids: Zondervan, 1997.

Scruton, Roger. *Art and Imagination: A Study in the Philosophy of Mind*. London: Methuen, 1974.

———. *Culture Counts: Faith and Feeling in a World Besieged*. New York: Encounter, 2007.

Scrutton, Anastasia. "Emotion in Augustine of Hippo and Thomas Aquinas: A Way Forward for the Im/passibility Debate?" *International Journal of Systematic Theology* 7 (April 2005) 169–77.

Seitz, Christopher R. "The Prophet Moses and the Canonical Shape of Jeremiah." *Zeitschrift fur die alttestamentliche Wissenschaft* 101 (1989) 3–27.

Sherry, Patrick. "The Beauty of God the Holy Spirit." *Theology Today* 64 (2007) 5–13.

———. "The Sacramentality of Things." *New Blackfriars* 89 (September 2008) 575–90.

———. *Spirit and Beauty: An Introduction to Theological Aesthetics*. London: SCM, 2002.

Sikka, Sonia. "On the Truth of Beauty: Nietzsche, Heidegger, and Keats." *Heythrop Journal* 39 (July 1998) 244–48.

Simon, Ulrich. "Balthasar and Goethe." In *The Analogy of Beauty: The Theology of Hans Urs von Balthasar*, edited by John Riches, 60–76. Edinburgh: T. & T. Clark, 1986.

Sircello, Guy. *A New Theory of Beauty*. Princeton: Princeton University Press, 1975.

Smith, James K. A. *Introducing Radical Orthodoxy: Mapping a Post-Secular Theology*. Grand Rapids: Baker Academic, 2004.

———. "Will the Real Plato Please Stand Up? Participation versus Incarnation." In *Radical Orthodoxy and the Reformed Tradition: Creation, Covenant, and Participation*, edited by James K. A. Smith and James H. Olthuis, 61–72. Grand Rapids: Baker Academic, 2005.

Smith, James K. A., and James H. Olthuis. *Radical Orthodoxy and the Reformed Tradition: Creation, Covenant, and Participation*. Grand Rapids: Baker Academic, 2005.

Smith, Mark S. "Jeremiah IX 9—A Divine Lament." *Vetus Testamentum* 37 (January 1987) 97–99.

Snyder, James. *Northern Renaissance Art: Painting, Sculpture, the Graphic Arts from 1350 to 1575*. Upper Saddle River, NJ: Prentice Hall, 2004.

Spieckermann, Hermann. "The Conception and Prehistory of the Idea of Vicarious Suffering in the Old Testament." In *The Suffering Servant: Isaiah 53 in Jewish and Christian Sources*, edited by Bernd Janowski and Peter Stuhlmacher, translated by Daniel P. Bailey, 1–15. Grand Rapids: Eerdmans, 2004.

Spiegel, James S. *The Benefits of Divine Providence: A New Look at Divine Sovereignty*. Wheaton, IL: Crossway, 2005.

Stackhouse, John. "The True, the Good, and the Beautiful Christian." *Christianity Today* January 7, 2002, 60–61.

Stafford, William S. "Imagination and Scripture: Seeing the Unseen." *Sewanee Theological Review* 50 (Christmas 2006) 154–65.

Stern, J. P. *A Study of Nietzsche*. Cambridge: Cambridge University Press, 1979.

Tertullian. *Against Marcion*. Translated by E. Evans. London: Oxford University Press, 1972.

———. *On the Testimony of the Soul*. Translated by Alexander Roberts and James Donaldson. Ante-Nicene Fathers 3. Peabody, MA: Hendrickson, 1994.

Thiessen, Gesa E. *Theological Aesthetics: A Reader*. Grand Rapids: Eerdmans, 2004.

Thiselton, Anthony. *The Two Horizons*. Grand Rapids: Eerdmans, 1980.

Bibliography

Thompson, John A. *The Book of Jeremiah*. The New International Commentary on the Old Testament. Grand Rapids: Eerdmans, 1980.

Thompson, Marianne M. *Colossians and Philemon*. Grand Rapids: Eerdmans, 2005.

Thrall, Margaret E. "The Suffering Servant and the Mission of Jesus." *Church Quarterly Review* 164 (1963) 281–88.

Tolkien, J. R. R. "On Fairy-Stories." In *Essays Presented to Charles Williams*, edited by C. S. Lewis, 38–90. Grand Rapids: Eerdmans, 1966.

Tolstoy, Leo. *What Is Art?* Translated by Richard Pevear and Larissa Volokhonsky. New York: Penguin, 1995.

Torrance, Thomas F. *The Christian Doctrine of God: One Being, Three Persons*. Edinburgh: T. & T. Clark, 1996.

Tracy, David. *The Analogical Imagination: Christian Theology and the Culture of Pluralism*. London: SCM, 1981.

———. "Literary Theory and Naming God." *Journal of Religion* 74 (1994) 302–19.

———. *On Naming the Present: God, Hermeneutics, and Church*. Maryknoll, NY: Orbis, 1994.

Treier, Daniel J. *Virtue and the Voice of God: Toward Theology as Wisdom*. Grand Rapids: Eerdmans, 2006.

Treier, Daniel J., et al., editors. "Introduction." In *The Beauty of God: Theology and the Arts*, edited by Daniel J. Treier, et al., 7–18. Downers Grove, IL: IVP Academic, 2007.

VanGemeren, Willem. "Prophets, The Freedom of God, and Hermeneutics." *Westminster Theological Journal* 52 (1990) 79–99.

VanGemeren, Willem, editor. *New International Dictionary of Old Testament Theology and Exegesis*. 5 vols. Grand Rapids: Zondervan, 1997.

Vanhoozer, Kevin. *Drama of Doctrine: A Canonical-Linguistic Approach to Christian Theology*. Louisville: Westminster John Knox, 2005.

———. *Is There a Meaning in This Text? The Bible, Reader, and the Morality of Literary Knowledge*. Grand Rapids: Zondervan, 1998.

———. "A Lamp in the Labyrinth: The Hermeneutics of 'Aesthetic' Theology." *Trinity Journal*, 8 (1987) 25–56.

———. "On the Very Idea of a Theological System: An Essay in Aid of Triangulating Scripture, the Church, and the World." In *Always Reforming: Explorations in Systematic Theology*, edited by A. T. B. McGown, 125–82. Downers Grove, IL: IVP Academic, 2006.

———. "Praising God in Song: Beauty and the Arts." In *The Blackwell Companion to Christian Ethics*, edited by Stanley Hauerwas, 110–22. Oxford: Blackwell Publishing, 2004.

———. *Remythologizing Theology*. Cambridge: Cambridge University Press, 2010.

———. "Theology and the Condition of Postmodernity." In *The Cambridge Companion to Postmodern Theology*, edited by Kevin Vanhoozer, 3–25. Cambridge: Cambridge University Press, 2003.

———. "What Has Vienna to Do with Jerusalem? Barth, Brahms, and Bernstein's Unanswered Question." *Westminster Theological Journal* 63 (2001) 123–50.

———. "What is Everyday Theology? How and Why Christians Should Read Culture." In *Everyday Theology: How to Read Cultural Texts and Interpret Trends*, edited by Kevin J. Vanhoozer et al., 15–62. Grand Rapids: Baker, 2007.

Vanhoozer, Kevin, et al., editor. *Dictionary for the Theological Interpretation of the Bible.* Grand Rapids: Baker, 2005.
Viladesau, Richard. *Theological Aesthetics: God in Imagination, Beauty, and* Art. Oxford: Oxford University Press, 1999.
Waldstein, Michael. "Hans Urs von Balthasar's Theological Aesthetics." *Communio* 11 (Spring 1984) 13–27.
Walford, E. John. "The Case for a Broken Beauty: An Art Historical Viewpoint." In *The Beauty of God: Theology and the Arts,* edited by Daniel J. Treier, et al., 87–109. Downers Grove, IL: InterVarsity, 2007.
Wallace, Daniel B. *Greek Grammar Beyond the Basics: An Exegetical Syntax of the New Testament.* Grand Rapids: Zondervan, 1996.
Ward, Graham. "The Beauty of God." In *Theological Perspectives on Beauty,* 35–65. Harrisburg, PA: Trinity Press International, 2003.
———. "*Kenosis, Poiesis,* and *Genesis*: Or the Theological Aesthetics of Suffering." In *Encounter Between Eastern Orthodoxy and Radical Orthodoxy: Transfiguring the World Through the Word,* edited by Adrian Pabst and Christoph Schneider, 165–75. Aldershot, England: Ashgate, 2009.
Warnock, Mary. *Imagination.* Los Angeles: University of California Press, 1976.
———. "Religious Imagination." In *Religious Imagination,* edited by James P. Mackey, 142–60. Edinburgh: Edinburgh University Press, 1986.
Webster, John. "The Church and the Perfection of God." In *The Community of the Word: Toward an Evangelical Ecclesiology,* edited by Mark Husbands and Daniel J. Treier, 75–95. Downers Grove, IL: InterVarsity, 2005.
———. "Resurrection and Scripture." In *Christology and Scripture: Interdisciplinary Perspectives,* edited by Andrew T. Lincoln and Angus Paddison, 138–55. Edinburgh: T. & T. Clark, 2007.
———. "Theologies of Retrieval." In *The Oxford Handbook to Systematic Theology,* edited by John Webster, et al., 583–99. Oxford: Oxford University Press, 2007.
Weinandy, Thomas. *Does God Suffer?* South Bend, IN: Notre Dame University Press, 2000.
———. "Does God Suffer?" *First Things* 117 (2001) 35–41.
Westermann, Claus. "The Role of the Lament in the Theology of the Old Testament." *Interpretation* 28 (January 1974) 20–38.
Westpahl, Merold. "Onto-theology, Metanarrative, Perspectivism, and the Gospel." In *Christianity and the Postmodern Turn,* edited by Myron B. Penner, 141–56. Grand Rapids: Brazos, 2005.
Wigley, Stephen D. *Karl Barth and Hans Urs von Balthasar: A Critical Engagement.* Edinburgh: T. & T. Clark, 2007.
Williams, Rowan. "Balthasar and the Trinity." In *The Cambridge Companion to Hans Urs von Balthasar,* edited by Edward T. Oakes and David Moss, 37–50. Cambridge: Cambridge University Press, 2004.
Wilson, Gerald. "Wisdom." In *New International Dictionary of Old Testament Theology and Exegesis,* 5 vols., edited by Willem VanGemeren, 4:1276–85. Grand Rapids: Zondervan, 1997.
Winke, Ross. E. "The Jeremiah Model for Jesus in the Temple." *Andrews University Seminary Studies* 24 (Summer 1986) 155–72.
Wippel, John F. *The Metaphysical Thought of Thomas Aquinas: From Finite Being to Uncreated Being.* Washington, DC: Catholic University Press of America, 2000.

Bibliography

Wittgenstein, Ludwig. *Lectures and Conversations of Aesthetics, Psychology and Religious Belief.* Edited by Cyril Barrett. Oxford: Oxford University Press, 1966.

———. *Notebooks, 1914–1916.* Translated by G. E. M. Anscombe. Edited by G. H. von Wright. 2nd ed. Chicago: University of Chicago Press, 1984.

Wolterstorff, Nicholas. *Art in Action: Toward a Christian Aesthetic.* Grand Rapids: Eerdmans, 1980.

———. "Beauty and Justice." Paper presented at the National Lilly Fellows Conference, Seattle, Washington, October 10–12, 2008.

Wright, N. T. *Justification: God's Plan, Paul's Vision.* Downer's Grove, IL: InterVarsity, 2009.

Yocum, John. "A Cry of Dereliction? Reconsidering a Recent Theological Commonplace." *International Journal of Systematic Theology* 7 (January 2005) 72–80.

Young, Edward J. *The Book of Isaiah: The English Text, With Introduction, Exposition, and Notes.* 3 vols. Grand Rapids: Eerdmans, 1972.

Zachman, Randall. *Word and Image in the Theology of John Calvin.* South Bend, IN: Notre Dame Press, 2007.

Scripture Index

Old Testament

Genesis

1–2	139, 194
1:2	133n11
1:27	119n80
3	139, 147, 195
3:6	38
11:1–9	150
14:18–20	172
15:6	168
15:18	168
17	168
17:2	168
18:22–33	99n18
24:14	98

Exodus

4	105
14:17	117
20:1–6	39
31:3	133n11
32	149, 150, 152
32:1–10	150
32:1–6	149
32:11–14	99
32:30–34	99, 99n18
32:13	98
40:34	117

Leviticus

17:11	120n82
20:26	76, 169

Numbers

11:29	133n11
12:6–8	98

Deuteronomy

1–34	168
9:27	98
34:5	98

Joshua

1:7	98
1:13	98
1:15	98

2 Samuel

3:18	98
11	149n66
13:15	149n66

1 Kings

8:53	98
8:56	98
11:34	98
14:8	86
19:4	99

2 Kings

8:19	98
9:7	99
17:23	99
18:12	98
21–25	105n35

Scripture Index

1 Chronicles

24:20–21	99

2 Chronicles

33–36	105n35

Psalms

1:2	47
19	130
19:1	194
22	111, 111n58, 112
22:1	111
22:8	111
22:9–10	111
24:1	119n80
26:8	117
34:8	47
37:4	47
45:62	102
51	149
96:3	117
103:2–5	119n79
110:4	172
112:1	47
145:16	47

Proverbs

8	170
8:27–31	173
9:6	170
9:10	111
23:26	47

Isaiah

1:10–31	99
1:11–20	46
6	99, 105
6:5	70, 146n56
11:1–10	103
25:8	138
33:6	173
37:35	98
40–55	97
41:18	103
42:1	123
44:24–28	119n79
49:1	101
49:4	101
49:6	101
50:4	101
52:7	174
52:13–15	103
53	73, 99n18, 102–104, 137, 137n29
53:1	103
53:2–12	103
53:2	73, 103
53:2b	102
53:3–12	101
53:6	102
53:10	102
55:8	137

Jeremiah

1	99
1:1–3	105
1:1	105
1:5–10	105, 168
1:5	111
1:8	108
2–3	106
2	106, 109
2:4–37	99
2:6	103
2:13	109
3:1–24	105
3:12	105, 110
4–6	106
4:18	106
4:20	106
4:23	106
5:1–5	105
7:6	113
7:25	113
8:5–7	109
10:17–22	105

Jeremiah (*cont.*)

11:3–4	105
11:18–23	106, 107
11:18–20	99
11:19	114
11:21–23	106
11:26–32	106
12:1–6	106, 107
12:5	110
13:14	105, 110
13:18–20	105
15:10–21	106
15:10–18	107
15:16	110
15:18	110
15:19–21	107
15:16	105, 108
16:2–4	106
17:14–18	106, 107
18:18–23	106
20:2	106
20:7–18	108
20:7–13	106
20:7–8	107
20:7	111
20:9	108
20:10	107
20:11–13	108
20:14–18	106, 107
23:1–2	105
23:24	119n80
24:7	106
26	106
26:15	113
26:20–23	99
32:39	173
33:21–22	98
33:26	98
37:1–3	109
37:6–10	109
37:11–16	106
37:13–21	109
38:1–13	106
38:1–3	109
38:4–6	109
41:16—44:30	106

Ezekiel

1:28	70
2	99
2:8—3:3	108
3:16–21	99
34:23–24	98
37:24–26	98

Daniel

10:9	70

Hosea

6	46
9:8	99

Amos

3:7	99
7:15	99

Micah

6:8	173

New Testament

Matthew

3:17	132
4:1	142n45
5:1–12	149
5:8	130, 148
5:14	77
12:34	186–87
13:11–17	116
13:15	186–87
16:15	172
16:20	115
17:1–3	123n93

Matthew (cont.)

17:5	44, 123, 142, 145, 168, 172, 193
17:6	70
17:9	115
22:37–39	44, 45, 172–73
23:13–36	46
23:29–37	114
23:39—24:1	113
25:11	47
26:10	172n34
26:39	132

Mark

9:6	70
10:45	114
15:34	111

Luke

1:14–17	133n11
1:78	160
2:39–53	133n11
4:1–13	123n93
4:14–21	114
4:14–19	133n11
9:23	135, 194
11:37–54	114
13:31–35	114, 172
22:19	192

John

1:1–14	56, 100
1:3	82, 194
1:14	142n45
3:8	145
3:16–17	144
3:16	159
4:20–26	46
4:20–24	38
4:34	132
6:38	132
6:65	44
7:39	133
8:42–47	143
10:17–18	138
10:17	159
10:18	159
11:1–46	143
12:20–33	146, 168
12:27–28	115
13:1	115
14:6	169n24
14:10	134
14:16–20	140
14:16	134
14:26	83n87, 191
15–17	141
15	140, 173
15:5	77
15:11	146
15:13	120n82, 135
15:26–27	137
15:26	133, 141
16:5–15	133
16:5–11	133
16:13–15	83n87
16:13	134
17	114–15, 131, 168
17:9–10	133
17:1	131
17:2	115
17:5	115, 132
17:10	132
17:14	163
17:17	188
17:18	188
17:21	132, 165
17:23	132
17:24	132
17:26	132

Acts

8:32	114, 172
9:4–9	70
17:8	94, 198
17:28	165

Romans

1:19	65
1:20–25	45
1:21	118
1:22–25	130
1:24	118
5:1–8	163
5:1–5	47, 172
5:5	164
6:4	115
7:22	47
7:23	178
8:9	117
8:11	117
8:15–16	117
8:18–25	130, 140, 191
8:19–23	160
8:20–22	139, 147, 194
8:23	117
8:26	117
8:27	118
8:34	114
9:2	118
10:15	174
11:25–26	116
12:1–2	86
14:15	118n75
16:25–26	117

1 Corinthians

1:27	104
2:6–9	116
2:7–10	117
2:10–16	116
9:24–27	189
11:1	172
12	174
13:4–7	160
15:51	116
15:54	138
16:14	118n75

2 Corinthians

1:1–5	163
1:6–7	120
3:18	19, 129, 161, 164, 174, 183, 187, 200–201
5:4	138
5:7	183
5:17	131, 168
5:18	140, 194
8:9	194
9:7	118
10:5	163, 178
12:9	104

Galatians

2:20	168
3	195
3:14	117n72
3:26	117n72
3:28	117n72

Ephesians

1:1–11	77, 88
1:3–14	78, 194
1:9	117
1:10	139
1:13–14	140, 191
1:18	189
2:12	191
2:13	117n72
2:14–18	194
2:14	191
2:15–16	117n72
2:20	191
2:21–22	117n72
3:5	117
3:9	119
3:15	172
5:1	149
5:2	114

Scripture Index

Philippians

2	155
2:1–18	86, 148
2:1–2	118n75
2:5–13	131
2:6–11	142
2:6	83n87
2:8	132
2:12	169n24
3:10	163
4:4	47

Colossians

1—2:5	18, 97, 116–20, 129, 171, 199
1:3–12	171
1:3	117
1:7	118
1:9–14	131
1:9–12	170
1:9–10	118, 140
1:11	78, 118
1:15–20	56, 100, 119, 119n79, 131, 194
1:15–17	139
1:15	118, 142n45
1:16–17	82
1:16	173
1:17	94, 198
1:18	138, 140, 191
1:19	119, 119n80
1:20	115, 119, 138, 173
1:21	189
1:22	141, 164
1:24	120, 163, 171–72
1:25–27	171
1:25	117
1:26	116–17
1:27	116, 138, 163
1:28–2:1	118
1:28	173
2:1–2	171
2:2	116, 118, 171
2:3	118
2:6	118
2:19	118n75
3:4	118
3:10	118, 140
3:12–14	135
4:8	186n84, 187

1 Thessalonians

1:6	149

1 Timothy

2:5	114

2 Timothy

3:12	120

Hebrews

1:1–4	56, 100
1:1–3	115
1:1	56, 96
1:3	82, 96, 139, 142
2:5–8	115, 173
2:8	115
2:9–10	164
2:9	115
2:10	115
2:11–18	114
4	149
5:1–10	114
7	172
7:25	172
9:12	172
9:13–14	120n82
11	189n97, 193
11:1–3	181n62

James

1:2–6	47, 172

1 Peter

1:16	76, 169
1:19	114

232

1 Peter (cont.)

1:21	115
2:9–10	171
4:13–14	163

2 Peter

1:16–21	123, 199
1:17	145, 168

1 John

1:5	144
4:7–21	140
4:7–16	132, 144
4:9–10	135

Revelation

1:8	138
1:17	70
1:18	138
7:12	78
4	46
4:8	191
21–22	140
22	139, 195

Subject Index

action
  ethical, xii, 164, 169, 181, 187–95, 198, 205
  human, xii, 54, 68, 74–78, 94, 198
aestheticism, 31n38, 32, 38–39, 41, 43, 61, 96, 100, 120, 180
aesthetics, xii, 23n2, 63, 175
  definition of, 27–28, 60
  and ethics, 53, 74–78, 79, 87–88, 93, 181, 198
  history of, 26–36
affections
  divine, 152, 157–59, 162, 200
  human, 24, 39n76, 44, 46, 47, 90, 158, 172, 180–81
Alston, William, 178–79
analogy of being, 55–56, 61n9, 63, 64n20, 81n81, 121–22
analogy of faith, 55, 63, 64n20, 81n81, 122
analogy of love, 64n20, 122
Anselm, 3, 7, 9, 10n31, 25, 127, 136–37, 196
Aquinas, Thomas, 3, 7, 11, 12n37, 25, 40n80, 61n9, 61n11, 121, 127, 152n76, 196
atonement, 120n82, 135–38, 172, 184
attunement, 72–73, 89, 132, 134, 143, 161, 163, 199, 202
Augustine, Saint, 3, 7, 11, 24, 46, 104, 124n97, 127, 142, 149–50, 157–58, 196
Avis, Paul, 175
Ayres, Lewis, 6

Bacon, Francis, 26, 28
Balthasar, Hans Urs von, 14, 16, 40, 43–44, 49, 51, 54–57, 93–96, 100–101, 113, 131, 141, 145, 147–48, 188
  aesthetic theology, 54, 60–61, 64n20
  analogy of being, 61n9, 63, 121–23
  and Barth, 62–63, 81
  beauty of Christ, 65–74, 144
  creation, 82–83, 84, 129–30
  fittingness, 134–36, 143
  Gestalt, 66–74, 142
  grace, 83, 84, 144
  I-Thou, 71, 88
  imagination, 179–80, 182, 183
  impassibility, 129, 153–57, 200
  kenosis, 82–83, 154–57
  revelation, 69–74, 82–83
  sin, 83, 85, 130
  theodrama, 74–78, 169
  theological aesthetics, 55, 59, 62–64, 78–90, 95–96, 128, 164, 197–98
  theology and life, 58–59, 77–81
Bargello Diptych, 17–19
Barth, Karl, xii, 19, 37, 43, 46, 49n113, 50, 62–63, 81, 85–86, 97, 121, 124n96, 128, 137n29, 141n41, 150, 152n76, 159n107, 172, 184, 185–86, 197, 202
Baumgarten, Alexander, 27–28
beauty
  anthropocentric, 53–54

235

Subject Index

beauty (*cont.*)
  call of, 192–95
  of Christ, 65–74, 93, 102, 123–24, 133–34, 138, 164, 174
  christocentric, 54–57, 80, 81–83, 96, 100, 130–31, 198
  and creation, 56, 81–82, 85–86, 89, 93–95, 96, 121–22, 129, 130, 136 139n36, 139–40
  of the cross, 16, 18n54, 104, 135, 137–38, 146, 168, 189–90
  dangers of, 36–39, 50n118, 100, 149–51, 178, 197
  demise of, 43–49
  and Enlightenment, 27–32
  eschatological, 80, 89, 138–39, 140–41, 144, 201
  of forgiveness, 194
  and form, 66–69
  and glory, 43n89, 61n9, 62n13, 64, 65n23, 97, 121–24
  and the good, 44, 48, 74–78, 80
  of holiness, 44–45, 132, 138, 144, 170, 172–73
  of the Holy Spirit, 133–34, 142n45, 144
  and humanities, x, 23
  and imagination, 16, 32, 33, 36, 39, 43, 49, 56–57, 58, 129, 174–87
  intellectual history of, 24–36
  and justice, x, xi
  objective, 24–26, 54–55, 61, 78, 142
  and Postmodernity, 32–36, 142
  and Protestant theology, 23, 36–43, 43–49, 50, 62, 174
  and romanticism, 31–32
  subjective, 27–32, 32–36, 60–61, 58, 78, 145–46
  and sublime, 52–53, 123n92
  suffering, 72–74, 80, 100, 102–4, 137
  theology of, 18, 51–57, 60, 78, 87–90, 137n26
  transcendental/iconic, 51–52
  trinitarian, xii, 16–19, 50–51, 94, 134, 137, 142n45, 144, 157–61, 165–74, 196
  and truth, x, xi, xii, 34–35, 44, 48

Begbie, Jeremy, 96n11, 139, 146n57
Benson, Bruce Ellis, 168n21, 193
Brueggemann, Walter, 106–7
Brunner, Emil, 185–86

Calvin, John, 39, 39n76, 103–4, 121, 140, 170–71, 189n94
Christ
  and the church, 72, 76–78
  and creation, 53, 56, 70, 94, 119–20, 122, 139
  death and resurrection, xii, 5, 17, 48, 80, 96, 115, 130–31, 135, 137–39, 147, 150, 153, 159–61, 163, 202
  Herrlichkeit, 16, 18, 56, 59, 65–74, 78, 80, 82–85, 90, 93–94, 100, 120, 122, 124, 128, 143, 198, 201
  incarnation of, 15, 46, 47, 56, 64, 71, 82, 113–16, 155, 188–90
  as King, 115, 129, 171, 173, 199
  mission of, 73, 77, 88, 93, 137, 143, 144, 171–74
  obedience of, 163
  personification of wisdom, 117
  presence of, 139–40, 192, 205
  as Priest, 114, 129, 171, 172–73, 199
  as Prophet, 113–14, 129, 171, 172, 199
  redemption of, 47, 84–87, 89, 94, 97, 119–20, 129, 163, 194–95
  revelation, 65, 70, 72, 82, 95–96, 100–101, 117, 123, 130, 133–34, 142, 160, 188

Subject Index

Christ (*cont.*)
  suffering of, 1, 4, 17, 18n54, 73, 79, 102–4, 111–12, 115, 131, 137, 159, 163, 164, 168, 196, 200
  Suffering Servant, 98, 102–4, 113–16, 129, 131, 142–43, 161, 172, 199–200
  Übergestalt, 16, 18, 54–56, 59, 65–74, 78, 80, 82–85, 90, 93–94, 100, 120, 124, 128, 143, 198
  union with, 6, 117–18, 135, 138–39, 140–41, 165, 170–71, 191
  wisdom of God, 48, 118–19, 171, 200–201
Christian life, x, 7, 15, 17, 78, 79–81, 83, 89, 185, 201
church, the, 17, 19, 24, 45, 72, 76–77, 79, 88–89, 133–34, 140–41, 142–44, 147, 163, 171–74, 188, 192–93, 199, 202, 203, 204–5
Clayton, Philip, 9, 10, 10n29
Clowney, Edmund, 95
Cole, Graham, 2n4, 88, 133n11, 159n106
Collins, Cecil, 48
compassion, divine, 16, 54, 88, 107, 110, 112, 151, 157–61, 162–63, 200
contemplation, 38, 60, 74, 88, 145, 169, 180
Cooper, John, 7, 11
covenant, 75–77, 98–102, 105–6, 109–10, 112, 114, 135, 148, 149–51, 152, 167n18, 168–70, 171–73, 187, 188, 191, 200
  and creation, 82, 84–86, 94, 122, 128, 139, 160, 198
creation
  goodness of, 69, 89, 119, 121, 130, 139, 148
  fallen, 130, 139, 147, 148,
  creative-redemptive, 64, 84, 94, 122, 128
Creator-creature distinction, 7, 12n37, 61, 80, 87, 89, 153, 157, 165, 170
Creel, Richard, 152

deism, 7–8
derelection, cry of, 97, 104, 111–12, 153, 157, 198
Derrida, Jacques, 32, 35–36
Descartes, René, 7, 9–12, 26–27, 59
doxastic practices, 178–79
drama of redemption, xiii, 16–19, 44, 47–48, 56, 74–78, 80–81, 88–89, 104, 109, 137, 145–46, 161, 163, 168–70, 196
Duhm, Bernard, 97, 103
Dyrness, William, 94–95

Edwards, Jonathan, 42n86, 51n119, 56n134, 132n8, 133, 186–87
Ehrenfels, Christian von, 67
election
  of God, 85, 93–94, 128, 131, 198
emotions
  divine, 151, 152–53, 157–58, 159n106, 162
  human, 27, 28, 153, 157, 158n102, 175
Enlightenment, 7–9, 12, 27–32, 36, 39, 48, 61n11, 175, 177, 197
epistemology, xi, 13, 86n101, 89, 178

faith, ix, 17, 25, 33n46, 53–54, 67n31, 71–72, 73, 74–75, 80, 84, 86, 104, 108, 122, 148, 164, 169, 171, 174, 183, 187, 200
Farley, Edward, 23, 33n44, 37, 42n88, 49, 53–54
Feuerbach, Ludwig, 12–13, 41, 127, 150, 197

237

Subject Index

Fiddes, Paul, 135n21, 157, 162, 166–67, 168n21, 170
fittingness, xii, 16–19, 41–42, 47–49, 55, 72–73, 88–89, 109, 115–16, 118, 130, 143–44, 149–51, 161, 163, 170, 173, 186, 188–90, 199, 202
    of Christ, 131–32, 135–38
    of the Spirit, 132–34
flourishing, human, xii, xiii, xvii, 19, 129, 131–32, 135–38, 139–41, 149, 164, 182, 189, 193, 196, 201–2, 205
form, 24, 40, 66–69, 88, 142, 144, 176–77, 199, 202
freedom
    divine, 7, 16, 23, 60, 65, 74, 75–76, 85, 86, 116, 119, 122, 128, 136, 145, 153, 156, 159, 160, 163, 184–85, 198
    human, 31, 75–76, 86, 128
Fretheim, Terence, 108

Gavrilyuk, Paul, 6, 8
Gestalt, 93, 100
    of Christ, 16, 71, 72–74, 78, 80, 82, 85, 88, 123, 137, 142–43, 186, 201
    definition of, 40, 40n79, 66–69
    of revelation, 69–72
glory
    and beauty. *See* beauty, and glory; God's beauty, and glory
    of Christ, 16, 17–18, 56, 65, 70–71, 80, 94, 100, 115–16, 119, 132, 139–40, 143, 155n88, 164, 173, 182, 187, 199
    and creation, 65, 70, 140, 164, 187
    hope of, 88–89, 118–19, 120, 130, 138, 144, 163, 171, 173, 191
    of God, 16, 18–19, 45, 47, 60, 63–64, 65, 70, 74–75, 76–78, 82, 85–87, 89–90, 94, 96, 113, 117, 120, 122–23, 130–31, 136, 138–39, 157, 169, 198, 202
    sublime, 122–23, 129, 141, 143, 145, 168, 199
    suffering, 17, 18n54, 96, 104, 120, 140, 163–64
    trinitarian, 71, 72, 89, 131–32, 134
God
    absence of, ix
    and atonement, 135–38
    attraction of, 123, 124, 146–47, 168–69, 178, 186, 194, 201
    beauty of, 36, 39n76, 50–57, 61, 87, 96, 100, 115–16, 128–29, 131, 136, 187, 196–200
    being is in becoming, 5, 6, 15, 51n119, 121, 167
    call of, 168–70
    and Christ, 16, 18, 62, 73, 77, 87, 95–96, 100, 103, 115, 123, 128–29, 132, 134, 140, 142–43, 198, 200–201
    and Christian doctrine, xi, xii, 42, 87–90, 128, 203–4
    and Christian witness, 46–48, 77
    and the church, 72, 76–77, 133–34, 142–44, 147–49, 173–74, 188, 192, 199, 204–205
    and creation, 51–52, 96, 121–24, 139n36, 139–40, 198
    definition of, 16, 97, 123, 132, 142n45, 199
    and discipleship, 53, 77, 80
    doctrine of, 3, 7, 15, 19, 43n89
    eschatological, 46, 89, 138–39, 140–41, 144, 147, 201
    faithfulness of, 98–99, 105, 110, 114, 151

God (cont.)
   and glory, 43n89, 62n13, 79n76, 97, 100, 121–24, 128–29, 135–38, 143, 199
   and God-world relation, 56–57, 61, 121–24, 141
   and holiness, 132, 169, 170
   holiness of, 76, 109–10, 132, 146, 169, 170
   and Holy Spirit, 51–52, 96, 100, 132–34, 140–41, 143, 148–49, 205
   honor of, 79n76, 136
   and human affections, 46–47, 145–47, 147–49, 149–51, 163–64
   human flourishing, xvii, 19, 140–41, 145–47, 147–49, 164, 170, 196, 200–201, 204–205
   and imagination, 19, 49, 174, 178, 183–87, 187–94
   and impassibility, 19, 83n88, 151–61
   and joy, 47–48, 88, 164, 172
   justice of, 77, 88, 102, 107–8, 110, 136, 158
   knowledge of, xii, 49, 56, 62n13, 86, 88–89, 96, 120, 118, 148, 197, 204
   and love, 44–45, 71, 73, 88–89, 132, 134, 143, 161, 169, 199
   objectivity of, 18, 142–44, 164, 169, 179, 186, 199, 201
   oneness and threeness, 2, 3, 6, 11–12, 23, 51
   participation. *See* participation, and God's beauty
   and prayer, 44
   and Protestant theology, 36–43, 43–49, 196–97
   relationality of, 18, 147–49, 149–51
   responses to, 146–47, 164, 170, 193–95, 199
   and Scripture, 202–3
   self-limiting, 1, 75, 79–80, 112, 162
   subjectivity of, 18, 145–47, 147–49, 149–51, 163–64, 186, 200–201
   and suffering, 96–97, 99–101, 102–4, 115–16, 116–20, 128–29, 130–32, 144, 146, 151–61, 163–64, 200
   suffering of, 1, 6, 104, 112, 153–54, 157, 161
   suffering glory of, 96, 104, 120
   and the tragic, 80, 88, 100
   and the Trinity, 44, 50–52, 56, 77, 87, 94–96, 128–29, 141–44, 145–47, 157–61, 165–74, 196, 198
   and wisdom, 48–49, 116, 120, 143, 146, 170, 199, 204–5
   wisdom of, 105, 108–10, 113–14, 118–20, 135, 137, 140, 143, 146, 161, 170, 171–72, 173, 189
   world relation to, 56, 64, 80, 86, 121–23, 128, 141, 165, 166, 199
   and worship, 43–46
God's beauty-in-act, xii, 16, 18–19, 97, 104, 124, 129, 161, 163, 196, 199
Goethe, Johann Wolfgang von, 32, 66, 185
Gouwens, David, 182n64, 190
grace
   covenant of, 85, 112, 169n26, 170n30
   and nature, 55, 55n132, 63, 65n25, 82, 84–85, 122n90, 185–86
   prevenient, 60, 83–84, 128
Green, Garrett, 185–86
Gregory of Nyssa, 24, 148, 149
Grenz, Stanley, 6n18, 12

Subject Index

Grudem, Wayne, 152n77, 177
Gunton, Colin, 3
Harnack, Adolf von, 6n19, 9n25
Harries, Richard, 142n46, 202–3
Hart, David Bentley, 49, 54n130, 123n92, 147, 199–200
Hart, Trevor, 176
Heidegger, Martin, 27, 32, 34–35, 36
Henry, Carl F. H., 176–77
Hodge, Charles, 13, 176
Hoekema, Anthony, 145
Holladay, William, 111
Holy Spirit, 16, 18, 44, 50–52, 73–74, 83, 95, 100, 118, 120, 121, 184, 185, 187
   as Beautifier, 133, 139–40, 164, 186
   and beauty. *See* beauty, and Holy Spirit
   bond of love, 132–33, 140, 143
   as communicative agent, 134
   as *communio*, 132, 141, 144
   fellowship of, 141
   gift, 133
   and God's beauty. *See* God's beauty, and Holy Spirit
   mission of, 133–34, 140, 143, 147, 173–74, 185
   power of, 25, 44, 74, 80, 100, 118, 134, 138–39, 140–41, 144, 148–49, 161, 163, 170, 171, 174, 178, 182–83, 186, 196, 205
Hume, David, 29–30

I-Thou, 68, 71, 143–44
iconoclasm, 38–39
imagination, xii, 16–17, 19, 44, 49, 58, 86, 128, 141, 163–64, 174–87, 196, 200
   central to human identity, 182
   creative, 175, 179–82
   demise of, 43–49, 128, 175–78

   as a disposition, 182, 190
   and emotions, 164n5
   eschatological, 191–92, 201
   and faith, 183–85
   and God's beauty. *See* God's beauty, and imagination
   Gospel-formed, 17, 163–64, 178, 183–87, 205
   and Holy Spirit, 16, 52, 184–85
   and human action, 180–81, 185, 187, 187–95
   human flourishing, 182, 187–95
   and human perception, 19, 39, 86, 148, 178–80
   intellectual history of, 27–36, 175
   limitations of, 178
   and memory, 190–91, 201, 204–205
   parabolic, 184
   passive, 179, 182, 183–87
   and Protestant theology, 18, 36–43, 49, 58, 129, 174–78
   and reason, 148, 164n5, 175, 177n48, 177–78, 187
   shaping of, 49, 164, 186, 188–87, 190, 202
   and understanding, 164, 175, 181–82, 183, 194
imago Dei, 53–54, 140, 170, 183
immutability, 2–4, 18–19, 83n88, 127, 129, 152, 152n76, 153n80, 156–57
impassibility, 2, 3, 4, 16, 19, 127–29, 151–61, 162–63, 196, 200
improvisation, 146n57, 193–95, 201
incarnate Beauty, xii, 16, 18–19, 123–24, 129–41, 146, 151–61, 164, 168, 183–87, 194, 199
incarnation, 38, 47, 50, 61, 63, 69–72, 81–83, 111, 113–16, 142, 172

Subject Index

Isaiah
  problem of, 102–4
Jenson, Robert, 5n14, 49, 51n119
Jeremiah
  embodied wisdom of, 104, 108–10
  laments of, 18, 97, 99, 106–8, 110–13, 198–99
justification, 60, 81n82, 84–85, 93–94, 128, 198

Kant, Immanuel, 26–27, 28, 30–32, 39, 52, 59, 62, 102n27, 123n92
Kasper, Walter, 160
Kaufmann, Gordon, 41
Kearney, Richard, 36, 175, 179n53
kenosis, 83n87, 200
  of Christ, 154–56
  divine eternal, 56, 60, 82–84, 129, 154–56, 200
Kerr, Fergus, 6, 6n19, 62

LaCugna, Cathrine Mowry, ix, 1, 4–6, 7n21, 12n37, 14, 151, 165–66, 196
laments, biblical, 18, 97, 99, 104, 106–8, 109, 110–13, 129, 199
Levering, Matthew, 156
Lewis, C. S., 47, 49n112, 204
Locke, John, 28–29
love
  and beauty, 142–44, 146n57
  of Christ, 18, 104, 135, 150, 168, 171, 173
  definition of, 71n46, 135
  of God, xii, 1, 5, 6, 15–17, 71, 112, 165, 169, 184
  and God's glory, 79n76, 131–32
  of neighbor, 77
  and obedience, 131–34, 159
  and prayer, 43–46
  self-giving, 5–6, 70, 78, 81n79, 82–83, 104, 135, 138, 144,
  146, 155–56, 159–60, 163–64, 168, 186, 196, 200
  suffering, 6, 110, 112, 132, 135–38, 151, 159–60, 162, 168
  trinitarian, 71, 73–74, 77, 80, 83n87, 89, 124, 131–32, 135–38, 143, 147, 160, 186
  unity of, 112, 131, 132n10, 140
Luther, Martin, 8n23, 39

MacDonald, George, 183–85
Maritain, Jacques, 154
Mascall, E. L., 180, 186n84
McFague, Sallie, 135n21
McIntyre, John, 183–85
metaphysics, 11, 24, 30, 40n80, 58–60, 64, 93, 121–22, 128–29, 165–66, 197
Milbank, John, 49, 52–53, 156
Molnar, Paul, 7
Moltmann, Jürgen, ix, x, 1, 3–15, 41, 79–80, 112, 151–52, 154, 166–67, 196
Murphy, Francesca, 30n31, 39, 89n105, 94n3
mystery, 18, 97, 116–20, 129, 137, 138, 147, 171, 199

Newman, John Henry, 177n48, 180–82, 186
Nietzsche, Friedrich, 27, 32–34, 35, 36

obedience, 110, 114, 128–29, 168n21, 187, 199
  joy of, 135
  of the Son, 18, 71, 73, 114, 131–34, 143, 146, 155n88, 159, 163
  of the Spirit, 132–34
Owen, Huw P., 2n3, 152

241

Subject Index

Pannenberg, Wolfhart, ix, 1, 3, 5n14, 7, 10, 14, 196
participation, 76–78, 88, 90, 120, 129, 138, 161, 164
  call-response, 188, 192
  covenantal, 112, 168–69, 170–71, 173–74, 187
  divine life, 44, 76, 138, 161, 164
  fitting, 173, 174, 188–90, 191, 197, 200
  imaginative, 190–95
  missional, 120, 151, 170–74
  ontological, 165–68, 170n30
perception
  human, 28, 53, 63, 67–68, 69–72, 74–78, 80, 85–86, 89, 95, 145, 147–49, 149–50, 178–83, 193
Postmodernity, 32–36, 39, 50, 100, 142, 175n41
Przywara, Erich, 61n9, 63, 64n20

Rahner, Karl, 11n34, 50n16, 65n25, 154
Rahner's Rule, 4–6, 15
realism, xi, 41, 49, 53, 178
redemptive-creative, 16, 18, 89, 119–20, 128, 129–31, 138–41, 187, 192–94, 198–200
revelation
  divine, 3, 9–12, 16, 40–41, 45–46, 55–56, 61, 63, 65, 69–74, 75, 81–82, 88, 96, 116–17, 137, 148, 162, 175, 179–80, 186, 201, 203–4
romanticism, xi, 31–32, 38n72, 61, 62n13, 68, 146, 179, 181, 193

sanctification, 60, 84–85, 93, 128, 198
Scarry, Elaine, x, xi, xii
Sherry, Patrick, 37, 39, 49, 51–52, 133–34
sin, 53–54, 60, 73–75, 80, 82–87, 89, 93–94, 100, 128, 130, 136–37, 139, 149–51, 154–56, 198
spiritual disciplines, 188
splendor, xii, 17, 25, 40n79, 46, 62n13, 65n13, 68–69, 72–74, 77, 79n76, 102, 132, 137–38, 141, 143–44, 151, 161, 163, 186, 196, 199, 205
Stackhouse, John, 176
suffering, 18, 97, 116–20, 129, 163, 171–72, 199–200
Suffering Servant, 196
  Isaiah, 97, 102–4
  Jeremiah, 100–102, 105–13, 128–29, 198
  Jesus Christ. *See* Christ, Suffering Servant
  thematic patterning, 18, 96–97, 97–113, 196
  wisdom of, 97, 105–10

theism
  classical, ix, 1–15, 58, 127, 151, 196–97
  relational, x, 1–15, 23, 58, 79–80, 97, 104, 112, 127–28, 151–52, 162, 165–66, 196–97
theological aesthetics, xi, xii, 15–16, 18, 26, 42–43, 50–51, 59–60, 62–64, 65–67, 68, 74, 77, 78–90, 134, 164, 169, 198
theological ethics, xi, 16, 18, 53, 59, 62, 74–78, 83, 87–88, 93, 169, 181, 198
theology
  aesthetic, 40–41, 48, 60–61, 175, 178
  after Balthasar, 87–90
  amorphous, 41–42, 48–49, 176, 177–78
  apophatic, 2, 9–10
  evangelical, 42, 176
  and life, x, xii, 15, 49, 58, 60, 79–81, 93, 127, 197, 205

Subject Index

theology (*cont.*)
  natural, 3, 10
  patristic, 2n3, 4, 25, 153, 157–59
  perfect being, ix, 1, 2, 7, 8–16,
    23, 41, 127, 129, 151, 175,
    177–78, 196–97, 204
  perfect-fit, 19, 178, 204
  Protestant, xii, 7, 23, 36–42, 49,
    58, 62, 174
  trinitarian, 4, 5n14, 16, 50–51,
    56
  without beauty, 43–51
theology, Christian
  Hellenization of, 3, 4, 6, 7, 127,
    151
  irrelevance of, x, 2, 7, 15, 58,
    127, 151, 196–97
theophany, 67n31, 70, 75–78,
  95–96, 108, 141
Tolkien, J. R. R., 47
transcendentals, x, xi, 15–16, 24,
  42, 44–46, 48, 50, 60, 63, 68,
  69n37, 70, 81–82, 87, 93,
  129–30, 141, 150, 177, 182
Treier, Daniel, 50n115, 89n105
Trinity, xii, 4, 7, 11, 15–16, 50–51,
  69–72
  dialogue within, 131–32, 142,
    144
  immanent and economic, 4, 5,
    6, 15–16, 152, 154, 156, 167,
    200
  life of, 165–74
  social, 5, 165–66
Triplex Munus Christi, 170–74, 200

Vanhoozer, Kevin, 10n31, 35n59,
  86, 123n94, 157n99, 189,
  192n103, 193n109
virtues, ix, 86, 88, 135, 148, 149n65

Ward, Graham, xi, 49, 53
Warnock, Mary, 164n5, 181
Webster, John, 90, 131, 138–39,
  165, 167
Weinandy, Thomas, 157
Westermann, Claus, 107, 111
wisdom, xii, 17, 18, 42, 43, 48–49,
  95–97, 105–20, 129, 135,
  137, 140, 143, 146, 150–51,
  170, 199, 202–3
Wittgenstein, Ludwig, xi, xii
Wolterstorff, Nicholas, xi, 38

Yahweh, Servant of, 98–99, 101,
  103, 105, 114

243

www.ingramcontent.com/pod-product-compliance
Lightning Source LLC
Chambersburg PA
CBHW050438240426
43661CB00055B/2429